Straight Talk

Oral Communication
for Career Success

Straight Talk: Oral Communication for Career Success has a fresh new approach that gives tools needed to communicate with confidence.

This text provides a thorough overview and hands-on practice in the speech communication skills essential for life and work success. Whether talking person to person, in a group, or in front of an audience, plenty of practical applications give hands-on experience in: practicing effective speaking, handling conversations, participating in teams, and gaining confidence in delivering formal and informal presentations.

This book also helps students prepare for competitive events, and includes a 5-Step Strategic Communication tactic, which students can immediately apply to practice their communications skills.

Paul R. Timm, Ph.D. is Professor of Organizational Leadership and Strategy at Brigham Young University.

Sherron Bienvenu, Ph.D. has taught for 22 years at Emory University's Goizueta School of Business in Atlanta. In addition, she has been a Visiting Professor of Management Communication in the International MBA Program at the Helsinki School of Economics (Finland).

Straight Talk

Oral Communication for Career Success

PAUL R. TIMM, PH.D.
AND
SHERRON BIENVENU, PH.D.

Routledge
Taylor & Francis Group

NEW YORK AND LONDON

First published 2011
by Routledge
270 Madison Avenue, New York, NY 10016

Simultaneously published in the UK
by Routledge
2 Park Square, Milton Park, Abingdon, Oxon OX14 4RN

Routledge is an imprint of the Taylor & Francis Group, an informa business

© 2011 Taylor and Francis

Typeset in Garamond by Wearset Ltd, Boldon, Tyne and Wear
Printed and bound in the United States of America on acid-free paper by
Walsworth Publishing Company, Marceline, MO

Library of Congress Cataloging in Publication Data
Timm, Paul R.
Straight talk : oral communication for career success / by Paul R. Timm and
Sherron Bienvenu.
p. cm.
1. Business communication. 2. Oral communication. I. Bienvenu, Sherron.
II. Title.
HF5718.T554 2010
658.4'52–dc22   010011439

ISBN13: 978-0-415-80232-1 (hbk)
ISBN13: 978-0-415-80197-3 (pbk)
ISBN13: 978-0-203-84292-8 (ebk)

SUSTAINABLE
FORESTRY
INITIATIVE

Certified Chain of Custody
Promoting Sustainable
Forest Management
www.sfiprogram.org

NSF-SFI-COC-C0004285
The SFI label applies to the text stock.

Contents

About the Authors vi

1 Introduction to the Straight Talk Model: Discovering a Strategic Approach 1

2 Define Context Before Speaking or Participating 25

3 Consider Your Media, Source, and Timing Options 55

4 Select and Organize Your Message Content 74

5 Enhance Your Message with Powerful Support Material 107

6 Deliver Your Message with Confidence and Impact 138

7 Contribute to Effective Meetings 168

8 Participate in Effective Conversations and Interviews 197

9 Evaluate Feedback for Continued Success 232

Reference Tool. 252
Notes 268
Index 271

About the Authors

Paul R. Timm, Ph.D., is a Professor Emeritus in the Marriott School of Management, Brigham Young University in Utah. He has written and trained extensively on management, communication, and customer-loyalty topics. He also teaches in the MBA program at Aalto University (formerly the Helsinki School of Economics) in Finland.

Sherron Bienvenu, Ph.D., taught for 20 years at Emory University's Goizueta School of Business in Atlanta. In addition, she is a visiting professor of Management Communication in the International MBA Program at Aalto University (formerly the Helsinki School of Economics) in Finland. Dr. Bienvenu has extensive consulting experience in organizations throughout the US and in Europe.

one

Introduction to the Straight Talk Model[1]

Discovering a Strategic
Approach

Communication is the only task you cannot delegate.
(Roberto C. Goizueta, Chairman and CEO, the Coca-Cola Company)

Discovering the Foundations of Message Planning and Delivery

Business people often feel so confident in their ability to communicate that they see little need to prepare. They have had success in past attempts to write or speak and assume that they can use the same techniques regardless of the audience or purpose. Without thinking the situation over, they rely on style over substance—or substance with no style—and the results are disastrous. So, if you have been told that you are articulate and smooth as a communicator, accept the compliment but beware. You can only go so far on "articulate" or "smooth." You still need to prepare for a speech, interview, meeting, or critical conversation. Or, if you have been told that your ideas are excellent, again, beware. An unfocused purpose, poor organization, or inarticulate delivery can ruin even a potentially powerful message full of excellent ideas.

This chapter will introduce you to the five-step strategic approach to professional communication. We call it the Straight Talk Model, which forms the blueprint for better communication, especially in the workplace. As you read, keep in mind that this chapter presents a very broad overview of the model. We will provide additional elaboration in future chapters.

Performance Competencies

When you have completed this chapter, you should be able to:

- Describe the five elements of the Straight Talk Communication Model.
- Explain the three factors that constitute a communication context.
- Understand how media, source, and timing options can impact communication effectiveness.
- Apply proven processes for selecting and organizing message content.
- Identify key variables that affect delivery of messages.
- Apply a simple pattern for giving and receiving feedback on communication behaviors.
- Use a Credibility Checklist to evaluate your own communication.

The Way It Is … Geoff Wings It

Geoffrey believed (people told him so in college!) that he had a great speaking voice and exceptional poise (classmates referred to him as very "cool"). His confidence and "gift for gab" (as his mother called it) proved useful in the early years of his career where he sold office equipment. After five years of selling, Geoff returned to school for an MBA and later landed a job as a mid-level manager for a large corporation. The future looked good.

Geoff's new employer was a cutting-edge organization that supported a belief in ongoing employee development by providing extensive training and designated mentors. Geoff's mentor was a division manager in his mid-fifties.

Although Geoff's day-to-day activities included interacting with his staff and leading meetings, he rarely had to speak before large groups. Until today—when his mentor decided it was time for Geoff to address a group of visiting clients to give a progress report on marketing efforts for a recently launched product. The audience for his ten-minute presentation was composed of 20 executives from Seoul, Korea. All were fluent in English and well-educated. Most had been to the US many times.

Unfortunately, Geoff relied on his natural charm and expended little effort in preparing his presentation. He greeted the group with a good-natured story about an Asian student he knew in college who was really good at math. He told his audience that he "wasn't going to bore them with a prepared 'speech' but rather just wanted to talk with them" and they "should feel free to butt in anytime with your questions." Then he rambled though a disjointed discourse on the new product. The listeners were courteous but unimpressed. Geoff's mentor was embarrassed.

Get the Big Picture: the Straight Talk Model (STM)

For some people, words like "strategy" and "model" conjure up images of academic jargon, of complicated but impractical theory. In reality, good strategies provide clarity and practical focus. They help people solve problems in functional, creative ways. The value of a systematic approach across a variety of communication situations (that is, the application of a strategic model) greatly increases the likelihood that you will get your message across effectively and efficiently. The model provides a foundation for Straight Talk.

The Straight Talk Model provides a working plan for the preparation and delivery of spoken messages. This five-step strategic process is suitable for all types of workplace communication and allows you to personalize your approach while following one basic, master plan. However, it also allows for plenty of creativity and opportunities to project your unique personality and makes you more credible and persuasive when you present, interview, share information, or interact in teams and groups. In short, the Straight Talk Model makes you a more effective communicator.

The STM includes the following five steps:

1   **Understand**: Define the context. Learn everything you can about the context in which you are communicating—the current situation, your target audiences, and your objectives with each of those audiences.

The term "audience" means anyone who could potentially read or hear your message, whether you want them to or not. Another term for audience is "constituency."

---

2   **Decide**: Consider your media, source, and timing options. Decide on the communication medium that is most appropriate and effective for your message, the best person to deliver that message, and the best time for the message to arrive.

3   **Choose**: Select and organize information. Select specific material that focuses on the needs and concerns of your target audiences, and then arrange your information so that it will meet your objectives with those audiences. Base your organizational plan on the information you have collected, first about the context and then about your media, source, and timing options.

4   **Deliver** your message. When it is time to deliver your message, do so correctly and appropriately—again based on your earlier analysis—with a confident, personal style.

5   **Evaluate** feedback for continued success. Give, gather, and apply feedback so that you may continue to learn and grow as a communicator.

By internalizing the STM, you will have access to a powerful tool for boosting communication effectiveness. Let's look briefly at each step of the model and begin the process of making this approach part of your mental toolbox.

Seek first to understand, then to be understood. (Stephen R. Covey, *Seven Habits of Highly Effective People*)

Step 1: Understand: Define the Context

Chapter 2 goes over the process of context analysis in more depth. For now, we want to introduce you to the term and overview some aspects of communication context that you should take into account for effective communication. When we talk about the communication context, we are referring to three key factors. These factors form the foundation for your strategic planning:

- The situation or problem that generated the need for you to produce a message (*Why* are you communicating? What's going on that requires a response or action?).
- Your target audiences (*To whom* are you communicating?).
- Your desired objectives with those audiences (*What* do you want your listeners to do or think?).

You greatly improve the odds of getting what you want if you thoroughly understand the situation, your audiences, and your objectives before you communicate. Even experienced communicators often fail to spend enough mental effort defining their situation, audience, and overall objectives. They prefer to jump into preparing what they want to say without sufficiently thinking about what their message receivers need or want. Might that be you?

In our opening story, Geoff seems to have misread his audience. His folksy approach and even his opening comments about his Asian classmate who was good at math (a widely overused stereotype) may have been disconcerting to his audience of Korean executives who probably expected something more formal or at least more clearly structured.

Defining the context is a critical step in any communication effort. In each situation you will need to start with specific knowledge about what you are dealing with, whom you are presenting to, and what you want them to do or think. In fact, defining the context may well be the single most important thing you can do to achieve your goals.

Pause for a moment here and consider the possible contexts we discussed above. In a few words, what is likely to be the most positive outcome? What would you want your audience to do or think in each situation?

For example, your responsibilities on the job might include persuading clients, informing colleagues, facilitating problem-solving meetings, delivering presentations, and evaluating employees. You constantly interview, whether you are looking for a new job, hiring new employees, or justifying your own existence to a new boss. So, to have a better chance of achieving your goals, start every communication process by gathering specific knowledge about what you are dealing with, whom you are presenting to, and what you want them to do. We repeat, defining the context may well be the single most important thing you can do to help you get what you want when you communicate.

Now, let's drill down a little deeper. As we look closer at the broader term "context," we should consider three major parts: our situation, our audience, and our objectives. Our strategic approach analyzes each aspect separately and systematically. We'll start with the existing situation because the situation usually creates the reason to communicate.

Define the Situation (What's Going On?)

A communication challenge lands on your desk: close a deal with a client, update colleagues, prepare a presentation, motivate or give negative feedback to an employee, lead a problem-solving meeting. Perhaps all of the above!

Wait! Step away from the computer. Don't start building that slide deck yet. First, why are you communicating? What's going on?

The first part of defining the context involves looking at the scope of the problem you are planning to communicate about, evaluating the external climate in which the problem exists, and evaluating the corporate culture (both yours and that of your target audience).

Unfortunately, no one is going to hand you a complete description of the corporate culture or a full explanation of the problems and issues surrounding a company's external climate. Your job as a professional communicator is to carefully research information that will help you develop your message. Thus, in order to define the situation completely, follow the steps explained in the next few sections.

Limit the Problem, Issue, or Task

This step may sound simple, but isolating the significant issues at the root of a problem is often difficult. Focus on the distinct cause of your message. Then, if necessary, break your problem into smaller parts and work on them one at a time.

For example, if you are preparing a proposal for a new product, it matters whether the interest in a new product is competition-driven or whether your company prides itself on being innovative. This initial catalyst for why you are investigating a new product will help you determine your criteria for effective persuasion. If you are wrestling with the need to "motivate" your work team, you need to target specific behavior changes you would like to see occur as a result of your communication.

Evaluate the Problem Within the External Climate

The external climate is a composite of business, economic, political, and social pressures being faced by similar businesses or organizations. While it may seem daunting to consider all these possible factors, it makes sense to give some thought to what's going on in the world that affects your specific problem. Look at the climate in which your particular communication problem or issue exists to determine how this climate affects the problem. For example, if you are working under conditions of an economic slowdown and considerable concern about job security, a message encouraging the launch of a risky new product may face much more resistance than in better times.

As another example: if your communication challenge is to negotiate an increased budget for your department, you should find out in advance how your projects and staff needs compare with other departments in the organization and in similar organizations in your industry and geographical area. This comparative data will be powerful support for your argument.

And here's a corporate example: investors might view a small high-tech company as risky or unlikely to generate an immediate profit. Or, the same company may project the identity of an exciting, high-growth organization. This viewpoint will change based on what is happening in the external climate. Often, the most important question to ask about external climate is: "What's going on with the competition?"

Whatever your topic, be aware of factors that influence the organization and your audiences. Find out what is going on in the specific field, in related industries, and in the local and global markets. Keep current on issues that affect you, and update your research regularly.

Evaluate the Corporate (or Organizational) Culture That Impacts on the Problem

Corporate culture refers to the predominant values, attitudes, and beliefs of the company/organization that are consciously or subconsciously agreed upon by most members and result in shared behaviors. Typically, culture is defined by the degree to which the organization encourages such things as innovation, risk-taking, attention to detail, productivity, people orientation, team utilization, aggressiveness, and stability.

These accepted attitudes and behaviors are often established by the leader of the group, such as the president of a company or the manager in a department. For example, the culture of the accounting department may be more formal, more detail-oriented, and less innovative than the culture of the marketing department, based on the personality and behaviors of the respective managers. Tangible indicators of culture found in an organization may include:

- Formal versus informal processes, communication, dress codes, etc.
- Task oriented versus employee oriented emphasis.
- Closed or tightly-controlled systems versus open or loosely-controlled systems.
- Results-orientation versus process-orientation.
- Normative environment (what ought to be) versus pragmatic (what is).

As you identify the elements of the corporate culture, you can adapt your own communication style to reflect the expectations of the organization and thus be more effective when you speak, write, interview, or work in teams and groups. For example, a communication strategy that would be appropriate in a small, informal, flexible organization might be completely inappropriate in one that is more formal and structured.

In case you're wondering—no, you're not being hypocritical or fake by adapting. You are not changing or deceiving. You are simply showing that you care enough about your audiences to make your messages more comfortable for them to receive. Your messages are still Straight Talk.

Activity: How Would You Describe the Culture of an Organization You Work In?

Select an organization (an employer, civic organization, academic institution, or a department) with which you are involved. Evaluate the organization on the following "agree–disagree" scales: 1 = strongly disagree, 2 = disagree, 3 = neutral, 4 = agree, and 5 = strongly agree.

My organization encourages and supports its members to be:

- Highly creative   1 2 3 4 5
- Formal when talking to each other   1 2 3 4 5
- Casual in dress and grooming   1 2 3 4 5
- Careful about following all rules or procedures   1 2 3 4 5
- Flexible about work hours   1 2 3 4 5
- Open to new, even offbeat, ideas   1 2 3 4 5
- Concerned with presenting a professional image   1 2 3 4 5
- Careful to maintain a chain of command   1 2 3 4 5
- Very detail oriented   1 2 3 4 5

How do culture elements influence the communication that occurs among members? Or with outside audiences?

Define Your Audience

The second part of defining the context includes identifying and learning about your target audiences. We all tend to inconsistently and inadequately analyze our audiences, which is another reason to get this part right—you will distinguish yourself and stand out. The more specific information you have about your readers or listeners, the better you can tailor your message to their needs and achieve your goals.

The most common mistakes people make are generalizing and assuming information about their audiences. Of course, sometimes you have to do those things if you really can't find the information you need, but generalizing and assuming should never be your default. Here are some steps you can take to ensure that your audience analysis is thorough.

Identify All Potential Audiences (Distinct or Overlapping)
This includes the primary audience, the hidden audience, and the decision-makers.

The primary audience is the actual individual(s) to whom you speak. These are the people sitting in front of you when you make a presentation, the individuals across the table in an interview, or the participants in your meeting.

The hidden audience is an indirect receiver of your message, such as a person who hears the message second-hand. This audience may not be directly connected with your communication purpose, but may have some power over your target audience. For example, a powerful hidden audience can be a spouse of your listener who has considerable influence at home. Other hidden audiences may be colleagues or friends with whom your target audience talks about work-related decisions. The challenge with target audiences is that they rarely have all the relevant information, so their input is likely to be biased. Nothing you ever do or say exists in a vacuum; any person with whom you interact in any way may later influence someone else who is important to you.

The decision-maker is your most important audience. This is the person who has authority to approve your idea, course of action, or project. Since audiences can overlap, the decision-maker might be your primary audience (hearing your speech or reading your letter) or your hidden audience (a senior executive from another department who hears about your message). The challenge with decision-makers is identifying them. Be aware of "gatekeepers" who say they are making decisions when they are really passing on your material to the real decision-maker.

A caveat here: it's not necessary to label each individual as "primary" or "hidden" or "decision-maker." These category names exist to insure that you recognize all the audiences who are—or might be—relevant for your communication strategy.

Learn About Each Audience

Focus on facts, attitudes, wants, and concerns. To do so, first gather both professional and personal facts about audience members, such as their age, gender, ethnicity, cultural background, education, job responsibilities and status, civic and religious affiliations, and their knowledge of your topic.

As our typical businesses become more global, it becomes increasingly important to recognize that individuals are influenced by their national cultures. For example, does your target audience's culture emphasize:

- Acting as an individual or a group?
- Maintaining power distance between members of a hierarchy? (Formality)
- Focusing on long-term versus the short-term time perspective?
- Rewarding competition or relationship building?
- Valuing risk-taking versus stability or caution?

These are just a few examples of cross-cultural differences. Remember that your target audience is composed of individuals and not stereotypes of their countries. However, national cultures do influence individual preferences and norms. Again, our opening story of Geoff's casual speech to a group of Korean executives probably violated some cultural expectations.

Next, discover your audience's attitudes about:

- You.
- Your topic.
- Actually being present as a receiver of your message.

As disillusioning as it may be, the reality is that many people would rather be somewhere else, with someone else, doing something else than listening to you. The hard questions that you must ask yourself are: what does my audience think about me? What do they think about my topic? What do they think about spending time listening to my message?

Next, determine exactly what your audience *wants* to learn. Be careful to avoid the problems of giving the audience too much or too little information. Your job is to balance between the two. Give your audience what they want to know before you ask them to meet your needs.

For example, a problem can arise when a supervisor tells employees only what they need to know to do their specific jobs, without regard for information that will motivate them to perform their tasks well. The employees might do as they are instructed, but without enthusiasm or commitment. What they may want to know is how the project will impact the company or how the customer uses the product. Keeping employees informed about the company in general makes people feel more a part of a team, even if the specific information is not absolutely crucial to their job performance. To put it bluntly, people always want to know what's in it for them. They probably won't verbalize this, but, ultimately, it's what they want most.

The real key [to marketing and communication] is simple: Your customers want to know *"What's in it for me?"* Tell them. If you don't do that, no amount of fireworks and freebies matter. (Daniel Will-Harris)

Finally, recognize consistent audience concerns. Most people you interact with on a regular basis express continuing interest in the same issues. For example, the company's financial officers may have a consistent need to keep costs down, while the production supervisor is always concerned about process efficiency. One manager may be consistently impressed by face-to-face client visits while another manager values attendance at internal meetings. This awareness of your target audience's consistent concerns should influence your decisions when you select information and prepare your messages.

Define Your Objectives With Each Audience

The third part of defining the context concerns your objectives with each of your audiences. Most messages, no matter how apparently simple, encompass three objectives:

- An overall goal.
- The specific purpose of the communication.
- Your hidden agenda.

Define Your Overall Goal

The overall goal reflects your ultimate purpose or long-term plan. You may not actually refer to this goal in your message, but you should recognize where your specific message fits in that overall plan. For example, getting a higher managerial position in your company might be your overall goal, but your specific purpose would be to impress a particular vice-president in a particular meeting. Try to tie individual, short-term communication events with your long-term goals.

In corporate communication, the mission statement of the organization often drives the overall goal. Therefore, the overall goal of your presentation about the budget for the next quarter would be likely to succeed if it reflects the company's commitment to increasing shareholder value, for example.

Identify the Specific Purpose of the Message

The specific purpose of the communication is what you want your listener to *do* after receiving your message. Identify the specific purpose by combining your needs with your analysis of the needs of the target audiences. Pay particular attention to your audience's level of knowledge about your topic. Remember that your primary audience may know a lot about your subject, but your decision-maker may need a review of the background information. Ask yourself, as a result of this communication, exactly what you want your listener to do.

The specific purpose of any communication is what you want the receiver to do.

One way of looking at your specific purpose in relation to your overall goal is to imagine a persuasive continuum from 0 to 10, where 0 represents your target audience saying, "I know nothing about this," and 10 represents "Yes! Let's do it!" You want to assess where your target audience is on the continuum so that you don't ask for too little or too much. You also don't want to waste time giving your audience detail on what they already know. Nor do you want to tell them more than they are ready to hear.

You are getting closer to a focused, persuasive message. You've looked at the big picture and learned everything you can about your target audience. Now you must use the material you have gathered to help you articulate your specific goal. The major questions are:

- Exactly what does my audience know about my topic?
- As a result of this message, exactly what do I want to occur?
- Exactly what does my audience want/need to know to move to that next step or make that next decision?
- How can I measure my success?

Acknowledge Your Hidden Agenda

Finally, as you clarify your intentions about your objectives with the members of your audience, keep in mind that you probably also have hidden agendas—personal goals you want to achieve but don't necessarily talk about. Everybody has hidden agendas, especially successful people. Each time you communicate, you have an opportunity to work toward your goals. Acknowledge this opportunity and factor it into your planning.

For example, one hidden agenda might be that you want your supervisor to recommend you for an annual performance award several months in the future. You wouldn't ask directly for that but, through your work, you can demonstrate the qualities that would qualify you for the award as you speak or interact in teams and groups. Another hidden agenda might be to gain additional training opportunities so that you can prepare for a career change. You probably won't announce this motivation, but you should acknowledge it to yourself in your own context analysis.

Step 1 of the Straight Talk Model is absolutely critical to success, yet it is often given short shrift by people too eager to get on with "communicating." Take the time to carefully think through all relevant information about your situation, audiences, and objectives. Such thinking will pay enormous dividends in overall effectiveness.

But, before moving on, here are a couple notes of encouragement. We expect that you may be concerned about how complicated this all sounds. First, we flesh out this process of context analysis in Chapter 2, so, if you are a bit confused and/or overwhelmed at the moment, clarifying ideas are coming. Second, we provide worksheets in various sections of the book that will remind you of key points and guide you along. Finally, and most importantly, *context analysis gets easier*. Really. After a couple of times through the worksheet, you'll discover how many of these points you automatically consider. You'll also recognize the "aha!" points—the questions you usually forget that offer interesting, relevant information. In the future, each time you analyze your situation, your audiences, and your goals with those audiences, you'll work faster and smarter.

Step 2: Decide: Consider Your Media, Source, and Timing Options

Now that you have given careful thought to understanding your communication context—the situation, your audience, and your objectives with those audiences—the next step of our Model reminds you to explore the "How?" "Who?", and "When?" options. The key questions to consider are:

- How should you send your message?
- Who should deliver the message?
- When should the message arrive?

If you fail to think through these options when you communicate, the meaning of your message might be drowned out by an inappropriate medium, disregarded because of an unacceptable source, or undermined by awkward timing.

In other words, you can destroy a powerful message if the wrong person delivers it in the wrong way on the wrong day. And here's the continuing lesson: *it's not about you.* It may be your idea, your proposal, or your résumé, but if you want your message to be effective, it can't be all about you. The decisions on the how, who, and when must be determined by the needs of your target audience.

Don't let the meaning of your message be drowned out by an inappropriate medium, disregarded because of an unacceptable sender, or be undermined by awkward timing. The next few sections outline these three sub-steps.

Select Media Options That Are Most Appropriate for Your Message

Never before in history have there been so many media choices.

Technology is providing an almost daily increase in media options. Emails, mobile phone calls, text messaging, and teleconferencing often replace traditional letters, personal visits, and meetings. Wireless technology has created communication accessibility that is practically unaffected by infrastructure, geography, or time zones.

Lots of choices should be good news, but the reality is that more options often mean that there are more ways to "get it wrong."

Each medium has certain advantages, disadvantages, and ground rules that make it more or less appropriate for a specific purpose.

Unfortunately, we too often make our choices about how to send the message based on our *own* communication habits—what's most comfortable for us—rather than on the preferences of our target audiences or the particulars of the situation. Alas, it's not about us.

For many people, the default medium is email, while others default to the phone. One may argue that email doesn't intrude and is therefore better, and the other counters that a phone call is more personal and is therefore better. Some managers call meetings for most communications, while others prefer one-to-one conversations. Each is right—and wrong—depending on what our particular target audience prefers.

Remember: your choice of medium is *not about you*—it's about your communication context: your situation, your target audience, and your goals with that audience.

Choose a Credible Source

Who you are always speaks louder than what you say.

You won't always be the best person to deliver a particular message. Perhaps someone else can be more effective than you. When determining the best source—the person best positioned to deliver your message—the most important criterion is the perceived credibility of that source by your target audience. In other words, who will your audience perceive as having the most experience, power, and concern for them?

A common mistake is to make decisions about the source based on our own needs, rather than those of the receiver. We naturally take ownership of a project and then want to see it personally through to completion by delivering the message ourselves to employees, supervisors, clients, and other decision-makers. Our hidden agenda (e.g., a desire to be impressive) may override the fact that someone else might be more persuasive with the target audience. In truth, someone with more perceived credibility in the eyes of the targeted receiver may be more effective in presenting your message.

This does not necessarily mean that you should hand over the presentation of your ideas or project to a person whose credibility may make a better persuasive connection. Another option is to ask the more credible person to introduce you and help establish *your* credibility with your target audience.

Weigh your source options carefully to maximize your potential for success, even if it takes a little "credibility by association."

The way to get things done is not to mind who gets the credit for doing them. (Benjamin Jowett)

Send at the "Right" Time

The timing of a message can have an impact on its effectiveness. For example, sending a thank-you note months late or delivering a "closing" sales presentation before the customer is ready to buy may have little positive effect. And—yet again—you should consider the needs of your audience in conjunction with your own communication goals when deciding when to send the message. Do not communicate only at your own comfort and convenience, but, more importantly, take into account the convenience, sensitivities, and needs of your audience.

Consider the sequencing and spacing of your messages, particularly with multiple audiences. Decide which audience should receive which message and in what order. Also consider how much time to allow between messages. The very process of selecting which audience to tell first communicates a strong message in itself.

For example, you wouldn't approach a vice-president with a question that your direct supervisor could answer. Conversely, the president of your company would be unwise to tell you about a policy change before telling your supervising vice-president or senior manager.

The Rule that Applies to All the Steps

Just remember that it's about *them*—your target audience. It's about *their* needs and *their* concerns. If you remember and apply this one simple rule, you are more likely to get what you want. Then, and only then, it can be all about you.

Step 3: Choose: Select and Organize Information

Chapter 4 covers details about selecting appropriate information and organizing your messages for maximum impact. For now, we discuss this as the third step in the Straight Talk Model.

After you have defined the context of your message and have considered your media, source, and timing options, you are (finally!) prepared to move on to the next step—selecting and organizing information. The next few sections introduce ways to effectively select and organize your information into a coherent, credible message.

Review Your Analysis of the Context

As we mentioned above, a common mistake of inexperienced business communicators is to prematurely jump ahead to selecting and organizing information. They overlook or ignore the first two steps in the model. These are the fly-by-the-seat-of-the-pants communicators. They may be able to get by with a lack of analysis some of the time; however, in today's professional environment, "getting by" does not provide you with a competitive advantage. And choosing the wrong information because of poor situation and audience analysis can seriously damage your credibility.

Thus, take a moment to ensure your assumptions up to now have been correct. If you have done all you can to understand the situation, your audiences, and your goals with those audiences—and if you have used that understanding to decide about media, source, and timing—then *now* you will select an organizational plan for your information that will help you meet your goals.

Compare Key Organizational Patterns and Select the Most Effective One

Compare key organizational patterns for the body of your message, select one, and include a complete introduction and conclusion. The introduction grabs your audience's attention, explains what's coming, and establishes the benefit for the receiver. The body of your message follows through on your stated plan. The conclusion summarizes and reinforces your main points and asks for action. Planning an organized message, complete with an introduction and conclusion, ensures that you follow through with the purpose of your communication.

Limit Your Main Points

Limit the information in the body of your message, focusing on material that offers specific, personal benefit to the individuals receiving the message. Too many people focus on the benefit for the organization, such as increased profits, rather than the benefit for the actual receiver, such as increased salaries or bonuses.

In addition, cognitive psychologists tell us that, on average, people can only remember between three and seven items. Busy business people are more likely to remember only three. If you give too many reasons to promote you or buy your product, your listener may only remember a few of them, and those may not be your most persuasive points. Fewer main points work better.

Enhance Your Message with Powerful Support Material (Visual Aids, Numbers, Stories, and Examples)

No matter how brilliantly you articulate key ideas, your audience will remember your points better when you use powerful support materials (discussed further in Chapter 5). Provide appropriate support with stories, visual aids, numbers, and examples. Stories work well because listeners become mentally involved picturing the events you describe. Examples and numbers make a message more memorable and concrete for your listeners. Good visual aids or props can also draw your audience into your presentation and make it more interesting to them.

Once again, the support material you use depends on your audience, situation, and objectives, in addition to your choices about medium, source, and timing. For example, you would not use cartoons in a serious presentation to bankers. You would not weave a long narrative in response to a request for a short email. You would not tell a humorous story if you were not comfortable doing so. *Always* make your decisions with your earlier analysis in mind.

Step 4: Deliver Your Message

In Chapter 6, we will get more specific about message-delivery techniques. Below is an overview of this critical aspect of the Straight Talk Model.

Once you have defined the context of your message, have considered your options, and have selected and organized your information, your success will largely be determined by your delivery of the message. This success will be affected by the spoken message, non-verbal cues (such as gestures and facial expressions), and, perhaps, visuals and graphics. If you have completed the previous three steps of the STM well, delivering your message will be that much easier. However, keep in mind that collecting your information and presenting it are equally important. A good, carefully developed message can be ruined by poor delivery. The following is a quick look at steps you can take to make your delivery more effective.

Develop Your Straight Talk Skills

Start with the basics. Learn to speak clearly and expressively. Developing your speaking, interpersonal, and group skills is a lifelong process of continual improvement. Actively look for opportunities to speak, share information, tell stories, and interact in teams and groups. Continually work to develop and display a professional visual image, such as how you dress, how you research and present your support materials, and how you design documents and visual aids.

Prepare Thoroughly (Rehearse Your Presentations)

Demonstrate the accuracy of your research and analysis with dynamic, articulate delivery. Rehearse presentations and edit visual aids. Be prepared to answer questions. Talk using your own words (but avoid grammatical errors and use common sense about slang or expletives). Avoid reading to your audience or mimicking another person's style. For other forms of communication such as interviews or team preparation, practice answering the types of questions or issues you may face.

Express Confidence in Your Topic and in Yourself

Show confidence in your material, based on your preparation. Stay in control even when things go wrong, such as unexpected interruptions or equipment failure. Let your audience know how sincere and enthusiastic you are about your topic. After all, you are the expert on this particular topic for this particular audience at this particular time. You have prepared.

Just one note about feeling less than confident: no matter how confident you are, at some point you are likely to experience speaker anxiety. "Stage fright" is normal; it's your body's adrenaline kicking in, which provides extra energy. In fact, we worry more about speakers who say that they are not nervous at all, since an audience might perceive a relaxed attitude as a *lack* of enthusiasm. We'll discuss some tricks for overcoming stage fright in Chapter 6.

Be Yourself (but Adapt Your Style to Your Audience and Situation)

Most importantly, be yourself. Allow your personality to show in all your communication. You are the most important part of your message, and your unique personality is your most valuable delivery skill. However, keep in mind that you may need to adapt your style to meet each audience's expectations in their organizational culture.

Step 5: Evaluate Feedback for Continued Success

Effective communication is an ongoing process of practice and improvement. Yes, you have to get feedback, and no, you won't get any better by communicating the same way over and over. If you always do what you've always done, you'll always get what you've always gotten. Feedback-based changes are crucial to improvement. No one can make constructive changes without getting feedback.

Improvement in communication skills is based on realistically evaluating feedback from your target audiences and trusted colleagues. Apply all four parts of the feedback process—giving, soliciting, and receiving feedback, and evaluating yourself with the Credibility Checklist—as briefly described in the following sections. We deal with this critical step in more depth in Chapter 9.

Give Feedback

There can be no positive change without negative feedback.

If you only offer positive feedback to other people, you are cheating everyone. The speaker will miss the opportunity to learn from matching your perceptions—what you heard—with his or her intentions—what the speaker meant for you to hear. You, as an evaluator, will miss the opportunity to learn from recognizing your own shortcomings that you may see in someone else's work.

Truly useful feedback points out a need for improvement and offers suggestions for how to make that improvement without discouraging the person who prepared the message. The following are some basic guidelines for giving good feedback:

- Describe something positive first (such as, "I can tell that you worked hard on this project and that …").
- Express constructive criticism in terms of "I" (such as, "At the same time, I didn't understand …").
- Give a specific example (such as, "For example, the comparison on the quarterly numbers wasn't clear to me.").

- Offer an option for a solution (such as, "Perhaps if you could show me that information on a chart …").
- Close with another positive statement (such as, "Overall, you are very persuasive. When you add the clearer charts, I think we'll be ready to present to senior management.").

Solicit Feedback

To be an effective communicator, you need to reach out for feedback. "So, how'd I do?," however, may not be the best question to ask if you really want thoughtful feedback. You may hear, "Fine" and feel better, but you won't get the information you need to learn and grow. Instead, ask open-ended questions that avoid single-word responses.

The following are three simple guidelines for soliciting the kind of feedback that will help you improve your communication:

- Identify individuals—people you trust—who can provide you with the candid feedback you need.
- Ask them *in advance* to evaluate your presentation, meeting participation, or planned conversation.
- Specify areas where you need them to pay close attention. For example: "I've been trying to sound more enthusiastic when I speak. Would you evaluate how I'm doing?"

Receive Feedback

Try to avoid unconstructive reactions, such as defending yourself, overreacting, disregarding, or blaming others. None of these reactions will help you improve as a communicator. Instead, use the following positive attitudes and behaviors:

- Develop feedback-receptive attitudes—be open, not defensive.
- Listen carefully to comments (take notes in detail, if appropriate).
- Ask for specific, clarifying information and examples, then repeat these back to the person giving the feedback for clarification.
- Notice non-verbal messages from your audience. (These can tip you off as to how well you are *really* doing.)
- Accept responsibility for any needs and changes, and correct in the direction of the evaluation—don't overreact.
- Recognize that whatever your audience perceives, real or not, is very real to them—show appreciation for their point of view (even if you don't fully agree).
- Thank the person for the feedback (even if it's hard to do).

Evaluate Yourself with the Credibility Checklist

Your credibility is your target audience's perception of you. The only *reality* is what that audience—the people to whom you communicate or the people with whom you interact—perceives. Your *intention* doesn't count.

Perceived credibility is the most powerful source of persuasion.

The most important element of your personal and professional communication strategy is to project credibility. If your audience perceives that you are credible—if they believe you, trust you, have confidence in you—you will be persuasive. And if you are persuasive, you will get what you want: you will achieve the objectives of your messages.

Your credibility is based on your audience's perception of four key characteristics—your goodwill, expertise, power, and confidence. These four characteristics make up the Credibility Checklist. This checklist is your way of confirming your decisions throughout the STM process.

Establish Goodwill

Goodwill is your audience's perception of your focus on them and concern for them—their perception of *what you think of them*.

This one is not only first, but if you don't pull it off, you won't have a chance with the other three. This dimension is about your audience, not about you. Goodwill is their perception of how much you care about them—how unique they are, how special they are, how important they are to you or your organization.

The perception of goodwill comes from carefully-selected information based on your analysis of your audience, situation, and objectives. So, obviously, if you haven't thought carefully about the people hearing your presentation, being interviewed, or participating in your meeting, you won't be successful on this dimension of credibility.

Demonstrate Expertise

This second dimension is your audience's perceptions of the *facts about you*. You will earn the perception of expertise through examples that demonstrate your knowledge, education, and experience. It's your chance to share the facts about yourself.

The good news is that facts are objective. The bad news is that the *perception* of facts is often *subjective*. Use the information you learned in your audience analysis to select the most relevant facts to share, based on each particular audience's interests and concerns. What impresses one person might not work with someone else. Expertise is also tricky because you don't want to come off as cocky or arrogant about what you know. (In an ideal world, we would all be eloquently introduced by someone else!)

Reveal Your Power

Power is the audience's perception of *what other people think about you.* You will achieve the perception of power with material that refers to your rank and illustrates your success. It's your opportunity to mention any recognition that would be meaningful to this particular audience.

Power (and the perception of it) can take several forms: personal power (the ability to control your own environment), interpersonal power (the ability to influence other people), and corporate power (the ability to mobilize resources). Depending on what you know about your audience, you can find many examples to increase the perception that you are powerful and therefore credible. Also, when it comes to power, success is "transferable." For example, an accomplishment as president of a volunteer organization illustrates leadership ability that you can apply on the job, such as organizing a work team. Or, work experience in any field applies to another field (e.g., when you change from engineering to marketing, you bring your understanding of the products with you). Success in any form indicates your experience with many relevant skills, such as decision-making or project management.

All that said, however, keep in mind that an individual's status, prestige, and success may be perceived differently depending on the specific culture of an organization, industry, or country. Be prepared to explain your examples in context, so that your target audience understands how powerful (and credible) you are.

Express Confidence

This dimension represents your audience's perception of how you present yourself, how sure you are of yourself. It's their perception *of what you think of yourself.* You will achieve the perception of confidence through excellent communication skills, which always include doing your homework and preparing messages tailored to your audiences' needs and concerns. Once your material is right, it's easier for you to feel confident. But you have to look confident, too.

Finally, if you project confidence, your target audiences will automatically perceive you higher on the other dimensions of credibility.

A Quick Review of the STM

Step 1: Understand. Define the context of your communication: the current situation, your target audiences, and your objectives with each of those audiences.

Step 2: Decide. Consider your "How?," "Who?" and "When?" options, and select the communication medium that is most appropriate and effective for your message, the person who is most credible, and the best time for the message to arrive.

Step 3: Choose. Use that understanding of your audience to select and organize specific information to meet your objectives. Put the right words in the right order with the right "stuff."

Step 4: Deliver your message with a confident, personal style.

Step 5: Evaluate feedback for continued growth and success.

The remainder of this book will amplify on the overview presented in this chapter. You have the big picture. Now, let's get into the details that make all the difference in developing your ability to apply Straight Talk in your professional communications.

Performance Competencies

After completing this chapter, you should be better able to overview and describe key elements of the Straight Talk Model, including:

- Understand and define the context of the current situation, your target audiences, and your objectives with each of those audiences.
- Consider your media, source, and timing options, and select the communication medium that is most appropriate and effective for your message, the person who is most credible, and the best time for the message to arrive.
- Use that knowledge to select and organize specific information to meet your objectives with your audiences.
- Deliver your message with a confident, personal style.
- Evaluate feedback for continued growth and success.
- Recognize that, by applying the Straight Talk Model to all of your important communications, you will be more credible and more per-suasive when you speak informally, present professionally, interview, or interact in teams and groups. Your audiences will perceive your communication as "straight talk," and you will achieve what you want.

What Do You Know?

Activity 1.1: A Rationale for a Model

Identify a communication situation you have experienced recently. This may have been a presentation you gave, a lesson you taught, an interview or exchange of information you engaged in, or even a discussion or dispute with your spouse or a friend. Based on what you have read in this chapter, list the kinds of information you had before communicating. Then list the facts or information you could have benefited from but you either didn't think of or could not get. How do the first two steps of the Straight Talk Model broaden your view of the need to plan before speaking?

Activity 1.2: Identifying the Communication Culture

The culture of an organization can impact on the way people communicate within that organization. List some key characteristics of the communication culture of an organization you belong to. What are some of the "rules" or unspoken assumptions about the ways its members communicate? Do cultural elements create any "elephants in the room" that no one talks about? If so, what are these? Be creative.

Reinforce With These Review Questions

1 The first step in applying the Straight Talk Model is to define the

   _____.

2 The three elements of communication context are:
   (1) _____, (2) _____, and
   (3) _____.

3 True/False—The external climate—which impacts the communication situation—is a composite of business, economic, political, and social pressures.

4 Name three typical indicators of organizational culture as described in this chapter: (1) _____, (2) _____, and
   (3) _____.

5 True/False—Effective speakers generalize and assume things about their audiences based on a quick look at demographic factors.

6 Name three kinds of audiences (some of which may overlap):
   (1) _____, (2) _____, and
   (3) _____.

7 True/False—Good communicators work to avoid having any hidden agenda.

8 True/False—Good communicators use the same media consistently rather than changing with various message types.

9 Name three kinds of support material you can use to amplify on main points of your message:
(1) _____, (2) _____, and
(3) _____.

10 True/False—Feedback, although occasionally useful, is not critical to building communication skills.

Mini-Case Study: Sophie's Poor Choices

Sophie is the newest employee at Allegiance Software, a fast-growing technology company. She has a degree in computer science and a track record as an exceptionally good programmer. She also manages to avoid the nerd stereotype by being very personable as well. In part because of her outgoing personality, Fred James, the company president, asked Sophie to host some important visitors for about a half-hour before they began official meetings. The visitors were potential investors and Fred wanted to make a good impression. Sophie was to give them a company tour and overview of facilities, staff, and products.

The day of the visit came too soon for Sophie, who had been working overtime to meet a programming deadline. The night before the visit, she and a programming team worked until almost 1 a.m. "Fortunately," she thought to herself, "I'm good at schmoozing people, so preparation isn't really that important."

Sophie's hosting duties quickly came unglued as the visitors asked her questions she had not anticipated—and she had no answers. Employees were unaware that she was bringing people into the departments, and the facilities looked cluttered with pizza boxes from last night's late work stacked on desks. To make matters worse, Sophie made a derogatory joke about a rival university that just happened to be the alma mater of one of the visitors. In short, the visit didn't leave a good impression, and Fred was furious when he heard complaints from the people he was most trying to impress.

Question

1 How should Sophie have used the Straight Talk Model to better prepare and communicate the company's message?

two

Define Context Before Speaking or Participating

Great communication takes more than knowing the result you want yourself. When you also focus on your listeners—and their needs—you connect in a way that makes things happen. You create an energy that helps everyone move forward together.

(Kim Rosenblum, Vice President, Creative Director, Nickelodeon)

Analyzing Audiences, Communication Situation, and Message Objectives for Straight Talk Messages

Effective workplace communication requires understanding your target audiences. The more specific that understanding is, the more likely you will succeed. The Straight Talk Model stresses the importance of defining the context for your messages, including the needs and wants of your target audiences. Many communicators use a shotgun approach, shooting in the general direction of the target and hoping to hit something. Professional, successful business communicators today must use a narrow, targeted focus—a rifle approach.

This chapter discusses the steps necessary to do a thorough, in-depth context analysis.

Too many communicators fail to analyze the context effectively, instead giving lip service to the notion of understanding their audience. When a message is important enough to merit preparation, defining the context must precede the other steps in the communication process. Simply put, it is critical to "engage brain before putting mouth into motion." Think carefully about the context as described in this chapter and you will greatly enhance the likelihood of communication success.

Performance Competencies

When you have completed this chapter, you should be able to:

- Recognize that career-damaging communication blunders arise from failure to accurately define the context before speaking.
- Describe and recognize the importance of the factors that comprise the communication context.
- Name seven characteristics of organizational culture that can have an impact on how a message is perceived in that organization.
- Distinguish among three groups of target audiences and explain why each audience may have different needs and wants.
- Use listening skills, observation techniques, and secondary sources to gather context information.
- Define the overall objective, specific purpose, and hidden agenda of any message.

The Way It Is ... Communicating Without a Strategy

Organizational communicators don't always get it right. In fact, there is no shortage of examples of "open-mouth, insert-foot" situations, most of which can be attributed to the failure to consider the communication context.

Careers of prominent people have been damaged or destroyed by misstatements such as unfortunate comments by talk show hosts or politically incorrect comments by actors or other prominent people. Racial insensitivity by celebrities such as Michael Richards (*Seinfeld*'s Kramer), anti-Semitic rants by Mel Gibson (*Braveheart*), misguided cleverness of Don Imus, and others have made front-page news in recent years.

But even among the less famous, failure to consider the audience has posed a trap. A lack of understanding of cross-cultural differences in meaning has provided amusement as well as miscommunication. A few examples:

- Managers at one American company were startled when they discovered that the brand name of the cooking oil they were marketing in a Latin American country translated into Spanish as "Jackass Oil."
- Proctor & Gamble used a television commercial in Japan that was popular in Europe. The ad showed a woman bathing, her husband entering the bathroom and touching her. The Japanese considered this ad an invasion of privacy, inappropriate behavior, and in very poor taste.
- A Japanese manager in an American company was told to give critical feedback to a subordinate during a performance evaluation. Japanese use high context language and are uncomfortable giving direct feedback. It took the manager five tries before he could be direct enough to discuss the poor performance so that the American understood.

- One company printed the "OK" finger sign on each page of its catalogue. In many parts of Latin America, that is considered an obscene gesture. Six months of work were lost because they had to reprint all the catalogues.
- Mountain Bell Company tried to promote its telephone and services to Saudi's. Its ad portrayed an executive talking on the phone with his feet propped up on the desk, showing the soles of his shoes—something an Arab would never do![1]
- VW introduced a new vehicle called the "Bora." In Iceland, the name translates into, essentially, rectum.

But we don't have to look to language differences alone to see failed context analysis. Sometimes, the whole message just doesn't resonate with the audience. For example, Wal-Mart attempt to put a smiley face on its somewhat tarnished image in 2007. The company had been battered by some negative publicity regarding employee relations. It responded by hiring heavy-hitting public-relations firm Edelman, which set about using tactics derived from political races to reverse public perceptions of the giant retailer.

Dubbing its campaign "Candidate Wal-Mart," the firm trumpeted all manner of new Wal-Mart initiatives: improved employee healthcare benefits, higher starting pay levels, new stores in downtrodden neighborhoods, reasonably priced organic foods, and a flat $4 fee for hundreds of generic prescription drugs. While the message content was quite persuasive, the theme just didn't work. As one wag put it, candidate Wal-Mart quickly became, well, the most popular politician since Spiro Agnew. By year's end, Wal-Mart suffered its first quarterly profit drop in a decade, saw same-store sales decline in November's run-up to the crucial holiday shopping season, and suffered a series of public-relations gaffes.[2] People did not respond well to the politician metaphor.

Northwest Airlines (now merged with Delta), while in bankruptcy in 2007, began laying off thousands of ground workers, but not before issuing some of them a handy guide, "101 Ways to Save Money." The advice included dumpster diving ("Don't be shy about pulling something you like out of the trash"), making your own baby food, shredding old newspapers for use as cat litter, and taking walks in the woods as a low-cost dating alternative.[3]

Context problems from hypocrisy of failing companies paying huge salaries to their leaders have become a staple of news in recent years. One example: dodging investors angry over the pay received by Home Depot chairman and CEO Robert Nardelli, who took home at least $120 million over five years as the company's stock price dropped 12 percent, Home Depot's board failed to show up at its annual shareholders' meeting.

The session was presided over solely by Nardelli, who sidestepped all questions ("This is not the forum in which we would address your comment") and cut the meeting short after half-an-hour. The event's negative fallout, highlighted by demonstrators wearing chicken costumes and orange Home Depot aprons, led Nardelli to announce days later that, for next year's meeting, "we will return to our traditional format ... with the board of directors in attendance." Nardelli resigned a few months later, walking away with another $210 million in severance.[4]

And, of course, we have examples from politicians. Phil Gramm, a former Texas senator, spoke as the late 2008 financial crisis spread to Main Street. He appealed to voters and their economic anxieties by calling them a "nation of whiners" and dismissed a troubled economy as a "mental recession."[5] To compound the fallout, Graham was campaign manager for presidential candidate John McCain at the time.

What is the common theme in all these kinds of communication blunders? In each case they reflect a failure to communicate with a carefully thought-out strategy. They reflect a failure to define the context.

Effective communication requires understanding your audiences. The more specific your understanding, the more likely you will succeed. The Straight Talk Model, around which this book is designed, stresses the importance of defining the context for your messages, including limiting your problem and evaluating it with regard to internal culture and external environment, identifying and understanding your audiences, and defining the objectives with those audiences—and then tailoring your message to them.

Will you always communicate perfectly? Of course not. But carefully processing information about the context and factoring it into your preparation will greatly enhance your likelihood for success. Don't use a shotgun approach, shooting in the general direction of the target and hoping to hit something. Use a narrow, targeted focus—a rifle approach—to hit a bull's-eye with your messages.

Understand the Three Factors of Communication Context

This chapter looks in-depth at the processes of context analysis for a given message. This step in the Straight Talk Model reminds you to learn everything you can about the context in which you are communicating. Specifically, this context includes the following:

- The *situation* or problem that causes you to produce your message. (Why are you planning to communicate?)
- Your target *audiences*: primary, hidden, and decision-makers. (To whom are you communicating?)
- Your desired *objectives* with those audiences. (What do you hope to accomplish with your message? What do you want your listeners to do or think?)

Understanding these three factors as you begin to prepare a message will provide a foundation for a successful communication strategy. Start with the existing *situation*—the conditions that create the motivation to communicate. For example, a required sales meeting report is a situation that triggers a need for your presentation of sales results. A scheduled performance review requires some information-gathering interviews. Assignments to explain new policies or to recommend an idea generate the need to communicate. Awareness of the specific situation provides a starting point for context analysis.

At the end of this chapter, you will find two Context Analysis Worksheets. One has been completed as an example; the other is blank for you to copy and use as you plan messages. Within each section of the chapter, we have also included the portions of the Context Analysis Worksheet that deal with the step of the Straight Talk Model being discussed. As you read through the material, try to fill out the portions of the worksheet, using a recent example in which you received or sent a message within an organization.

Define the Situation

Three tasks comprise the process of defining the situation:

1 Limiting the problem.
2 Evaluating the problem within the external climate.
3 Evaluating the corporate (or organizational) culture that affects the problem.

Figure 2.1 shows the portion of the Context Analysis Worksheet that deals with this process. We look at each of these tasks in the following sections.

CONTEXT ANALYSIS WORKSHEET

[Defining the situation]

How should I limit the problem or topic of my message?

What factors in the current business (or organizational) environment may influence my audience's response to my message?

What key elements in the corporate (organizational) culture should I take into account as I prepare my message?

FIGURE 2.1 "Situation" Portion of Context Analysis Worksheet

Limit the Problem

People can go on and on about almost any topic—there are an infinite number of things that can be said even about the most mundane issue. To illustrate this point, we know a professor who stands before his class, holds up a piece of chalk, and asks the class to respond to the question, "What could you say about this piece of chalk?" Once the students begin to respond, they identify a wide range of topics associated with a simple piece of chalk. They suggest talking about uses for chalk, descriptions of its shape and size, the comparative advantages of chalk versus ink markers, its chemical composition, and even the history of the chalk industry. In short, any number of topics for messages could come from focusing on even a simple object. And, of course, most of what could be said is irrelevant to a speaker's purpose. Limiting the scope of your message is critical to good communication.

Because overload is one of today's most pervasive communication barriers, your first challenge when speaking is to isolate the specific issues that you want to address. You can make this decision by focusing on the distinct reason for the message. What happened that caused you or someone else to call this meeting? What's going on? Focus first so that you reduce the risk of babbling later.

For example, if a labor union in your industry is threatening a strike, you might choose to limit your discussion to the current dispute and your opinions about how to resolve it. You should probably avoid discussing the history of labor relations, the pros and cons of having a unionized company, or the personalities of individuals involved. These are givens. Don't get sidetracked off-topic, even if the detour may be interesting to you. Limit your message to information that may best solve the problem or address the concerns of the situation—in this case, limit the topic to issues that may have an impact on the decision to strike.

Evaluate the Problem Within the External Climate

As a professional, you know the value of being well-informed about your business. As a communicator, the best way to evaluate the external environment is to be current on what is happening in your specific industry, in related industries, and in the local and global markets that influence your organization. Watch business television, review websites that cover relevant news, read and clip articles from workplace publications, and subscribe to relevant news sources in order to stay well-informed about issues and events that could affect your and your target audience's organization. Commit to staying abreast of what is happening.

A lack of awareness is illustrated in our opening examples. The communicators should have been aware of the possible negative effects of their messages.

Evaluate Aspects of the Corporate Culture that May Impact on the Problem

The culture of an organization derives from its shared attitudes, beliefs, and meanings, which result in shared behaviors. Recent research summarized by Stephen P. Robbins shows seven primary characteristics that capture the essence of an organization's culture.[6]

- **Innovation and risk-taking.** The degree to which employees are encouraged to be creative, innovative, and to take risks.
- **Attention to detail.** The degree to which employees are expected to exhibit precision, careful analysis, and attention to detail.
- **Outcome orientation.** The degree to which management focuses on results or outcomes rather than on the techniques or processes used to achieve those outcomes.
- **People orientation.** The degree to which management decisions consider the effects of outcomes on people within the organization.
- **Team orientation.** The degree to which work activities are organized around teams rather than individuals.
- **Aggressiveness.** The degree to which people are aggressive and competitive rather than easygoing.
- **Stability.** The degree to which organizational activities emphasize maintaining the status quo in contrast to growth or change.

Key Dimensions in Assessing National Cultures[7]

Organizational cultures are influenced by the national cultures of the people in the organization. With growing globalization and ethnic diversity in companies everywhere, awareness of national culture tendencies becomes increasingly important. (Failing to be aware can lead to the kinds of blunders described in the examples in our "Communicating Without a Strategy" section near the beginning of this chapter.)

Dutch researcher Geert Hofstede has spent his professional career studying the impact of national cultures. His work studied data looking at work-related values of more than 100,000 employees in 40 countries. He found that managers and employees differ on five value dimensions of national culture. As you read these, think about how each might influence a person's communication behaviors.

- **Power distance.** Some cultures put strong emphasis on social classes or socioeconomic levels. People in higher positions would rarely be approached by those in lower circumstances. These class differences are quite rigid. Conversely, some cultures put little emphasis on such status and treat all people equally. The culture of the United States exhibits lower power distance.

- **Individualism versus collectivism.** Some cultures accept or encourage individualism. Others frown on it, instead stressing the value of collective behaviors. People who rate individualism highly tend to look after themselves and their families; people who rate collectivism highly tend to belong to groups and look after each other in exchange for loyalty.
- **Quantity of life versus quality of life.** Quantity of life is the degree to which the society values the accumulation of material things, skills, and attributes. Quality-of-life cultures focus on the value of relationships and showing concern for the welfare of others.
- **Uncertainty avoidance.** Some cultures value predictable and stable structures (individuals tend to become nervous and stressed when the routine is upset). Others encourage innovation and risk-taking, even when it may undermine traditional ways of doing things.
- **Long-term versus short-term orientation.** Some cultures are simply more patient than others, looking to the long term rather than pressing for more rapid changes.

Define Your Audience

The second step in defining the communication context includes identifying and learning about your target audiences. The more specific information you have about your listeners, the better you can tailor your message to their needs and achieve your specific purpose. The most common mistakes we make are generalizing and assuming things about our audiences. The Straight Talk Model provides questions to ask about your audiences that will take you beyond generalizing and assuming. Figure 2.2 shows the portion of the Context Analysis Worksheet that deals with this step.

Identify All Potential Audiences (Distinct or Overlapping)

Inevitably, your message will have more than one audience. Don't risk failure by assuming this is not the case. Let's take a moment to consider three kinds of audiences you are likely to have—primary, hidden, and decision-makers.

- **Primary audience.** The primary audience is easy to identify because they are the individual(s) to whom you address your message—the people "sitting in front of you" when you speak. The primary audience is critical to the success of your communication. However, you should

CONTEXT ANALYSIS WORKSHEET

[Defining the primary audience]

Who is my primary audience (actual receiver of my message)?
- What do I know about him, her, or them personally and professionally (age, gender, educational level, job responsibilities, status, civic and religious affiliation, knowledge of subject, and cultural background)?
- What are his, her, their key attitudes
  - About me?
  - About my subject?
  - About actually being there receiving my message?
- What does my primary audience *want* to know about my subject?
- What is the *consistent concern* that I always hear from such primary audiences?
- Exactly where is my audience on the Persuasion Continuum?
- Therefore, exactly what is my goal with my primary audience?

[Defining other possible audiences]

Who is My Hidden Audience?
- What do I know about him, her, or them?
- What is the *consistent concern* of my hidden audience?
- What is my goal with the hidden audience?

Who is the Decision-Maker?
- What do I know about him, her, or them?
- What is the *consistent concern* of the decision-maker?
- What is my goal with the decision-maker?

FIGURE 2.2 "Audience" Portion of Context Analysis Worksheet

not limit your audience analysis to just these people. In almost every case, you need to think about other audiences as well.

- **Hidden audience.** The hidden audience is composed of those people who influence your primary audience or your decision-makers. Because of their influence, this audience may not be directly connected with your communication purpose or process but may have some power over you. For example, your supervisor may not directly observe your message but is likely to hear about it. Another example of a hidden audience may be a supervisor in another department who has had her eye on you for a possible promotion. A powerful hidden audience may be your target listener's spouse or significant other, who influences the listener's decisions—and is totally outside of your control.

- **Decision-maker.** The decision-maker is your most important listener(s), even in situations in which this audience gets information second-hand from your primary audience. In the workplace, this is likely to be your boss. Your work associates may be the primary audience, but the boss will be the one evaluating your job performance. Similarly, someone outside the primary audience may well make a final decision on your proposal. (Often, organizations observe a chain of command, limiting formal communication with only one's immediate boss. He or she then takes your ideas to his or her boss who holds the authority to decide. In such cases, the decision-maker may not even hear your message first-hand.)

An example of these three types of audiences might be illustrated by a situation in which customers come to your office for a sales presentation. Your primary audience is that group of customers. Your hidden audience might be your division manager, who tends to drop in on sales presentations and who has power over your career advancement. Another hidden audience might be colleagues of your customers who have had some experience with you or your company. Your decision-maker may be someone in the customer's organization who did not attend your presentation but who will make a decision based on the reports of the employees who did attend.

This may all seem complicated, but these are the realities of the business world. Communicators who simplify too much and think only of the obvious primary audience in front of them often fail to accomplish their objectives. The Straight Talk Model reminds us to think through some of these complexities.

Learn About Each Audience

Focus on the facts, attitudes, wants, and concerns of each audience. To the extent possible, learn as much as you can about each audience using the kinds of questions on the Context Analysis Worksheet. Make an effort to focus on the following four activities:

1 Gather personal and professional facts.
2 Consider audience attitudes.
3 Evaluate audience "wants" and your "needs."
4 Look for consistent concerns.

Gather Personal and Professional Facts
Some key information about your audience may include age, gender, education level, cultural background, religious preferences, personal values, job responsibilities and status, as well as their knowledge of your topic. Although this data may not all be readily available, work to consider these and any other personal information that may be useful in better understanding your audiences. Let's look a bit more closely at examples of the potential value of some such data.

- **Age, gender, and education level.** Your message may be phrased much differently for an audience of young, ambitious, entry-level employees than for a group of senior managers. Younger, ambitious audiences may be more likely to be motivated by opportunities to make more personal income or develop their careers, whereas senior managers may find that less relevant. Also, marketing research into various generations reveals wide differences about what works with each. For example, "Generation-Y" (people between 25–40 years of age, generally) responds far better to visual, symbolic images, and less well to text. Giving a long, wordy handout will probably be a waste of paper when dealing with Gen-Y audiences.[8]

Communication Expectations of "Net-Generation" Audiences

The first generation to come of age in the digital age has been dubbed the "Net Generation." This age group relates to technology far differently than their baby-boomer parents. They are comfortable acclimated to life in today's high-speed, interactive world. They also adhere to a set of norms that are transforming work and the ways we communicate at work—not just the mechanical, technical aspects of communication, but the underlying psychology as well.

One workplace norm cited in Don Tapscott's excellent book, *Grown Up Digital* is the notion that "teamwork is not just motherhood." Tapscott contrasts the boomers who grew up with hierarchies—at home, at school, at work. The Net Generation is not turned on by status or hierarchy. They want to do challenging work, but don't necessarily want organizational responsibility. "Their dream job gives them chances to work on problems or dilemmas no one knows how to solve and offers them lots of great people to work with."[9]

Net-Genner norms also assume that they can and should speak up without regard for organizational position and that the company should always be transparent with them. These norms are not commonly accepted by older workers or by workers from some national cultures.

Context analysis that misreads these kinds of audience norms run a significant risk of producing ineffective communication.

Recognize, too, that your gender can influence communication effectiveness. Studies consistently show that men and women often communicate differently. And even when they communicate the same way, men and women are often perceived differently by their target audiences.

- **Cultural background, religious or ethical beliefs, and personal values.** A person's national culture as well as the cultures their families may have brought with them through the generations have an impact on their values and, thus, on what motivates them. Similarly, people who are involved in religious activities may base their thinking on how an idea fits with their view of ethics or appropriate behavior. Personal values about such things as physical fitness, intellectual activities, social or political activism, family concerns, and use of financial resources can color the way people receive and process new information.

- **Job responsibilities and status.** People from different levels in an organization may look at issues in different ways. In traditional organizations, the higher the position a person holds, the more likely he or she will be managing complex problems and taking a larger view of recommended actions. Lower-level employees may see issues through the lens of their limited experience or their immediate department. However, as modern organizations become less hierarchical and more team-oriented, this distinction between so-called levels becomes blurred. Many of today's organizations downplay status differences and work hard to be sure employees throughout the company are fully engaged in multiple aspects of the business.

- **Knowledge of your topic.** How much people already know about your topic will impact on how you should develop your message. If your audience has sufficient background experience, you can probably move more quickly through your material or ask for a greater commitment to your objectives. If your audience knows little about your topic or seems confused, you will have to provide appropriate background before you can persuade.

Knowing about the demographics, values, attitudes, and predispositions of your audiences can give you hints as to how listeners may react to what you say. For example, as we mentioned, older workers may be more loyal to the ways things have always been done and might be resistant to changes you are recommending. They tend to be less adaptive to technology, for example. Audience members who are active in religious organizations may respond well to your recommendation of a charitable activity or your discussion of ethical issues. People in lower levels of responsibility may resist additional overtime work, whereas higher-level personnel may accept the need to work longer hours in order to maximize their bonuses.

Be careful, however, to remember that these generalizations are just that—generalizations. Communicators run the risk of stereotyping when they take an oversimplified view of groups of people. Ultimately, the best option is to interact with people as individuals, not as categories.

Think carefully about past experiences with the people to whom you will communicate. If you don't know your target audience personally, talk to others who do. Then, the longer you work with individuals, the more you are likely to know about them. Finally, consider your experience with similar people in similar situations.

Review all pertinent information and make notes. Seriously. Take the time and effort to make notes about potential audience members. Ask questions. Don't assume an oversimplified view of a group of people is accurate. Then make your best guesses about how they are likely to respond to your ideas or proposals. You cannot predict with 100 percent accuracy how people will react, but the more information you have, the better your predictions will be.

Consider Audience Attitudes Toward You and Your Topic

How does your audience feel about you, about your topic, and about being there to listen to you? Honesty may force you to acknowledge that your audience really doesn't want to deal with you or your topic. They may prefer to not hear your presentation, work with you in a team, or attend your meeting. They may be busy and uninterested and resent having to spend the time on this issue.

A classic example (which we can verify) is when a company hires consultants to teach presentation skills. The consultants need to ask themselves questions such as, "What are likely to be our audience's attitudes about us or the topic of our message (i.e., attending a training program)?" Most employees know little about the consultants personally, and they may hate the idea of going to a "speaking course." They may have a desk full of work and a to-do list a mile long, and they may resent their bosses telling them to attend. They may fear such a course—after all, public speaking has been rated as the number-one human fear by surveys. (Death is apparently second!) Honest consultants would probably conclude that their primary audience would rather be thrown into a pit of snakes than attend speech training. The consultants' work is cut out for them well before getting into the actual content of their training course.

Realistic audience analysis prepares you for handling reluctant message-receivers and likely listener objections. As disillusioning as it may be, you *will* face times when your audience would rather be somewhere else, with someone else, doing something else, rather than talking with or listening to you. Don't assume that just because it's part of their job to receive and respond to your message that they really care. Anticipate their specific needs and give them something to *motivate* them to care.

Evaluate Audience "Wants" and Your "Needs"

After facing the potentially cruel realities of listener attitudes toward you (what's not to like??!), your next step is to determine exactly what your audience wants to know. Your job is to give them their "wants" before you ask them to do something that meets your "needs." In other words, you must satisfy their information hunger before you ask them to change their beliefs or behavior. Until you tell people what they *want* to know, they will never hear what you *need* them to know to fulfill the purpose of your message.

For example, your task may be to develop a presentation and a series of follow-up meetings with employees to explain changes in job responsibilities after a company reorganization. The employees, however, may not be willing to focus on the details of their job descriptions until you tell them about the security of their jobs or the status of their benefit plans. Satisfy your audience's information needs first.

Look for Consistent Concerns

Most people with whom you interact regularly express continuing interest in some key issues or themes. In today's world, the threat of terrorism has become a consistent concern for business that had never seriously considered it a few years ago. Similarly, computer hackers or viruses are relatively new consistent concerns that were less common a decade ago. Recessions, economic downturn, increasing regulation, undesirable publicity, the perception of unethical behaviors or wasteful spending ... the list goes on. (Sorry to be so depressing.)

Remember, too, that each individual in your target audience might have his or her own consistent concerns. For most people, job security, personal safety, opportunity for satisfying work, and the need to balance work and personal lives are ongoing concerns. In addition, various functions in a company have different consistent concerns. For example, employees with financial responsibilities usually will have questions about cost, Human Resource professionals express interest in personnel issues, and the Public Relations team watches image and reputation. Of course, politicians have a consistent concern about being re-elected, and, along that same line of thinking, most organizations have their own kind of "corporate politics" that create underlying, consistent concerns.

Define Your Objectives With Each Audience

The third element of defining communication context is to specify your objectives with each of your audiences. Most messages, no matter how apparently simple, encompass three objectives: an overall goal, a specific communication purpose, and a hidden agenda. Figure 2.3 shows the portion of the Context Analysis Worksheet that focuses on this step. We will look at each of these objectives in the following sections.

CONTEXT ANALYSIS WORKSHEET

[Defining objectives with each audience]

- What are my objectives with my primary audience?

- What are my objectives with other possible audiences?

FIGURE 2.3 "Objectives" Portion of Context Analysis Worksheet

Define an Overall Goal

The overall goal is your long-range plan or major desired result. For example, a student's overall goal might be to graduate with a specific degree or prepare for graduate study. The overall goal for an employee seeking a job might be to match his or her experience and skill set with the needs of a socially conscious company. An entrepreneur might want to launch a new business. An overall goal for a career would probably be to move into higher levels of responsibility in an organization or to build the company to a certain size. In corporate communication, the overall goal is often based on the mission statement of the organization. For example, the overall goal of a presentation about the budget for the next quarter might reflect the company's commitment to increase the value of its stock, or your luncheon speech at a civic club might focus on the president's initiative to "give something back" to the community.

While companies are not always faithful to their stated intentions, mission statements are intended to be an expression of an organization's vision and values—what it cares about and where it is going. Some companies do a good job of identifying—and talking about—their core values and how these impact the company. David Neeleman, the founding CEO of JetBlue Airways (a remarkable success story in a difficult industry) took frequent opportunities to recite the company's core values in speeches and interviews: "For our company's core values, we came up with five words: safety, caring, fun, integrity, and passion. We guide our company by them."[10] Such statements define the constant concerns of the company's leaders. The overall goal of any communication within that company should involve being congruent with these core values.

Here is the Coca-Cola Company's mission statement for stakeholders:[11]

> The Coca-Cola Promise: The Coca-Cola Company exists to benefit and refresh everyone it touches. The basic proposition of our business is simple, solid, and timeless. When we bring refreshment, value, joy and fun to our stakeholders, then we successfully nurture and protect our

brands, particularly Coca-Cola. That is the key to fulfilling our ultimate obligation to provide consistently attractive returns to the owners of our business.

The audience for this mission is all the company's stakeholders—employees, investors, customers, the media, the public—well, yes, just about everyone who knows about Coke. The values here are stated explicitly: refreshment, value, joy, fun, and attractive returns. These words were obviously carefully chosen by those who then crafted this mission statement. The "ultimate obligation" of "attractive returns" is a powerful way to state the company's vision and keeps the values stated in context.

Any communications from or within Coke are strengthened by consistently adhering to and reinforcing these values, these overall goals. The same principle applies to your business or organization.

Identify the Specific Purpose of the Communication

The specific purpose of a message depends on your needs and on your analysis of target audiences. Ask yourself, *"Exactly what do I want to occur* as a result of this message?" Failing to articulate a specific purpose is an all-too-frequent pitfall for ineffective communicators. For example, in the job-search process, the specific purpose of a cover letter or telephone contact may be to get an interview. The specific purpose of a first interview is to be invited back for a second interview. The specific purpose of the quarterly budget briefing might be to clearly explain each department's need to cut expenses and get them to take action that will do so. The specific purpose of a CEO's presentation at an annual shareholder meeting would be to explain past performance, preview future actions, and keep people enthusiastic about their investment in the company.

Be realistic about how much you can accomplish with a single communication attempt. Persuasion, especially, is a process that is seldom fully accomplished with one message. Most audiences consist of people with various levels of willingness to accept your ideas. Often, the best a speaker can hope for is to move the listener a little closer to the overall goal—to move people through the "sales cycle"—the steps customers typically go through before actually buying. If, for example, you are in the market for a new computer, an effective salesperson would move you through the sales cycle by:

- Initiating or establishing contact with a potential customer.
- Giving you information about the computer orally and offering a brochure.
- Inviting you to see the computer in the store or a demonstration room.

- Encouraging you to try the computer, using some of its features.
- Preparing the paperwork for the purchase.
- Delivering and possibly installing the computer.

Each of these actions is a step in the sales cycle. A typical buyer would go through all the steps. Each step in the process has a specific communication objective: to move the target audience to the next step.

The Persuasion Continuum

Since your goal in functional communication is most often to persuade others, you need to be realistic about your chances. The process of your communicated message can be visualized as a continuum from 0 to 10, where 0 represents, "I know (or care) nothing about this," and 10 represents, "I'm ready to sign on the dotted line!" (Or, 0 is, "Who is this Pat person applying for the Senior Manager position?" and 10 is, "Let's hire Pat for the job!")

Communicators hurt their effectiveness when they assume that their audience knows or cares more than they actually do and asks those audiences to move too quickly up the continuum. You must work to accurately assess where your audience is on the continuum, and then set a reasonable, specific objective. You generally can't get from 0 to 10 in one message. A more realistic goal would be to move them from complete ignorance to partial knowledge of an issue. For example, your specific purpose might be to take your audience from a "0" ("We don't need interns in our department") to a "3" ("An intern would be a low-cost solution for the extra help we need on our summer projects"). This is much the way a car salesperson moves a customer from browsing through the lot ("2"), to sitting inside a car ("4"), to taking a test drive ("6"), to going inside to discuss terms ("7"), to signing a contract ("10").

Acknowledge Your Hidden Agenda

Finally, as you specify your objectives, be honest about your hidden agenda—personal goals to which you are aspiring. Although the term often connotes some level of duplicity—some way of deceiving others—it need not be interpreted in such negative terms. Everybody has hidden agenda. This is perfectly normal.

For example, your business-related hidden agenda may be to be perceived by your co-workers as a leader, to earn a promotion, to move to another department, or to be considered for additional training or opportunities. If you acknowledge these intentions and factor them into your planning, you can make a conscious effort to include information that would demonstrate your leadership potential or value to the company. Make this part of your context analysis and planning. Remember that every time you speak—in any situation—you have the opportunity to nudge your target audiences toward the goal of your hidden agenda. Successful people always have this in mind when they communicate.

Gather the Information You Need

The process of defining your communication context requires gathering good information and using that information to tailor your message. This is where all the parts of your Context Analysis Worksheet come together. Getting the information necessary to complete this worksheet is not always easy, but it is always worth the effort. The good news is that this preparation part of the model becomes easier and faster with practice. The more often you ask the questions, the sooner you will learn which ones are intuitive defaults for you and which ones need extra effort.

The most common information-gathering approaches are listening, observing, and reading secondary sources. Let's talk a bit about each of these.

Use Listening as an Information-Gathering Technique

Ironically, of the four basic communication skills—reading, writing, speaking, and listening—only listening is rarely taught in formal classes. Yet, of all the communication skills, listening may actually be the most important. So, if you think you are a lousy listener, it's not all your fault, and you are not alone! In any case, it deserves more attention than it typically gets.

Some people think that listening is passive—it's really just a matter of sitting back and letting the talker have his or her say. In reality, it is a highly active mental process that takes two forms: *support listening* and *retention listening*. Support listening consists of giving people enough feedback so that they thoroughly express their thoughts. Retention listening emphasizes techniques for capturing information from what is said. Let's look at each listening approach.

Use Support Listening

The intent of support listening is to learn what a person thinks and feels. When gathering information with support listening, avoid speaking except to encourage the other person to elaborate. (Yes, this can be difficult! Most of us prefer to jump in and "share" our thoughts.) Support listening seeks to draw out people's feelings and ideas by using non-evaluative responses such as the following:

- **"Go on" comments.** "Uh-huh" is the simplest kind of oral response and consists of saying "uh-huh" or "hmmm" as other people talk to encourage them to continue to clarify their thoughts. Open questions that cannot be answered with a simple "yes" or "no" statement are also useful.
- **Content reflection.** Repeat, mirror, or echo the statement made by another person in the form of a question. Be careful you don't use a tone of voice that implies a judgment. You simply repeat what was said in essentially the same words and wait for further elaboration or clarification.
- **Non-verbal encouragement.** Let the speaker know that you are focusing on him or her. Make eye contact. Nod your head (but recognize that the speaker could perceive an "I'm listening" nod to mean "Yes"). Be aware of non-verbal behavior that could discourage the speaker.

For example, a corporate executive who was often interviewed on camera tended to create little frown lines between his eyebrows when he concentrated. He looked angry, which was not the image he wanted in the media. His communication consultant advised him to adopt a new "listening face"—raising his eyebrows slightly instead of knitting them together. When he remembers to do that, he is sending the non-verbal message of being receptive to questions rather than being annoyed by them.

Suppose you are gathering information from a customer about an unpleasant experience they had. If you reflect their comments using support listening, it may sound something like this:

CUSTOMER: I am very disappointed with the service I am getting from your company. It sucks.

YOU: You're disappointed with our service. I'm sorry to hear that.

CUSTOMER: I'm about ready to look somewhere else.

YOU: Hmmm. (nodding)

CUSTOMER: Yes, I thought you'd provide a replacement unit when mine is in for servicing without any hassle.

YOU: You want a replacement while yours is being serviced.

CUSTOMER: Yeah, it's too much of a hassle to have to shut down while you guys do maintenance.

YOU: Uh-huh. I understand why you would feel that way.

By using message-reflection and support-listening, you gained additional information about the reason for the customer's unhappiness. Now you can offer ideas that may solve the problem and save the customer. If you had not listened carefully, you may have jumped to inaccurate conclusions about the causes of his dissatisfaction. Reinforcing with support listening rather than challenging ("Our service is actually very good!") can tip you off to the kind of message that can persuade the customer ("We can arrange for a replacement unit and will do so to keep you as a satisfied customer").

Use Retention Listening

Retention listening calls for techniques that help you remember and use information you hear. The following are some tips for improving your retention:

- **Minimize distractions.** Concentrate on the speaker. Force yourself to keep your mind on what the speaker is saying, and avoid multitasking. Trying to do other things while listening simply does not work.
- **Recognize opportunities.** Do your best to find areas of interest between yourself and the speaker. Ask yourself, "What's in it for me? What can I get out of what this person is saying?" Identify the speaker's purpose. Is this person trying to inform you, or persuade you, or is he or she perhaps just trying to entertain you?
- **Stay alert.** Avoid daydreaming. If the person you are listening to is a bit boring, force yourself to stay alert. If your thoughts run ahead of the speaker, use the extra time to evaluate, anticipate, and review.
- **Listen for central themes rather than for isolated facts.** Too often, people get hopelessly lost as listeners because they focus on unimportant facts and details and miss the speaker's main point.
- **Take notes efficiently.** The simple process of writing key ideas as you hear them helps you retain information. People are often flattered when you convey that their ideas are worth jotting down.
- **Plan to report the content of a message to someone within 24 hours.** This forces you to concentrate and to remember. It is a good practice technique.

Use Observation as an Information-Gathering Technique

You can observe a great deal by watching. (Yogi Berra)

Much of the information needed to tailor your communications can be gathered by observation. This is particularly true when considering the corporate culture (many facets of which are readily observable) and the external climate. We learn about these things by systematically observing and carefully reading.

Of course, be aware that you may not get good information based on one or two haphazard observations. A better technique is to plan to systematically observe in certain ways over a period of time so that what you see is more likely to be common occurrences, not fluke behaviors. Multiple observations of the same or similar behaviors are better than just one look. If you suspect a problem or sense that an issue needs to be researched, make the effort to observe relevant behaviors systematically.

For example, if a particular product in your company's product line is not selling as well as it should, you may schedule systematic observations of customer behaviors. Select random times to observe how people look at or touch the product. Observe customer traffic patterns in your store. Do people seem to walk past the product without looking at it? Are customers hesitant to pick up the product or look more closely at it? Do they seem to react negatively when they see the price? Is the packaging hard to hold or so dull that people don't seem to notice it? These are the kinds of questions that can be answered in part by observation of customer behavior.

Observations of employee behaviors can reveal needed information. Increases in absenteeism and turnover (people quitting), or decline in work quality or willingness to work "over and above," are good indicators that something is amiss in working conditions or job satisfaction. Be sure to observe specific *behaviors* and not make guesses about attitudes or "morale."

Read Secondary Sources as an Information-Gathering Technique

A secondary source of information is an article, report, statistic, or other document already written about a topic. Researchers often look first at such sources to see what has already been discovered rather than starting from the beginning and repeating someone's efforts. Reading such printed materials or studying information on the Internet are excellent ways to gather information about the context of your communication. In the past, reviewing secondary sources required library research, but today your "library" exists in cyberspace. With the Internet you have a wealth of information available at the stroke of a few keys.

Searches often start with a few keystrokes into Google or similar search engines. Often, longer strings of search terms get more targeted results. For example, typing in the phrase "employee morale" is unlikely to get very specific information. A phrase such as "assembly line employee morale and productivity" would probably be better.

With a little effort, you can become very familiar with the kinds of issues facing any industry or company. Use this secondary information to enrich your knowledge of the company or industry and to better define the context of your message. If your research reveals that the industry is facing serious profit problems due to increased competition, for example, you need to consider that fact as you plan your messages.

You can also gather a lot of information about individual audience members. Again, using a search engine such as Google, simply type in the name of a target listener and see what comes up. People need not be famous to be listed.

If your listener has written articles, been listed on the company Web page, or engaged in various activities, there is a fairly good chance that he or she will show up on Google. Incidentally, if you are planning an interview, you would be foolish to not Google the other party before meeting. (This applies regardless of which side of the table you are on—interviewer or interviewee.)

Use the Context Analysis Worksheet

Figure 2.4 is a completed Context Analysis Worksheet for a business presentation. The speaker's assignment is to prepare a persuasive presentation encouraging workers in the company to accept a proposed company reorganization. Let's see how this might look.

CONTEXT ANALYSIS WORKSHEET

How should I limit the problem or topic of my message?
Stick to proposed consolidation of marketing and sales only. Avoid discussion of future possibilities.

What factors in the business environment may influence the audience's response to my message?
Consolidation of functions has led to reduction in force at some companies; marketing people feel superior to sales reps—see selves as the "big thinkers"; sales reps see marketers as "pie-in-the-sky" thinkers who don't know how tough it is to get out and really sell.

What key elements of corporate culture should be taken into account as I prepare my message?
Marketing seen as "elite"; successful sales reps make a lot of money (commissions) which creates resentment.

Who is my primary audience (actual receiver of my message)?
Employees of the affected departments.

What do I know about him/her/them personally and professionally (age, gender, education, job responsibility and status, civic and religious affiliation, knowledge of subject, cultural background)?
Sales guys are younger (age 25–33), 75% male, more brash, big egos—see marketers as support but not all that sharp; current marketing manager is in 60s, his staff in 40s or older. Marketers have advanced degrees, sales people only bachelor degrees or less; sales guys don't always understand marketing; mktg people seen as theoretical but no hands on selling skills; sales people more active in civic activities; marketing manager is very active in church work.

What is his/her/their attitude about me?
Both factions see me as a possible hatchet-person. I have less tenure with company than most, came from a competitor; they may not trust me. I am seen as a favorite of the CEO and as having strong ambitions to become top executive. They fear I am more concerned about me than them.

About my subject?
Most see that marketing and sales have not been working well together—seem to butt heads. Some kind of change may be welcome although any change is potentially threatening.

How does audience feel about being there to receive my message?
The sales people hate most meetings that take them away from their outside customer calls; they have a short attention span.

What does my audience *want* to know about my subject?
All parties want enough details about how it'll affect them personally.

What is the *consistent concern* that I always hear from my audience?
Fear of job insecurity; need to stay competitive to ensure organizational and personal success.

Exactly where is my audience on the persuasive continuum?
They have had some negative experiences with organizational changes in the past and may be hesitant to make an immediate commitment.

Therefore, exactly what is my goal with my primary audience?
I want them to evaluate and give constructive feedback about this proposed consolidation; be willing to have a conversation.

Who is my hidden audience?
My boss, the Board of Directors, families of impacted employees.

What do I know about him/her/them? What consistent concerns do they have?
Have a general trust that the company will do the right and ethical things. Wants to keep employees engaged. Values cooperation, no unnecessary boat-rocking.
Boss and Board want innovation and cost-effectiveness to boost profits. Families want secure income, family members to be happy, engaged at work (not grumpy)
Some concern about "too many changes, too fast."

What is my goal with the hidden audience?
Project security; reassure that core values are at the heart of the proposed change.

Who is the decision-maker?
Need buy-in from all departments (eventually) to succeed. Target opinion leaders first.

What do I know about him/her/them? What are their consistent concerns?
Key people (opinion leaders) share company vision and goals generally. Some want the number of changes to slow down so we can "catch our breath."
Want to be seen as loyal; maintain trust of others—not seen as the boss's lap dog.

What is the goal with the decision-maker?
Gain enthusiastic acceptance of the planned change (or a slightly modified version).

What is my hidden agenda?
To look like a capable, effective leader—a skilled negotiator who may be ready for advancement in the company.
To maintain friendships and goodwill with employees.

Other observations:
Highlight that Jones is in agreement even though he may stand the most to lose.
Don't ignore that competition X is trying to hire sales people like ours—we don't want to lose any.
Consolidation really will be a win-win.

FIGURE 2.4 A Completed Context Analysis Worksheet for a Business Presentation

Figure 2.5 is a blank Context Analysis Worksheet that you may photo-copy for your own use. This worksheet pulls together all the separate work-sheet elements you have seen throughout the chapter. As you review it, be sure that you understand what information should be placed in each section. If you are unclear about any section, review the material in this chapter.

CONTEXT ANALYSIS WORKSHEET

How should I limit the problem or topic of my message (immediate issue)?

_____

What factors in the current business environment may influence the audi-ence's response to me message?

_____

What key elements of corporate culture (both mine and theirs) should be taken into account as I prepare my message?

_____

Who is my primary audience (actual receiver of my message)?

_____

What do I know about him/her/them personally and professionally (age, gender, education, job responsibility and status, civic and religious affiliation, knowledge of subject, cultural background?

_____

_____

What is his/her/their attitude about me?

_____

About my subject?

_____

How does audience feel about being there to receive my message?

_____

What does my audience _want_ to know about my subject?

_____

What is the _consistent concern_ that I always hear from my audience?

_____

Exactly where is my audience on the persuasive continuum?

_____

Therefore, exactly what is my goal with my primary audience?

_____

Who is my hidden audience?

_____

What do I know about him/her/them? What consistent concerns do they have?

_____

_____

What is my goal with the hidden audience?

_____

Who is the decision-maker?

_____

What do I know about him/her/them? What are their consistent concerns?

_____

_____

What is the goal with the decision-maker?

_____

What is my hidden agenda?

_____

Other observations:

_____

_____

_____

_____

_____

FIGURE 2.5 A Blank Context Analysis Worksheet

Performance Checklist

After completing this chapter, you should be better able to use key principles of oral communication and avoid some common pitfalls. Specifically, you should now understand that:

- Message effectiveness is dramatically affected when you take the time and make the effort to carefully define the context for your business messages.
- The communication context consists of the specific problem or issue, the audiences, and your specific objectives with each audience.
- Limiting the problem, evaluating the external climate, and evaluating the corporate (or organizational) culture are important planning activities.
- Factors such as age, gender, and national cultures have an impact on people's work values.
- Key dimensions of different national cultures include power distance (status differences), individualism, quantity of life (materialism), uncertainty avoidance (versus risk-taking), and long-term versus short-term orientation.
- Three groups of target audiences should be considered as you define your context: primary, hidden, and decision-makers. These may be different people who have different informational needs and wants. These groups can also overlap.
- Context-analysis information can be gathered by careful listening, systematic observation, and review of secondary sources.
- Two types of listening can be effective: support listening and retention listening.
- The Context Analysis Worksheet is a useful tool for planning any message.

What Do You Know?

Activity 2.1: Defining the Context

Complete a Context Analysis Worksheet for one of the following situations.

1   You have been asked to give a sales presentation to introduce a new product or service to a target audience of potentially profitable buyers. The product or service is revolutionary and your audience is unfamiliar with the technical aspects of it.
2   You want to prepare a message advocating a zoning change that will permit your company to build a youth recreation center in an area where several senior citizen apartment complexes are located. The residents are upset about possible disruptions to their quiet neighborhood. You will present this to the seniors at their activity center.

3 You are preparing a presentation advocating the abolishment of a department or product line your company currently has. Your primary audience is the CEO and Executive staff. The CEO often speaks about "streamlining" the company. Her favorite phrase is, "Good is the enemy of great and we need to be great."

4 You have been asked to speak to a university student entrepreneurs club that focuses on teaching people how to start and run their own businesses. Your company occasionally provides support for launching potentially profitable businesses but these grants are very scarce and highly competitive. Your audience will be about 100 students. Most are juniors or seniors at a four-year college of business.

Activity 2.2: Determining How Well Others Define Their Contexts

Do an Internet search of current business sources to find companies that have recently experienced unfavorable publicity (www.money.cnn.com is a source we used for several of the "business blunders" we highlighted at the beginning of the chapter. But don't stop there). These cases may be companies whose products are defective, whose service practices are substandard or unethical, or whose sales results are declining sharply. In short, the company faces a crisis.

Review the ways the company communicated with their various audiences in light of the material discussed in this chapter. Prepare a brief oral report (three minutes or less) on why these companies have been effective or ineffective in dealing with the crisis, and how they have used or failed to use effective context analysis.

Activity 2.3: Gathering Information on Corporate Culture

Recently hired employees are a valuable resource for information on the corporate culture in which they work. As newer employees, they are often just figuring out the culture. Interview one or more recently hired people in your organization to gather information about how they see the organization's corporate culture. Design questions that you can ask to discover the seven primary culture characteristics of the company:

- Innovation and risk-taking (example question: "Can you tell me about a time when an employee was rewarded for innovating thinking or risk-taking?").
- Attention to detail.
- Outcome orientation.
- People orientation.

- Team orientation.
- Aggressiveness.
- Stability.

Prepare a summary report on your findings. Then analyze how effectively the organization's communication behaviors seem to reinforce the culture (or not).

Activity 2.4: Practicing Listening Skills

Prepare to interview a business executive—preferably someone in a higher-level position than yours—to explore ways in which communication strategy has contributed to his or her success. Thoroughly researched the organization and the person before the interview. Outline the specific information-gathering sources you will use for this interview.

- **Company.** List the name of the company in which you would like to conduct the interview.
- **Listening strategy.** During the interview, what information do you hope to gather? When will you begin gathering information? Who can be sources of information?
- **Support questions.** List some open-ended questions you will ask. Describe how you will reflect the content of this statement: "When I graduated from college, I thought that all that strategy stuff was only theoretical. But once I began working in business, I realized that I needed to use communication strategy on a daily basis."
- **Retention tactics.** What will you do if there is a noisy distraction in the hallway? What materials will you bring to ensure that you can take notes? How will you locate central themes? What form will your "report" take and when will you prepare it?
- **Observation strategy.** What opportunities will you have to observe the organization? Whom will you observe? When will your observation begin?
- **Secondary-source strategy.** What secondary sources are available to you? List at least four. Where will you find them? When will you access the sources? How will you let your interviewer know that you have researched the company?

Activity 2.5: Analyzing Your Peer as Your Audience (a Classroom Activity)

This activity is helpful if you are using this material in a class. Since your peers will make up the audience for your in-class presentations, it is helpful to analyze your peers. Pair up with a classmate and analyze him or her as an audience member, including personal and professional facts, attitudes, "wants," and consistent concerns. Complete a Context Analysis Worksheet detailing what you have discovered in your analysis. Prepare a copy of your worksheet for the class or team to discuss. Write an assessment of the accuracy of your analysis based on the discussion of your worksheet.

Reinforce With These Review Questions

1 Name the three factors that constitute the communication context: (1) _____, (2) _____, and (3) _____.

2 True/False—Limiting the topic of a message is critical to communication effectiveness.

3 True/False—The culture of an organization is a constantly changing feature that need not be considered when communicating.

4 Name three kinds of target audiences that should be considered as we define the context for a message: (1) _____, (2) _____, and (3) _____.

5 True/False—Focusing a message on the audience's needs and concerns is far more important that focusing on your own needs.

6 True/False—Typically, your objectives are the same with all audiences.

7 True/False—An overall goal is often different from the specific purpose of a message.

8 The chapter discusses two forms of listening. These are _____ listening and _____ listening.

9 Name three ways we can gather information about our audiences: (1) _____, (2) _____, and (3) _____.

10 True/False—Context analysis is fundamental to effective communication.

Mini-Case Study: Why Are You Telling Us This?

International Week was billed as an excellent opportunity for executives from around the world to come to a major European MBA school to learn and share ideas. More than 100 mid-level executives flew into town for the event. They came from across Europe, North and South America, and Asia. All were currently engaged in or had recently completed MBA studies.

Following the first day's get-acquainted activities and social opportunities, the attendees were bused from the conference hotel across town to the host school for a "welcome" session. The school's Rector greeted them warmly in a fairly formal speech in the school's main auditorium. He then announced that a cocktail reception and light supper would be served. But first, several leaders of the University wanted to "say a few words."

What followed was a 20-minute "update" about what was going on at the university, complete with multiple PowerPoint slides. The Associate Rector over Business Studies programs delivered an elaborate description of the school's undergraduate and MBA programs encompassing full-time local students and several international and online options. She told the audience in considerable detail the requirements of each program, and offered anecdotes about successful student experiences. She also proudly trumpeted accomplishments in earning accreditation and of individual faculty.

The visiting guests listened patiently at first, but as the speeches droned on, they became visibly bored. At one point, a visitor from Korea (a nation whose culture stresses politeness) leaned over to his classmate and asked, "Why are they telling us all this? I already have my MBA."

Questions

1   How does this brief story illustrate ineffective context analysis? Where did the school go wrong?
2   What are some ways this "update" could backfire with the current audience?
3   What cultural expectation may have been violated by this presentation?
4   If you felt a need for such an update, how might you have communicated this information differently?

three

Consider Your Media, Source, and Timing Options

Sometimes just waiting one day to present an idea can make all the difference in the world. For great ideas to turn into great solutions, they have to fall on ears that are ready to hear them.

(Carol Gallagher, *Going to the Top*)

Selecting Options Before Communicating

Never in history has a communicator had so many choices of media. The options selected can and will have an effect on message impact and communication success. Before creating the content of a message, Straight Talk communicators think carefully about media as well as the available source and timing alternatives. To go forward without such forethought is a formula for potential disaster.

Performance Competencies

When you have completed this chapter, you should be able to:

- Recognize the advantages and disadvantages of using different communication media, source, and timing options.
- Describe how communication media trigger certain expectations in message receivers, present trade-offs between efficiency and effectiveness, and have unique capabilities.
- Explain the distinction between communication efficiency and communication effectiveness.

- Select appropriate media based on characteristics such as speed, feedback capacity, hard-copy availability, message intensity and complexity, formality, and relative costs.
- Describe some ways to mix media to improve effectiveness.
- Determine the most optimal source and timing options for your messages.
- Explain how media, source, and timing options are determined by the audience; "it's not about you."

The Way It Is . . . Wilbur Jackson's Outburst

In an employee meeting, Wilbur Jackson, the department manager, announced the following:

> Okay, people, I have one other thing to announce, and it is not open to discussion. I'm only going to say it one time, and I expect things to improve. It has recently come to my attention that department employees are taking excessively long coffee breaks. These violate company policy. Employees caught taking more than 15 minutes in the morning and afternoon will be terminated. If things don't improve, the coffee break room will be closed. I trust you will obey policy in the future regarding this matter.

With that said, Wilbur walked out of the room without a further word.

What problems do you see with this little speech? You could cite its tone and its abruptness, but a more basic problem arises from Wilbur's decision to make this speech in the first place. It is an ineffective communication medium for this message. Wilbur chose the "easy way" to deal with a problem and, in so doing, probably created more problems than he solved.

Suppose that you work for Wilbur and that you have been very careful to limit your coffee breaks to less than 15 minutes. Further, suppose that you often forego breaks to meet the demands of your job. How would you react to this announcement? Suppose Wilbur's message came shortly after you had put in large amounts of volunteer overtime to meet heavy production demands. How would that make this reprimand even worse?

A critical step when initiating a message is to consider media, source, and timing options. The term "media" refers to the channels or mechanisms for conveying a message. Each medium has certain characteristics, advantages, and disadvantages that make it more or less effective under various circumstances. "Source" refers to who can best deliver the message (it's not always the person who organizes the words), and "timing" involves selecting the optimal moment(s) to deliver the message to reduce the likelihood for distortion.

In short, this phase of the Straight Talk Model focuses on these questions:

- How should I send my message?
- Who should deliver my message?
- When should the message arrive?

If you fail to consider these questions when you communicate, the meaning of your message might by obscured by an inappropriate medium, disregarded because of an unacceptable source, or undermined by awkward timing. Wilbur basically got everything just a little wrong.

Be Aware of Media, Source, and Timing Choices

Although this book focuses on oral communication, let's briefly consider the broader question of media selection. Never before has a communicator had so many media options available, ranging from face-to-face to computer-mediated communication tools. Traditional media such as presentations, letters, memos, interviews, meetings, and telephone calls are now supplemented with faxes, email, teleconferencing, Web pages, videos, and DVDs, to name a few. You can use any (or all!) of these combined to get ideas across. Effective communicators evaluate the pros and cons of each option in relation to the message context (the situation, their audience, and their objectives with those audiences). Less-effective communicators too often make choices out of habit or based on what's easiest instead of considering the needs and preferences of their target audiences.

Media "Richness" and Options

Media richness theory (Daft and Lengel, 1984) describes the capability of a communication channel to convey a variety of cues. By "information richness," or "media richness," we refer to the channel's level of synchrony, the availability of social cues, the ability to use natural language (as opposed to text or symbols), and the ability to convey emotions using the channel.

Face-to-face (FTF) communication is richer but also more expensive. Computer-mediated communication (CMC) lacks social cues and non-verbal expressions, and uses text language instead of natural language. It is typically judged as being "less rich" on the media richness continuum. Adjusting to the advantages and limitations of multiple media options is an important part of effective communication.

(Kristen Campbell-Eichhorn, Candice Thomas-Maddox, and Bekelja Wanzer, Interpersonal Communication: Building Rewarding Relationships (Dubuque: Kendall/Hunt Publishing, 2008), pp. 372–733)

Note:
Levels of synchrony refers to the ability of both parties to interact freely such as in a conversation as opposed to being limited to asynchronous exchanges when only one person at a time can communicate. The availability of social cues refers to such things as facial expressions, dress and grooming, and the like. Use of natural language rather than type or symbols also impacts the ability to convey emotions using the channel.

Evaluate Media Options

Your choices from the many media options can dramatically impact your message's outcome. An otherwise effective message can fall flat (or even backfire) if you use an inappropriate medium.
Each communication medium:

- Triggers certain expectations in the message receivers.
- Presents a trade-off between efficiency and effectiveness.
- Has unique capabilities.
- Plays within certain "ground rules."

The combined effect of all these media characteristics is that the medium you select for a particular message becomes a part of the message—it conveys information about the message.

The media you select become a integral part of message effectiveness.

Consider Your Receivers' Media Expectations

People expect certain types of messages to be communicated via certain media. Habits of communicating develop and become the norm. With this in mind, a communicator may try using a different medium or combination of media to give a message extra impact. If, for example, a change in work schedule is normally posted on a bulletin board, a supervisor may get better audience attention by calling a meeting or talking with each worker individually about an unusual change. Similarly, a letter sent to a worker's home will have a different impact than will a general public-address-system announcement. Customers who expect little or no follow-up after a sale may be impressed by a personal, handwritten note. Apply creativity, a consideration of media characteristics, and some educated guesses about likely effects of messages, and you may see some real opportunities to develop an interesting and effective media mix.

Maintain awareness of the problem of communication overload. We are all bombarded with an enormous number of messages every day. We awake in the morning to messages from our clock radio. We watch the morning TV news, drive to work and see billboards and hear more radio messages, etc. The average person is targeted with thousands of messages every day. We develop expectations about how we are likely to receive certain types of messages. "Violating" those expectations—that is, using a different medium than is normally used—can provide a way to break through communication overload. For example, suppose that you typically get your information about traffic conditions from the radio, but on a particular day while stuck in traffic, you are approached by a police officer who gives you information about an alternative route. This would be a case of violating expectations with an alternative medium (personal contact versus radio) to break through with a message.

Communication-overload problems require us to select media carefully to cut through message clutter.

Consider Media Efficiency and Effectiveness

Media choices have cost implications. In a broad sense, we can best calculate costs by distinguishing between communication *efficiency* and communication *effectiveness*.

Communication efficiency is a simple ratio between the resources expended to generate a message (including time, materials, and effort) and the number of people to whom the message is sent. To improve efficiency, we simply increase the number of people reached or reduce the message preparation costs. A large group presentation, mass mailing, or broadcast TV ad can be efficient.

Communication effectiveness, however, is quite another matter. To remember the four-part definition of communication effectiveness, use the acronym RURU. Communication may be said to be effective when a specific message is:

- Received by its intended audience.
- Understood essentially the same way by the recipients as intended by the sender.
- Remembered over a reasonable period of time.
- Used when appropriate occasions arise.

The dilemma for the message-sender is that, in most cases, the communication methods that are most efficient are least effective, and vice versa. In almost every case, for example, face-to-face conversation with individuals is the least efficient, least convenient, and most costly method of communicating. It is also often the most effective. And, for some types of messages, including Wilbur's problem with the coffee breaks, it is essential. Wilbur's efficient announcement results in a shotgun approach that is likely to hit the wrong people (violating effectiveness condition number one, above) by striking the innocent as well as the guilty. This could cause huge resentment. Straight Talk generally requires communication effectiveness, with efficiency being secondary.

Communication effectiveness and communication efficiency are different.

Another efficiency-versus-effectiveness example comes from a business manager in a large corporation, who tells this story:

> I once attended a meeting that was called by the general manager for about 200 employees, mid-level managers, supervisors, and office staff. A meeting room was rented at a hotel near the main office, since we had no conference room large enough. The purpose of the meeting was for the general manager to explain, in a broad sense, the need to economize in our everyday operations. After stating that need and explaining how it related to the company's profit picture, the executive asked if anyone had any comments or suggestions.
>
> One secretary spent approximately ten minutes explaining how she had developed a system to save paper clips and make scratch pads out of used paper. Several others took the opportunity to impress the boss with their success stories at recycling containers or cutting down on photocopying.
>
> But no one seemed to notice the cost of that meeting! By the time the people drifted back to their offices, the company had spent over 300 employee-hours in direct labor costs alone. In addition, the company incurred the cost of the meeting room and the cost of reduced efficiency back at the offices while all the supervisors were gone. The company also faced the incalculable cost of possible lost business or customer resentment created when people wanting to speak to an employee simply had to wait until the meeting ended.

What was the return on this communication investment? Participants learned that the company would like to make a profit (a real eye-opening notion!), and they picked up some tips on saving paper clips and making scratch pads. The corporation used a thousand-dollar medium to convey nickel-and-dime ideas. The point, of course, is that selection of appropriate communication media can have a considerable effect on communication costs and effectiveness.

In some cases, of course, a message is very simple or not important enough to discuss in individual, face-to-face interaction. In many cases, organizational size or complexity forbids it. You need to strike a balance between efficiency and effectiveness.

Avoid choosing a medium out of habit, without considering the merits or drawbacks of possible alternatives. Avoid selecting what is easiest for *you* to do—rather than thinking about the preferences of your audiences. For example, you may prefer to email extensively because you are at your computer all day. Or perhaps you prefer to work with your cell phone, drop in on people to talk in person, or call frequent meetings. These media may be fine as long as you choose purposefully, not just out of habit.

Choosing a medium out of habit rather than considering the characteristics of each medium can reduce effectiveness.

Consider Media Capabilities

Each medium has specific advantages or disadvantages based on its capabilities and limitations. Let's look at some of the capabilities of business communication media that make one preferable to others in a given situation.

Speed

The speed of a medium depends on several factors, including preparation time, delivery time, and assimilation time (the time it takes for the receiver to comprehend the message being delivered). A letter is generally slow getting from sender to receiver (although overnight services have reduced delivery time), but an oral presentation of the same information may take considerably more preparation time. The time-consuming work of producing a videotape or slide presentation may be offset when repeated showings can efficiently present the same information to many audiences. Normally, the spoken word is faster than a print medium, except when we are comparing a formal oral presentation with a handwritten note.

Feedback Capacity

The amount and promptness of feedback are important media considerations. Written media elicit no feedback from your audience while you are writing the message. By the time you get a response, it is too late to adjust and clarify the original message. Telephone conversations provide immediate feedback in the form of questions, comments, tone of voice, pauses, hesitations, and so on. Face-to-face communication situations provide all this plus other, non-verbal feedback in facial expressions, body movements, and postures.

Media with high feedback capacity generally are more robust but also may be more expensive.

Hard-Copy Availability

Whether a tangible, permanent record of the message is *normally* retained or not is another media characteristic. Ordinarily, interviews, informal conversation, and telephone messages leave no record. (Of course, these can be recorded, but that is not routine practice in most organizations.) Email messages can be easily printed or maintained in electronic files, but otherwise do not leave an easily accessible hard-copy. Written communications such as letters, reports, and most memos are often maintained on file. An informal note, however, may be discarded and is therefore usually a non-record medium. Of course, a non-record medium can have advantages where candid, "off-the-record" expression is called for. Putting it in writing seems to make the message more formal or "official," a situation that may also call for less openness in expression.

Message Intensity and Complexity

Some media are more appropriate for conveying complex or highly intense messages. A high-intensity message may be one that conveys unpleasant information or in some way plays upon the receiver's emotions. Examples are messages that criticize the receiver's behavior or complex information about price changes or legal interpretations. Likewise, persuasive messages that require careful explanation of underlying reasoning are often best communicated by a medium that can carry complex data in a relatively structured format. Typically, a formal letter, a carefully planned oral briefing with handouts, or a written report would meet these requirements. Casual conversation or a brief memo would be less appropriate.

Formality

Some media are more appropriate for formal occasions, and others fit well in informal settings. A letter of congratulations to an employee seems more formal and has a rather different effect than, say, a casual, unplanned remark conveying the same information. The letter makes it official. An informal handwritten note sent to the board of directors by a worker may be considered out of line. When a message is intended for internal consumption only (within the organization), its format may be less formal than if it were to be publicly disseminated. For this reason, memos are used internally, while written correspondence sent outside the organization takes the form of letters—a slightly more formal format.

Table 3.1 summarizes key characteristics of some common communication media. The bolded items suggest characteristics that may be the most significant reason for choosing a particular medium.

Consider Media Mixing: a Sound Alternative

Bear in mind that you are certainly not limited to the use of a single medium for a given message. Often a combination of several media does the job very nicely, since the disadvantages of one medium can be offset by another. For example, the slow-feedback characteristic of written media can be offset by an accompanying oral medium. Table 3.2 suggests some ways to combine commonly used media to offset such disadvantages.

Combining several media can reduce limitations of one medium and enhance communication.

Experiments studying the effects of combining media have produced inconclusive results, primarily because of the difficulty of accounting for all possible variables—especially non-verbal ones. Nevertheless, some tentative findings have emerged. In one classic experiment, specific factual information was transmitted using each of the following media or combinations of media:

- Oral only.
- Written only.
- Posted on a bulletin board.
- The grapevine (no formal message sent).
- Both oral and written.

Several days after the messages were delivered, researchers tested the recipients to see how much content they could accurately remember. The results showed that the written-plus-oral message combination resulted in the greatest retention. Oral exchange alone was second in recall accuracy, followed by the written message used alone. The bulletin board was next, and the grapevine came in last.[1]

In a later study of communication within a company, researchers asked supervisors to rate the effectiveness of (1) written, (2) oral, (3) written and then oral, and (4) oral and then written communication for different types of situations. In general, the oral-followed-by-written technique came out best. Supervisors saw it as most effective for situations that required immediate action, passed along a company directive, communicated an important policy change, reviewed work progress, called for praising a noteworthy employee,

TABLE 3.1 Characteristics and Costs of Business Communication Media

Medium	Speed	Feedback Capacity	Hard-Copy Available	Formality	Can Handle Complex or Intense Messages	Cost Including Time, Technology
Informal FTF conversation	**Fast**	High	No	Informal	No	Low
Telephone conversation	**Fast**	Medium	No	Informal	No	Low–medium
Voice mail (phone message)	**Fast**	Low	No	Informal	No	Low
Formal oral presentation	Medium	Medium	Maybe	**Formal**	**Yes**	Medium–high
Informal note	Medium	**Low**	Yes	Informal	No	Low
Memo	Medium	Low	**Yes**	Either	Possible	Medium–high
Email message	Fast	Low	**Yes**	Informal	Possible	Medium
Fax	**Fast**	Low	Yes	Either	Yes	Medium
Letter	Slow	Low	Yes	Formal	**Yes**	Medium–high
Formal report	Very slow	Low	Yes	Very formal	**Yes**	High

TABLE 3.2 Combining Media for Effectiveness

Medium	Major Limitations	Supplemental Media
Conversation (phone or live)	No record; little non-verbal feedback with phone use	Record notes; send additional written material; tape record
Formal oral presentation	Preparation time; no record	Written handouts; outline of presentation; supplemental readings
Informal note	Low feedback; may look overly casual or unimportant	Telephone or conversation follow-up; insert with printed card
Memo	Low immediate feedback; medium often overused	Telephone follow-up to check for understanding
Email	Informal; may get lost among overload	Follow-up hard-copy or supplemental information; telephone or conversation follow-up
Formal report	Preparation time; low feedback; cost of printing, etc.	Meeting or presentation to discuss, clarify, and provide/receive feedback

or promoted a safety campaign. The written-only technique was judged best for passing along information that required action in the future or was of a general nature. An oral-only message was suggested for reprimands or to settle a dispute among employees.[2]

Some Media Choices in Management Communication

The following presents a brief review of the kinds of communication tools used in organizations. This listing represents popular use, not necessarily the optimum use of communication tools. The intent of this listing is to create awareness about the breadth of options available to today's communicator. (Since this book focuses on oral communication, we have omitted most written and electronic media from this list.)

To Convey Job-Related or "For-Your-Information" Messages

- Announcements of policy or procedural changes.
- Instructional interviews, performance reviews briefings, or training sessions.
- Announcement to explain personnel reassignment, promotions, appointments, etc.
- Supervisory briefings (routine, perhaps daily).

To Motivate Employees

- Celebrations of company or individual accomplishments with congratulatory speeches, motivational briefings.
- Open houses, family nights (programs including tours of the plant, exhibits, demonstrations, samples, and refreshments), and alumni or retiree activities.
- Recreational and social activities (such as athletic leagues, picnics, and outings).

To Convey Upward Feedback

- Advisory councils, focus groups, or similar groups to identify employee or customer concerns.
- Grievance interviews where employees or customers can speak face-to-face with a company representative.
- Exit interviews (interviews with employees who are leaving the company attempting to understand why they are leaving or what concerns they have about the company).

- Feedback systems that allow employees and customers to communicate with organizations and receive responses to their complaints, complements, suggestions or questions (may use written, electronic, or oral media).

These listings represent only a sample of tools used in organizations to communicate and create understanding. The professional seeking success at Straight Talk should objectively consider the many media and tools available and seek consistency of message across their use.

Use Multiple Media and Tools, But Speak with One Voice

One common organizational challenge is to consistently "speak with one voice." By this we mean that message-consistency is critical. Conflicting messages can arise from simply not thinking about the impact of a message. At best, this is seen as inconsistent; at worst, as hypocrisy. One does not have to look far for inconsistencies. Companies who trumpet that "their employees are the most professional in the business" and then communicate to them as though they needed micro-managing send a mixed and confusing message. Organizational leaders who quote a mission statement valuing low cost to customers who then waste money on personal perks or ostentatious living fail to speak with consistency. You get the picture.

Effective professional communication requires speaking with one voice, keeping message content and organizational focus consistent, or, at least, not in obvious conflict. Use of a variety of media and sources for messages can make that "one voice" goal tricky. Nevertheless, consistency of messages can elevate the organization's credibility as well as communication effectiveness.

Professionalism requires "speaking with one voice." Consistency strengthens messages.

Choose a Credible Source

Sometimes, you won't be the best person to deliver a particular message—even if you had the idea, designed the project, or identified the need to communicate. Perhaps someone else will be more effective than you. When selecting the source—the person to deliver your message—the most important criterion is the perceived credibility of that source by your target audience. In other words, whom will your audience perceive as having the most experience, power, confidence, and concern for them? (We discussed credibility in Chapter 1 and will provide more detail in Chapter 9.)

A common mistake—once again—is to make decisions about the message's source based on our own needs rather than those of the receiver. We naturally take ownership of a project and then want to see it personally through to completion by delivering the message ourselves to employees, supervisors, clients, and other decision-makers. Our hidden agenda (e.g., perhaps a desire to be impressive) may override the fact that someone else might be more persuasive with the target audience. In truth, someone the target receiver sees as having the highest perceived credibility will be more effective in presenting your message.

Perceived credibility of the message source impacts on effectiveness. Sometimes you are not the best source for your message.

As hard as this is to swallow, sometimes you might not be at the right organizational position, age, gender, experience level, or any number of other possible disqualifiers to be the most powerful source of your message. You might have gone to the "wrong" school, majored in the "wrong" field, served in the "wrong" branch of the military, or currently support the "wrong" political party, based on the perceptions of your target audience. Be open to these possibilities. Sometimes it needs to be someone else.

However, this does not mean that you should necessarily hand over your ideas or project to a person whose credibility affords him or her better opportunity of making a persuasive connection. Another option is to ask that credible person to introduce you and help establish your credibility with your target audience. Then you can take it on your own.

Again, choosing to have someone other than yourself do a briefing or pitch should not be seen as diminishing you in any way. Weigh your source options carefully to maximize your potential for success, even if it takes a little "credibility by association."

A recent example of unfortunate choice of source we saw was an auto manufacturer who was announcing some "green" initiatives that targeted young buyers of fuel-efficient cars. The spokesman for the company was (and we want to be charitable here) an overweight man in late-middle-age with a 1980s hairstyle and even older glasses. This may seem trivial (and perhaps even a bit catty), but the guy simply did not look the part of a trendsetter. He undoubtedly had the organizational rank and position, but he did not fit the aspirations of his target audience.

If your intention is to communicate functionally—that is, to get your receivers to do something—the cold fact is that someone else may do it better than you. Set aside your ego and enlist them into the effort.

Consider Your Timing Options

Poor timing decisions can ruin even the most carefully crafted message. This can occur when we communicate at our own convenience rather than being sensitive to our audience. Timing of messages can also have a dramatic effect on their acceptance and understanding. The following sections offer some suggestions for making the most of media.

When should the message arrive for maximum impact? The old joke about "engaging brain before putting mouth in motion" can remind us that it is often unwise to blurt out our thoughts without considering whether this is an appropriate time to share them. The same principle holds for prepared messages; improper timing can diminish their effectiveness. For example, giving a sales pitch for a product the customer does not yet need is usually a waste of time. Calling to thank someone for a gift months after you received it won't win you much goodwill, and giving a progress report briefing before you have progress to report will have little positive effect. Similarly, teaching an advanced application for a software product will do little good if the audience doesn't understand the basic uses.

Consider audience wants and needs in timing messages.

Don't just communicate at *your* convenience. Be sensitive to whether your audience is mentally prepared, capable of understanding, and available (physically and psychologically) to receive your message.

Be Aware of Competing Audience Concerns

Trying to communicate when people are preoccupied with personally important or emotional matters will be tough. In such situations, the listener may be psychologically unavailable—his or her mind is elsewhere.

Sometimes leaders deliver their messages at poor times. Some examples:

- A district manager sent an email message to subordinates asking them to call his secretary to schedule a meeting to talk about "performance issues." The email arrived at 6 p.m. on a Friday, giving the receivers all weekend to wonder and worry about this vaguely threatening message.
- A department leader told a subordinate that his contract was not going to be renewed on a day that marked the three-year anniversary of a tragic auto crash that killed the man's wife and daughter.
- A political blunder came to light when timing of a publicity photo shoot involved a low-flying aircraft in New York—on September 11, the day commemorating the eight-year anniversary of the terrorist attacks on the city.

You can best avoid such timing mistakes by striving to know your audiences, considering possible symbolism associated with the date, and being sensitive to their needs. Put yourself in their shoes and ask, "Is this a good time to receive such a message?" You can't always get it right, but applying this Straight Talk Model can boost the chances of avoiding miscommunication.

Avoid Communicating When You Are Upset

Many of us have fired off an indiscrete comment, made an angry phone call, or spouted off in a meeting while upset. And many of us have had to eat our words later. If a situation prompts you to send an emotionally charged message, write or draft your thoughts, but hold on to them for a day or two. Letting the message ferment and then editing it carefully can help you avoid embarrassment and serious credibility damage. The same principle applies in oral communication. Rehearsing a message may be both appropriate and prudent.

Sometimes good timing calls for judicious postponing.

Be Aware of Message Sequencing

Your decisions about timing can be further complicated when you communicate with multiple audiences or need to repeat the message. You need to consider the sequencing and spacing of your messages:

- Who should you talk to first? Second? Third?
- How much time should you allow between messages?

Companies normally expect messages to go through channels of authority. You would not, for example, go directly to a senior executive with a question that your immediate manager could answer. Conversely, the senior director should not tell you about a decision before telling your manager. In advertising or promotional campaigns, give careful thought to the frequency of broadcasting the message. Too much repetition may be annoying; too little may fail to imprint the message on potential buyers.

Also, certain audiences should receive information before others. For example, an employee who is being promoted or reassigned should get this message before others do. The supervisor of that employee should announce changes to the people involved in advance of a public announcement. Violating these timing issues can lead to embarrassment and the feeling of being "out of the loop" in the organization.

Remember One Little Rule

Just remember that *it* (message effectiveness) is all about them—your target audience. It's about their needs, their preferences, and their concerns. If you remember and apply this one simple rule, you are more likely to get what you want. Best communicators work to see the world through the eyes of their audiences.

Performance Checklist

After completing this chapter, you should be better able to apply some principles for selecting the best media and timing options for your message. Specifically, you should now understand that:

- Each communication medium triggers certain expectations in the message receivers, presents a trade-off between efficiency and effectiveness, and has unique capabilities.
- Efficiency and effectiveness are different and should be weighed in your media decision. Communication efficiency is a simple ratio between the total costs of a message and the number of people reached by that message. Communication effectiveness is determined by the degree to which a message is *received* by the intended audience, *understood* correctly, *remembered* for a reasonable period of time, and *used* when appropriate occasions arise. (The acronym "RURU" can help you remember this.)
- A communication medium operates within a generally accepted set of ground rules. These ground rules play a large part in determining the medium's effectiveness in a given situation.
- Mixing several media can offset the disadvantages of one of them, resulting in more effective communication.
- Consider timing options for your message by being aware of your audience's competing concerns, avoiding communicating when upset, and being sensitive to message sequencing.
- A wide range of communication tools is available to you. Creativity and innovation will help your message stand out from the massive amount of information bombarding people today.

What Do You Know?

Activity 3.1: Experiencing Media Choice Problems

Recall an experience you have had in which you received a message through an inappropriate medium. Describe in a memo to your instructor how that media choice damaged the effectiveness of the message. What medium would have been better? Why?

Activity 3.2: Recognizing Media Ground Rules

List eight communication media you use regularly. Then, articulate at least three ground rules for each medium. Finally, identify the most important characteristic that would cause you to choose each medium.

Media I Use	Ground Rules	Strongest Reason for Use
1		
2		
3		
4		
5		
6		
7		
8		

Activity 3.3: Applying Media Choices in Your Class

If you are using this book in a class, prepare an informal presentation to your professor detailing the role that each of the forms of media will play in your relationship with both your professor and classmates. Address peer-related issues of team projects, peer feedback, and study groups. Address instructor-related issues of graded assignments, individual questions, and feedback.

Reinforce With These Review Questions

1 True/False—Media selection can mean the difference between accomplishing your communication objective and not.

2 True/False—Media choices involve trade-offs between efficiency and effectiveness.

3 Of these two, efficiency and effectiveness, which is more important? _____.

4 When defining communication effectiveness, what does the acronym "RURU" stand for?
   R: _____,
   U: _____,
   R: _____,
   U: _____.

5 Name the five characteristics of communication media that make one preferable over others: (1) _____, (2) _____, (3) _____, (4) _____, and (5) _____.

6 True/False—Choosing a medium because it is easy for us to use is an appropriate strategy in most cases.

7 True/False—Audiences almost always face competing concerns which may impact on their ability to receive your message.

8 True/False—Mixing media can offset the disadvantages of some.

9 True/False—The timing of a message has little impact on its effectiveness.

10 True/False—Sometimes it is important to have someone other than you deliver a message, even if it's your idea.

Mini-Case Study: Straight Talk Model Applied

The medium that communicators choose for their messages sends important signals to the receivers. In the case of Wilbur Jackson in our opening story, he chose a brief announcement given to the larger group without an opportunity for feedback. The effect was to convey some possible unspoken messages, such as:

- This message isn't very important. If it were, I'd present it more formally and allow discussion.
- You are not important enough to receive this information from me personally.
- I am too busy to convey this information to you in a more personal way.
- I don't care about the appearance of my message; this "quick-and-dirty" approach is good enough.
- This matter is so urgent I had to sacrifice personalizing and professionalism to get out the information quickly.
- This is routine information that you will readily understand.

Unfortunately, Wilbur apparently gave little thought to the medium he chose. In failing to look at his options, he failed to consider the fact that the medium itself makes a comment about the contents of the message.

Questions

1 How would you have recommended that Wilbur handle the message he needed to communicate?
2 What can he do to remedy the situation with his employees?
3 What does this example say about the importance of media selection?

four

Select and Organize Your Message Content

When you've got a thing to say, Say it! Don't take half a day.... Boil her down until she simmers, Polish her until she glimmers.

(Joel Chandler Harris)

Selecting and Arranging Appropriate Information

Once you understand your context (your situation, target audiences, and goals with those audiences) and have considered and selected the best medium, message source, and delivery time, organizing the message becomes the critical task. Effective workplace communication requires a sensible arrangement of clearly stated ideas. A haphazard or illogical arrangement of even good ideas will reduce the likelihood of communication success. The Straight Talk Model provides time-tested patterns of arrangement that, although not fool-proof, greatly improve your ability to convey persuasive arguments, clear directives, and uncomfortable or bad news.

Communicators who "shoot from the lip," rather than pre-plan their approach, forfeit one of their most powerful tools—psychologically sound messaging strategies.

This chapter discusses the steps necessary to select and arrange message content to maximize its impact on your audience.

Performance Competencies

When you have completed this chapter, you should be able to:

- Choose an overall select-and-organize approach for your messages.
- Recognize and apply the power of stories to create mental images for your audiences.
- Identify the key ingredients in effective informative, persuasive, and bad-news messages.
- Understand the distinction between features and benefits.
- Justify different patterns of arrangement for various types of messages.
- Identify key factors that may damage goodwill in bad-news messages.
- Apply several "quick-and-dirty" patterns when you have limited presentation time
- Explain how the principles of organization covered in this chapter can be applied to long presentations.

The Way It Is ... Disorganized Speech(es)

Disorganized speech is a symptom of several psychological disorders. Examples of these symptoms include "loose associations" (also called tangential speech)—when speech moves quickly through multiple topics—and, the more serious disorder, Schizophasia (called "word salad"), which may include confused and repetitive speech and/or the use of unrelated words or words without meaning.[1]

We don't mean to get all clinical on you, but the symptoms of such psychological maladies are not unlike some speeches we have heard. The results can be very similar: difficulty in understanding. In fairness, most people are not totally unorganized, but many can improve the logical organization of messages by applying some simple patterns of arrangement.

Don't let your audience question your psychological health. Organize your messages.

"Good morning, my name is Dennis, and I'm here to talk about the budget for the next fiscal year, and here's my first slide ... blah, blah, blah, blah, ... Are there any questions? No? Well, then, uh, thank you."

Yawn.

Is what you hear (and then, unfortunately, model) most often something like this?

This chapter finally gets to the part of oral presentations where some less-effective communicators begin! Too frequently, people start putting together the ideas they want to convey before (or instead of) thinking through the many elements of the communication context or media, source, and timing options. By thinking about what we want to say before thinking about possible audience reactions, we set ourselves up for failure. If we sound like we are repeating ourselves, we are! But this is a significant problem that requires the reinforcement of repetition. (Sorry if it sounds like we are over-discussing this, but it is a significant problem.)

Review Your Decisions about Context, Media, Source, and Timing

As you face the task of selecting and organizing ideas for your message, take the time to review the context of your message. Specifically, jot down relevant facts about the situation, your audiences, and your objectives with those audiences. Your Context Analysis Worksheet will remind you of all the questions you need to ask yourself. Failing to have a clear picture of this context makes it nearly impossible to succeed as a communicator. Remember, the most successful communicators focus their thinking on their audiences' viewpoint.

The traditional (and our "default") position for any message is that it must have an effective introduction, body, and conclusion that are appropriate for the situation, audience, and objectives. To produce these elements, you must first be clear about your main objective, or what we also call the "big idea." In functional communication, the big idea is what you want your reader or listener to *do*, *think*, or *feel* as a result of getting your message. It answers the question, "As a result of this communication, exactly what do I want my audience to do?"

The "big idea" on any message is what you want your listener to do, think or feel—the specific goal of one message opportunity. Be clear about what you hope to accomplish.

If you don't have a clear, hoped-for outcome, or if you don't take the time to consider your audience, the big idea of your message will be unclear, and your message won't be functional. If you don't know what you are trying to accomplish, your reader or listener won't either.

Choose an Overall Select-and-Organize Approach

Selecting information to put in a message is a natural outgrowth of defining the context. In other words, you will discover questions that need to be answered as you apply the Straight Talk Model and gain a clear picture of the situation, audiences, and your objectives. The model-guided inquiry results in answers about what your message receiver needs or wants to know. This determines the specific information you need for your message to succeed. Try to assume the perspective of your various audiences and antici-pate any questions they would likely ask about your topic. A complete and effective message answers all the receivers' potential questions.

Before choosing a specific pattern of organization—a specific way to arrange the information you have selected—first consider two important questions:

1   **How much time do you have?** You either have ample, allotted time, or you don't. Have you been asked to present a report in a meeting when you have 20 minutes on the agenda, or will you have to give the same information to your boss as you walk down the hall? Will you have an hour to talk to employees about a change in policy, or will you have to persuade someone during a brief encounter? Can you facilitate an exten-sive problem-solving meeting, or do you need to quickly gather key data and make a decision? Your messages, therefore, are either traditional (with a complete introduction and conclusion), or they are "quick-and-dirty."

2   **What is your purpose?** Some experts would like to make this hard, but the simple truth is that, when you communicate, you are either inform-ing, persuading, or delivering bad news. Arguably, a longer message may have several of these elements, but the big idea is likely to be one of the three.

Let's talk first about the traditional situation where you have sufficient time to develop a fairly extensive presentation or briefing. We'll get back to the all-important "quick-and-dirty" communication situation a bit later in this chapter. For now, assume you have the luxury of a select-and-organize approach that includes an introduction, body, and conclusion.

Organizing the Traditional Message

In situations when you have adequate preparation and presentation time, you can take advantage of a fully developed traditional message that includes an introduction, a limited number of main points, and a conclusion. The intro-duction grabs your audience's attention, explains what's coming, and estab-lishes the benefit for the receiver. The body of your message follows through on your stated plan. The conclusion summarizes and reinforces your main points and asks for action. Whether you are writing or speaking, planning an organized message, complete with an introduction and conclusion, ensures that you follow through with the purpose of your communication. Let's take a moment to review the nature and functions of introductions and conclusions.

Introductions: Attention-Grabber, Benefit, Agenda

An effective introduction must grab the audience's attention—it must pry your listeners away from competing messages or distractions, engage their interest, and focus their attention on you and your message. You accomplish this by using some type of appeal that sparks their interest by offering or implying an advantage they can receive from listening to you. In addition to grabbing attention, an effective introduction should tell listeners about the benefits they will gain by listening to you and describe the agenda for the rest of your message.

Start With a Great Attention-Grabber

Becoming comfortable with delivering an attention-grabber is often the greatest obstacle for speakers to overcome, but gaining audience attention is the first step in any successful presentation, meeting, or even conversation. Based on your context analysis, develop appeals that suggest listener benefit. By listening to your message, the audience may receive something beneficial or avoid a loss with regard to their desires for success, power or status enhancement, self-satisfaction, or curiosity.

You have many, many options. The only rules are that the attention-grabber must (1) relate to your topic, and (2) relate to the audience. Some options include:

- A startling statement (if it supports your argument).
- A rhetorical question (if you are sure your audience would answer the way you want).
- A quotation (if you can deliver it smoothly—obviously not an issue in writing).
- A story (if you have time).
- A humorous anecdote (as long as it's not a joke that would insult someone in your audience).
- A compliment, thank-you, or reference to the occasion or the reason for the message.

Avoid attention-grabbers that sound apologetic, might offend, employ gimmicks, or are too self-deprecating. And no, your melodious voice, your contagious energy, your artistic presentation folder, or your attractive slides layout will not count as an attention-grabber. You must have excellent material, too. Well, actually, you must have excellent material *first*.

Table 4.1 shows you some positive and negative appeals that may gain audience attention.

Tell Your Audience What You Are Going To Talk About

In addition to grabbing an audience's attention, introductions should also lay out an agenda for the rest of the presentation. Letting people know what you

TABLE 4.1. Positive and Negative Attention-Getting Appeals

	Success	Power and Status Enhancement	Self-Satisfaction, Happiness, Fulfillment	Curiosity
Positive appeals	Acting will lead to success in accomplishing goals. *Examples*: "You can break into the million-dollar sales club …" or "I'll show you tips for remodeling your home and saving thousands of dollars."	Acting will improve power and status. *Examples*: "Do you want to master the art of negotiation?" or "Let me show you how to dramatically improve your ability to [add a skill] with just a few tips."	Acting will lead to a sense of satisfaction. *Examples*: "I can show you how to achieve your goal of becoming your own boss," or "I want to talk about ways of boosting your life satisfaction and happiness."	Acting will answer questions the audience would like answered. *Examples*: "How would you like to know your competitor's exact sales strategy?" or "I can show you some little-known key indicators that will guarantee …"
Negative appeals	Not acting will lead to the failure to accomplish goals. *Examples*: "Can you be satisfied with another average sales year?" or "Let me show you how to avoid the mistakes many home-repair people make …"	Not acting will cost the loss of power or status. *Examples*: "Are you coming up short in negotiations?" or "Here is why continuing to do [X] as you have been doing it will destroy your ability to lead."	Not acting will lead to dissatisfaction or missed opportunity for the audience. *Examples*: "How much longer will you work to make someone else wealthy?" or "Do you feel trapped in a rut?"	Not acting will leave important questions unanswered. *Examples*: "Is what you don't know about the competition killing you?" or "Have you ever wondered how hackers can get into your computer?"

plan to cover provides "content preview" and helps listeners to prepare mentally to receive your message. Such previewing may also describe what you *will not* be discussing, thus limiting the scope appropriately. For example, a speaker may say something like, "I will deal with only the three most popular product alternatives identified by our customers based on July's research survey." Or, "My briefing today will bring you up to date on the Harris Street construction, but I will not be discussing other new branches."

Clarifying an agenda (what you plan to cover—your content preview) and, of course, tying that agenda into audience benefit (what's in it for you) almost always makes a presentation, meeting, or interview clearer for listeners. It helps them focus on what you want to communicate about.

Make It About Them
(We know you are surprised to read this!) Remember the importance of answering your audience's question, "What's in this for me?" At the same time, it's easy to assume that they realize the benefit because that benefit is obvious to you. Never assume about benefit; put it in.

It's also easy to fall into the trap of stating a benefit for the company but not for individual readers or listeners. So, ask yourself, "Why, specifically and personally, should my audience listen to me speak or read my written message?" Then tell them exactly that.

Conclusions: Summary, Action Step, Final Statement

You have four last things to do in the conclusion of our message: tell your audience what you want them to remember, answer any questions, tell them what you want them to do, and leave a great impression.

What Do You Want Them to Remember?
Summarize the essence of the main points, not the headlines. In our many years of experience, the biggest mistake that we have noted is the tendency to summarize only the solution. Include the problem, too. Be sure you remind your audience of *all* the most important points in your *entire* agenda.

Do You Want Your Audience to Ask Questions?
This is a good place to put Q&A. You can also take questions *before* your summary or *after* your action step, but always end with *your* prepared final statement, not an unprepared answer to a random question.

What Do You Want Them to Do?
Be specific here so there is no misunderstanding about your expectations. Review your introduction and confirm that the action step here in the conclusion reflects your stated purpose.

What Do You Want to Leave with Your Audience?

This is your last chance. Save your most memorable words. Repeat your slogan. Show the picture of your ideal world as a result of your proposed solution. What you show, what you say, and how you say it should be a triple-powered display that insures you have made your point.

Yes, there is a worksheet, appropriately titled "Outline Worksheet," which will lead you through the process of designing a traditionally organized message.

Never End with a Q&A

A common mistake that many speakers make is to conclude a presentation with a question–answer session. While this can be useful in getting audience input, it runs significant risk and should never replace a final statement.

One of your authors (Sherron) had an experience that indelibly reinforced this principle. As a communication consultant with a major defense contractor, she was invited to the first public flight of a new fighter jet. The event was an enormously important milestone for the company, for the customer, and for international security.

The day was beautiful; the atmosphere was energized and patriotic; the flight exceeded expectations; and, as a final treat, the test pilot entered the event tent to answer questions from the eager audience.

He was obviously the best expert on this new airplane, and his media trainers had prepared him to handle every possible question about its capabilities. He was engaging and passionate and, well, just brilliant.

Then, someone announced that there would be one more question, thanked everyone for coming, and apparently disappeared, leaving the test pilot alone to answer the last question. A woman whom no one recognized stood up, and in one very long question, asked about everything negative associated with war, defense spending, and labor unions. The pilot simply could not answer.

No one was there to back him up. No final statement for after the Q&A. No perfect ending to that perfect day.

The lesson: always end with prepared comments that reinforce your message. Don't let this important emphasis position—the last thing your audience hears—be controlled by someone else. Prepare a powerful final statement.

Always use the final statement to reinforce your message.

Now let's look at some typical patterns of arrangement for the body of various types of messages.

Patterns of Arrangement for Positive, Routine Request, and Informative Messages

Positive and routine messages answer simple questions for listeners. Typical examples are requests for basic information, brief progress reports, or answers to interview questions. They convey information, update people, and/or provide good news. Receivers of such messages are likely to be happy—or at least not unhappy—to get them. You typically do not get significant push-back or objections when you deliver such messages. However, remember that you are always persuading just a little—you always want to change your audience in some way, even if it is to improve their understanding in some small way.

Criteria to Apply to Positive, Routine Request, and Informative Messages

In short, these types of messages can put the "big idea" right up front. Then include appropriate information that is complete and direct. The selected information should be organized to get directly to the main point and then follow with clarifying details (as needed) and a friendly close. Applying the following criteria to your messages will greatly improve your chances for success.

Be Complete
Make sure you provide enough information to accomplish what you want your listeners to do, think, or feel. If you are inviting people to an activity, for example, be sure to include its location, time, date, and what to bring or wear. If your message conveys a change in a procedure—one which the listener is not likely to resist—tell the receivers exactly how to make the change. If your message reports information, be certain that you include all the relevant information.

One way to check for completeness is to anticipate any questions the listener may have, and then proactively answer them. Use of the time-tested journalist's criteria of "who, what, when, where, why, and how" provides a good checklist. Example: if inviting all Accounting Department Supervisors (who) to meet (what) in the conference room (where) to discuss the Q4 budget (why) and reminding them to bring data comparing Q2 and Q3 results (how) pretty much covers it.

Be Direct

The intent of good-news or routine messages is to tell people something they are glad to hear, or, at worst, are neutral toward, so you can put the big idea up front and not worry about getting a negative emotional reaction. Then follow the big idea of the message with other relevant, subordinate information that clarifies details. Example: "Congratulations, Bill Warner. You are our sales leader for the month of June with 23 net new units sold."

If your informative message calls for elaboration—is more than a brief thank-you or routine request—help your receiver digest the details of your message with a clear introduction (attention-grabber, agenda, purpose, and benefit for the receiver), and then elaborate with one of these patterns:

- **Chronological order.** Organize supporting information items as they occurred in time. Example: "We have initiated a three-step strategy that calls for additional print advertising beginning on May 3, a TV marketing blitz during fall sweeps in November, and an aggressive telemarketing effort in early December."

- **Problem–solution.** Tell your audience what problems you faced and how you propose to resolve them. Example: "We experienced a drop in sales for Q1 and Q2 primarily as a result of insufficient sales staff to handle incoming orders. By mid-Q3 we will have three additional sales reps trained and fully active."

- **Topical or spatial order.** Progress systematically from one topic or place to another. "We opened the Glendale branch in January followed by the La Crescenta branch in May. Our next branch opening is scheduled for November in Tucson."

- **Cause–effect.** Tell your audience what happened and what caused it to happen. Example: "The time spent with the government auditors took key personnel away from our community-service initiatives."

Select and Organize Information for Persuasive Messages

Persuasive business messages are *action*-oriented. They seek to get listeners to *do* something they normally would not do without some prodding. The message's effectiveness can often be judged by the action that results. The effective sales message sells. The effective collection message collects. The effective policy-recommending presentation wins approval or further consideration. The persuasive interview lands a job or promotion. The persuasive presentation sways opinion or moves people to action. The communicator's job is to motivate listeners to expend the effort to change in the desired direction. Thus, the more you know about the audience's needs, wants, and motives, the more likely such motivation will occur.

Persuasion involves getting people to do something they would not otherwise do.

Criteria to Apply to Persuasive Messages

Most persuasive messages need to involve audience emotions to be successful. In sales training, you may hear the expression "Sell the sizzle, not the steak." It's the emotion of savoring the steak that causes people to buy (unless they are vegetarians, of course). Stories and vivid examples that stimulate the senses trigger emotions and motivation. Appeal to listener wants or needs, and relate the features of your product, idea, or proposal to specific audience benefits. Applying the following criteria to your messages will greatly improve your chances for success.

Persuasion almost always requires triggering listener emotions.

Generating Buy-In

A former senior correspondent and anchorman at CNN, Mark S. Walton draws on his rich communications background to help leaders master the language of leadership with his book, *Generating Buy-In*. Walton describes "buy-in" as getting understanding, commitment, and action from others in support of a person, idea, proposal, product, service, or organization. He explains that buy-in is the essential emotional ingredient needed for any collaborative effort to be successful. Buy-in is an indication of successful persuasion.

Leaders know they can get buy-in by recognizing situations that call for renewed commitment from others, creating strategic stories that generate enthusiasm, and calling for action to get the job done. These are the key ideas Walton explains.

- **The human mind thinks in stories.** Telling strategically created stories that project a positive outcome is essential for generating buy-in.
- **Capture people's emotions, not just their intellects.** Stories that provoke an emotional response in others help get buy-in. Simply providing heaps of information won't do the trick.
- **Follow the rules when creating persuasive stories.** Go step-by-step as you determine your objective, establish your storyline, target your audience's agenda, and call your audience to action.

- **Follow the Rule of Threes**. "When people ask me about this company, I tell them three things," says Steve Ballmer, CEO of Microsoft. The mind retains information best when it's presented in a group of three.
- **Use real-life examples**. Vivid, authentic examples influence decision-making more than abstract information, and are more helpful in generating buy-in.

(Mark S. Walton, Generating Buy In, published by Executive Book Summaries, P.O. Box 1053, Concordville, PA 19331. © 2004)

Use Information That Appeals to the Audience

One of the best ways to overcome resistance to your solution is to select information that addresses anticipated objections your audience may have. For example, suppose you wanted to propose that your department upgrades its computer technology. An obvious objection that comes to mind is the cost. Another objection might be the time needed to train department personnel on the new systems. Now that you have anticipated these objections and as many other possible objections as you can discover from your audience analysis (perhaps hidden agenda such as a vested interest or emotional connection to the old systems), you can address them in your message. You might overcome these objections by showing how the cost will be offset by increased efficiency or additional capabilities, for example.

Show your audience what personal benefit they will gain by doing what you want them to do. The recommended computer system, for example, may lead to increased company success, which will impact on employee bonuses. Many persuasive requests fail when the communicator forgets to phrase ideas in terms of the audience. Always think "WIIFM?"[2]

Use Information That Links Features to Benefits

Persuasive appeals work best when the benefits of what you are advocating relate closely to audience needs. If you have carefully analyzed the context of your message (and, hopefully, completed a Context Analysis Worksheet), you should have a pretty good picture of what benefits are attractive to your audience. But don't assume that listeners automatically connect the dots. Make the feature–benefit linkage clear.

Features and Benefits

A *feature* is simply some aspect or characteristic of your product, service, or idea. A vehicle may have a powerful engine; a vacuum cleaner may come with clever attachments; a package-delivery service may guarantee against breakage at no cost. These are features. A *benefit* is a "what-this-means-to-you statement."

To maximize the persuasive impact of features, these should be phrased in terms of the benefit your audience will get from them. For example, the truck can take you up the steepest gravel road; the vacuum can get disease-carrying dirt out of hard-to-reach places; intact delivery of your products will eliminate customer complaints and help your company be more profitable. You sell ideas and products with audience benefit. The skillful persuader alludes to the product's features only as they relate to audience benefits. Use the phrase, "and what this means to you" in showing the linkage your audience needs to see.

Say—or at least think—"what this means to you" when linking features to benefits.

Patterns of Arrangement for Persuasive Messages

Because persuasion, by definition, seeks to get people to do something they otherwise would not do, we usually prefer an indirect approach. An indirect approach leads up to the requested action and thus reduces the likelihood of turning off the receiver before you present the big idea. The opposite—a direct approach—would be like starting out saying, "I want to sell you some insurance." The indirect approach establishes some need before getting to that point (the big idea of the message). Occasionally the direct approach may be effective when your audience is predisposed to listen objectively to your proposal, when your proposal does not require strong persuasion, or when the audience prefers that you get to the point. But, in most persuasion, listeners need to hear the reasoning first.

Once again, if you have time, the ideal organizational strategy would include a complete introduction and conclusion. In your introduction, remember to include an attention-grabber that engages your audience, an agenda that describes what you are going to talk about, and a very specific benefit statement that articulates exactly "what's in it for them" to listen to you talk.

One caveat about the agenda, however, is to not give away too much. Remember, "I want to sell you some insurance" is likely to be off-putting, not enticing. Instead, your agenda might be more generic, such as, "I'm going to talk about critical financial concerns for our families and businesses and then how to protect them."

Select and Organize Information for Persuasive Messages

Traditional persuasive messages often organize around a clear and specific description of the problem or need that underlies the persuasive attempt.

Once the need is clarified, the message presents a series of possible solutions, identifies the pro/con of each of these, and then recommends the best alternative. If you have a preconceived notion of which alternative would be best, it usually makes sense to present the less-favorable ideas first, leading up to the preferred option. Sales people often do this using the good–better–best presentation much like the old Sear's advertisements for home appliances.

We recently heard an excellent presentation from a retirement-fund manager describe three good options. For each option she described its advantages and limitations objectively. The third happened to benefit her company more than the other two but also seemed to be the best choice. Her even-handed enthusiasm for all three alternatives gave her good credibility and, although the company did select her third option, they did so enthusiastically because of the fair-minded presentation.

A traditional decision-making model taught in organizational behavior courses (and elsewhere) also provides good guidelines for arranging a persuasive message if you have ample time. The steps in this model are:

- Define the specific problem or need.
- Identify the decision criteria. This step describes the characteristics of an optimal decision. For example, "the best solution to this problem would cost less than $50,000" or "would impact on no more than 20 employees" or "will enhance our reputation as an environmentally conscious company."
- Allocate weight to the criteria. For example, the $50,000 criterion is more important than the number of employees affected, and the environmental reputation would rank third among our criteria.
- Identify possible alternatives.
- Evaluate each alternative in light of the ranked criteria.
- Select or recommend the best alternative.

Fleshing out each of these steps for your audience adds credibility to your recommendation and gravitas to your decision.

Keep in mind, however, the persuasive continuum we discussed as a part of context analysis. Be realistic about where your listener is on that continuum. He or she may not be ready to go for your ultimate "big idea" but, rather, can be persuaded to move to a next step in the persuasion process. In other words, you can rarely go from zero to ten. People who sell, for example, luxury automobiles or other high-ticket items are realistic about common steps in the sales cycle. Their persuasive message may be to get you to test drive a car or to attend a demo of a piece of equipment. It would typically be unrealistic to get a person to sign a deal based on a single persuasive message.

Select and Organize Information for Bad-News Messages

Sometimes you need to convey information your audience does not want to hear. When this is the case, you need to make a cost decision: is softening the message and maintaining goodwill with your audience important enough to expend some extra effort and cost in communicating with them? The alternative is to be blunt about the bad news and, if their feathers get ruffled, so be it. Of course, there is often potential damage to relationships when communication is too direct or perceived as insensitive. A tactful, carefully arranged bad-news message may take a bit more effort but is likely to at least mitigate any negative impression your receivers have toward you or your organization. The payoff in maintaining goodwill may be worth the effort.

Criteria to Apply to Bad-News Messages

The bad-news message gives audiences information they probably would rather not get. These messages may refuse requests or convey disappointing, embarrassing, or even possibly hurtful information the receivers would rather not hear. While conveying such messages are sometimes necessary, the way you communicate can make a difference in how your listeners perceive and react to you. If you come across as overly blunt or insensitive, you may be seen as a poor communicator, and relationships can be damaged. If you are overly vague or sound tentative, you may be seen as indecisive or weak. Your credibility can be damaged.

The ideal outcome is for your listener to conclude that, "I am disappointed (or upset, or even angry) about the message, but if I were in the sender's position, I would probably make the same decision." If you communicate effectively, receivers will understand why you needed to give the bad news and will respect you for doing so with compassion and class.

The ideal response to a bad-news message is for the listener to think, "I would probably make the same decision."

Have Empathy

Before preparing bad-news messages, empathize with your listeners. Put yourself in the shoes of your listeners and applying sensitivity in selecting the information you deliver. Based on your analysis of the context, you should have some sense of what kinds of information will work best. If, for example, you are communicating with a business person and must refuse a request because it would damage your profitability, use an appeal to the value of maintaining a profitable company. The receiver should understand that line of reasoning. On the other hand, if you are communicating with someone who may not understand basic business needs (e.g., to be profitable), you may refuse a request on the grounds that it would be unfair to others. Most people understand the value of fairness and will accept that as a reasonable rationale for a decision. Look for common values that your listeners would relate to.

Appeal to values you share with listeners.

Be Clear

Although conveying bad news is seldom pleasant, you need to be clear. Some speakers try to be so sensitive to their receiver's reactions that they never really get to the point—they never actually give the bad news. Sometimes they try to sugarcoat the negative information so much that the receiver doesn't "get it." For example, telling a job applicant that he did not get the job should leave no doubt about your decision. Saying, "the position has been offered to another applicant" may seem clear to the communicator but could leave ill-founded hope in the mind of a receiver who may not know if only one position was available or if the other applicant has officially *accepted* the job. They may think they are still in the running, although that is not the message the speaker wants to convey. If you fail to make the bad news clear, you run the risk of leading people on. When the finality of the bad news eventually hits them, they will be more disappointed than ever.

Avoid being so empathetic that your message becomes vague. Be clear about the decision you made.

Be Clear in Conveying Bad News

An example of lack of clarity posed a problem in a small training company owned by Brian and Glenn. Because of the success of the company, a steady stream of people approached the business owners and expressed a desire to become trainers for the seminars and workshops the company offered.

When people applied for jobs as trainers, Brian was constantly optimistic, implying that the company would be delighted to hire the applicant. His need to be well-liked caused him to avoid directness. He inevitably led them on with vague promises and stalling tactics rather than being direct in telling people possible bad news.

Glenn then found himself having to play the role of the "bad guy." He found himself facing unhappy would-be trainers when they got tired of waiting for a definitive answer from Brian. Although Glenn also likes being well-liked (who doesn't?), he was more frank when people were not going to be hired. The outgrowth of this is that Glenn—the one who was candid with applicants—has far stronger credibility than Brian, who told people what they wanted to hear. The moral of the story: bending over backwards to "save" people from receiving bad news can damage your credibility. Be clear in all your communications—even the bad news.

Pattern of Arrangement to Apply to Bad-News Messages

This one basic pattern for delivering bad news has two very important options:

1 You can use it alone ("quick-and-dirty"), or you can add a complete introduction and conclusion ("traditional"). We will show you the Q&D version later in this chapter.
2 You can switch steps three and four. Give the bad news and then explain the reasons (direct approach), or explain the reasons first and then give the bad news (indirect approach).

Your decision about which approach to use should depend on your context analysis. Your hidden agenda may play an important role. If you want to maintain goodwill with the person getting the bad news, you may prefer the indirect approach—unless you know that your listener prefers to get negative news directly. In our experience, most people are comfortable with a direct approach at work, but they both use and appreciate a softer, indirect approach in personal situations.

The traditional "bad-news" pattern of organization includes six key elements:

1 Buffer.
2 Transition.
3 Reasons.*
4 Bad news.*
5 Alternative.
6 Optimistic close.

*Steps 3 and 4 may be reversed depending on your guess about listener preferences.

Now, let's look at the parts of this approach pattern for presenting bad news. Each step in the approach is highlighted in the message shown below and is discussed in detail in the following sections.

Example of a Message to Refuse a Request

Thank you for your interest in the kinds of employee motivation programs we are developing here at Synectic Systems and for your request to speak to your group in November. (*Buffer*)

Although I welcome such opportunities with young people, (*Transition*) after checking my travel schedule for the remainder of the year, I find that I have a conflict with the November 19 date you mentioned. I will be attending a conference in New York and will not return until November 22. (*Reasoning and refusal*) May I suggest an alternative? (*Alternative*)

Dr. Elliott Anderson has recently joined our organization. He brings excellent academic background and seven years' industrial psychology experience with a major manufacturing organization on the West Coast. He is eager to know more people in the area and has indicated a willingness to talk with your group on November 19.

Elliott is an excellent speaker, and I'm sure you'll enjoy his presentation. (*Optimistic close—makes the alternative easy to accept*) You can reach him via email at EAnderson@XYZcorp.com. I have asked him to look for a message from you to confirm his availability and to get more information about the topic you want him to address.

Again, thanks for thinking of us to speak to your fine group.

With my best regards,
Karina Powell, VP, Consumer Marketing

Let's look a little closer at this message.

1 Use a neutral or mildly-positive buffer. The buffer sentences present neutral or positive information with which the listener is likely to agree. The speaker's comments about "appreciating [the listener's interest" is an example of such comments. Often this buffer thanks listeners for their interest or makes other complementary statements with which anyone would be likely to agree. This buffer is designed to get the listener into the rest of the message—to avoid a premature turnoff before you've had a chance to explain the reasoning behind the bad news. One caution: the buffer should not sound so encouraging that it misleads the listener. Keep it vaguely positive or neutral.

A buffer that is too positive may create false hope for listeners.

---

2 Make the transition. Once you have offered a buffer, step 2 is to transition carefully into your reasoning. A transition may be just one word (especially if you have not been misleading). Its purpose is to connect thoughts and prepare the receiver for what is to follow. Some experts recommend that you avoid using "but" or "however," especially if these may sound like an abrupt shift in tone. We find that "and" with a smile works with most of our corporate clients.

3 Present your reasoning. Bad-news messages should be based on your best reasoning and make sense to your audience. If you are successful, your audience will either agree with the bad news or at least understand *why* you decided as you did. Remember the ideal outcome: the receiver will think, "I'm disappointed, but I would probably make the same decision if I were in his or her shoes."

The information you select to present should be factual, logical, and clear. If your decision is based on prudent reasoning, you should have no need to sound apologetic. It's okay to express regret or acknowledge the listener's disappointment, but apologizing too strongly undermines the perception that you made a sound, albeit unpleasant, decision.

Don't apologize for a well-thought-out decision, even if it is bad news for the listener.

In our example, the speaker had to refuse the request. The reasoning is simple—she will be out of town. In other cases, you may need to convey more detailed reasoning. For example, an employer refusing a job applicant may want to explain in more detail about the job requirements and why the candidate's skills do not meet the specifications for that position.

Express specific reasoning clearly and unapologetically.

4 Give the actual refusal or bad news. Be tactful but conclusive. In our speaker example, the fact that Ms. Powell will be in another city makes it clear that she cannot speak to that group. In some cases, the finality of the refusal may not be quite so clear. The actual refusal or bit of bad news should be carefully worded and clear so that there is no misunderstanding on the part of the audience. Some people feel that they soften the blow by phrasing the bad news in the passive voice ("Your request must be denied") versus active voice ("I must deny your request"). Passive voice tends to separate the action from the doer of the action, which is only rarely acceptable because it sounds like the speaker is unwilling to take responsibility for the decision.

Note that the other option to using this pattern is to offer the reasons first, and then give the bad news. Make this choice based on your audience analysis—how your audience would most appreciate hearing the news—not on what is most comfortable for you.

Another subtle way to soften the blow of bad news is to position the actual refusal so that it naturally receives less emphasis. The positions of strongest emphasis are at the very beginning and the very end of each paragraph you speak—your first words and your last. Your refusal or bad-news phrase would be best positioned toward the *middle* of the message for de-emphasis. Placing the bad news between the reason and the alternatives provides this opportunity.

The first and last words of a message tend to be emphasis positions. Don't put the bad news there.

---

5 Offer an alternative. Look for a way to give the bad-news recipient some alternative to his or her original request. Our example, of the Vice-President with a scheduling conflict does this very effectively and sends a powerful message about her willingness to make her refusal less painful by offering another speaker. Any alternative should be explained in a positive tone, conveying the assumption that it will be accepted.

Also, when offering an alternative, make it easy for the listener to accept. In some cases, communicators simply toss the ball back to the person making the request. They may say something like, "If some other date would be acceptable or if another person from our company could be of help, please contact me again." That would fail to achieve closure—the problem remains unresolved. If you offer an alternative, follow through on the new idea. Don't just give the problem back to the requester and start the whole cycle over again. Offering a lesser alternative should not be used as a way to avoid saying no. It should only be used when you genuinely want to offer an option to the person to whom you are giving bad news.

6 Use an optimistic close. Once the refusal or bad news has been clearly and tactfully conveyed, deliver an *optimistic close*. The intent of such closing remarks is to further repair any damage to goodwill that may have occurred. Use this as an opportunity to express confidence that a good business relationship will continue. Our speaker example expresses appreciation for being invited to speak.

Do not apologize. Since your decision has been based on sound reasoning, there is no need to apologize. In fact, the effusive apology may cause your audience to question the reasoning, wondering if you feel guilty for some misdeed. Instead, confidently express a desire to maintain a favorable relationship with the message receiver.

As you can see, the bad-news message requires more thought and effort than the routine informational message or a relationship-damaging, "Sorry. No can do" with the reason "It's company policy." The payoff comes from projecting a favorable, caring image, and not being seen as an insensitive communicator.

Quick-and-Dirty Inform and Persuade

As promised, we will now show you some quick-and-dirty patterns of arrangement. These can be easily memorized and applied when you have little preparation time and/or a limited presentation time available.

STARR

One of our favorite patterns of arrangement can be easily remembered with the acronym "STARR." We elaborate a bit more on this below because it is one of the most effective ways to quickly organize a useful and coherent response for information. For example, let's say your boss asks you for a quick progress report while she is on the way to another meeting. Pull this organizational pattern out of your communication arsenal when you need a sure-fire, on-target weapon for delivering basic information. There's no reason to be left standing alone in a hallway, mouth open, pen raised, and point unmade.

Use this pattern in response to questions like, "How's the project coming?" Try it in an interview when someone asks, "Give me an example of a time when you ..." Applying STARR reminds you to cover the situation overall, your task, your actions, your results, and your recommendations. STARR helps you *get to the point*.

The STARR Questions

Here's a set of questions to guide you through your preparation.

Situation
Exactly what does my target audience want to know about the situation or issue at hand? Then, what do I *need* them to know? Briefly define the situation for your audience. You should assume that they do not know as much as you do. You should also assume that they do not *care* about it as much as you do. Don't waste your time here. Balance what you believe they want with what you think they need.

Task
What is (or was) my responsibility? Tell your listener or reader your understanding of your assignment. In some cases, this might be your overall job description. Usually, you only need to describe your specific responsibility for this one particular project.

Action
What did I (or my team) do? Explain the process that you followed, step-by-step. Remember to practice the use of active language; say, "We did this and then we did that," not "This and that were done" (by whom?).

"But," you may object, "I can't 'brag'!" Well, actually, you can (briefly). If the question was about the update on Project ABC, and that's your project, then the only way to accurately describe what's going on is to talk about yourself. Humility is over-rated.

Results

What did I (or we) accomplish? What was the outcome of your action? This is the point when the information becomes important and when you can elaborate (finally!).

- **Be specific.** Articulate exactly what happened as a result of your actions.
- **Show the result.** Yes, *show.* This is the place to reinforce your message with a visual aid. A picture of the product. A graph of the ROI. An email from a satisfied customer. Your audience doesn't even have to actually *read* it; just having it in your hand is enough.
- **Make it about them.** Remind your audience "what's in it for them"— why your results benefit *their* corporate or professional goals.

Recommendations

How can I (we) apply what I (we) learned? Review what you learned (specifically if you are using STARR to answer an interview question). Suggest how that knowledge might contribute to the future success of the project or the company.

Note about recommendations: sometimes your audience does not expect you to suggest recommendations, and they might perceive you as overstepping if you do so. However, most of the time, even if your audience does not expect recommendations, they will perceive your contribution as "taking initiative"—a very good professional strategy on your part.

A quick review: STAR(R) stands for "situation," "task," "action," and "result." (If applicable, the second "R" stands for "recommendation.") Apply this pattern for a progress report by describing a situation you or the company faced, what task this situation required or what your specific task was, what action you took, and what finally happened as a result. Here is one more brief example.

- **Situation.** The department's sales results on high-margin products were dropping for three consecutive months. Sales people seemed too eager to sell the base model which had lower profit margins.
- **Task.** My assignment was to find a new incentive program that would motivate sales people to tell customers about our newer, more-sophisticated products.
- **Action.** I offered small but immediate cash bonuses for getting an appointment and giving a demo of the latest products.

- **Result.** Sales of high-margin units increased by 15 percent in October.
- **(Recommendation).** We should use similar cash incentives to target specific products that best impact our bottom line.

So, when you have only a couple of minutes to inform or explain, remember: define the situation, describe your task, explain your action, show your results, and, if appropriate, offer recommendations.

The ANSA Pattern

In theory, successful persuasion is simple. All you have to do is help your listeners get an answer to their questions or problems. The key word is "answer." With a little accent (Paul says it's New England; Sherron says it's Southern), answer becomes ANSA, which stands for:

Attention
Need
Solution
Action

Admittedly this is a bit corny, but corny can be memorable (like those awful commercials that you can't get out of your head). We want you to remember not only the four parts to the approach but also the key to successful persuasion—providing *answers*.

ANSA provides a proven pattern for organizing a persuasive message.

The ANSA pattern can work in almost any persuasive message and especially when you are "on the fly"—in the elevator or in the hall or on the way to the parking lot—any time you need to be convincing in a hurry. We will discuss each part as isolated steps in a four-step sequence, but these parts often overlap. Sometimes, when the need is obvious, more emphasis is placed on getting attention and convincing the reader your product or idea really is the answer. With this understanding clearly in mind, let's look at each part of the ANSA approach separately.

1 Gain audience *attention.* In this "quick-and-dirty" situation, try a simple statement of the topic or reference to the occasion, a startling statistic, a rhetorical question, a quotation, a definition, or a story. To work best, these techniques need to appeal to specific audience needs by implying or offering some benefit. Such benefits are *persuasive appeals*. Categories of persuasive appeals are widely used in communication to get listener attention. Some examples are appeals to the listener's needs for

- Success.
- Power and status enhancement.
- Self-satisfaction, happiness, fulfillment.
- Curiosity.
- Security.
- Actualization or empowerment.

These attention-getting appeals may be phrased positively or negatively. Positive appeals focus on what the message receiver stands to gain; negative appeals accentuate what the audience might lose if they do not pay attention to your message. Examples of such appeals were presented in Table 4.1, back on page 79.

Finally, attention-grabbers when you are in "quick-and-dirty" mode must be zingers—fast and dramatic. For example, don't use a quote from Thomas Jefferson. Instead, try something such as, "George says we're losing customers at the downtown store." Don't tell a story unless it's very short. And don't ask a question unless your audience knows it's rhetorical, or you may lose your precious time listening to the other person talk.

2 **Develop the** *need*. Often the attention-grabber combines interest-creating information with a description of a problem. Television commercials often follow this pattern, presenting an unpleasant situation in such a way that we can identify with the victim of, say, embarrassment, discomfort, disappointment, or failure. Our reaction may be to empathize and feel the discomfort of some similar emotions.

Why Does Need-Agitation Move the Reader to Action?

Psychologists explain this in terms of balance theory. People prefer to be in a state of psychological balance or equilibrium; they want perceptions to fit together, to make sense, to seem rational, to be comfortable. You create feelings of tension and imbalance when you expose a problem your listener can identify with. If strongly felt, this is agitating. To reduce this agitation or tension, the audience will try to restore psychological balance. If your message is effective, that restored balance comes about by doing what you, the persuader, suggest.

Therefore, expose a problem with which your audience can identify, and then make it relevant to his/her own situation. If your listener or reader has little knowledge of the problem, you may choose to use most of your time on this step. Sometimes, when the need is obvious, place more emphasis on getting attention and convincing the audience that your product or idea really is the answer.

3 **Offer a** *solution* **to the problem.** Once you have your listeners' attention and have helped them identify a personal need, your job is to explain how to satisfy that need. You can best do this by giving the listener a solution. To convince your audience that you really do have the solution, you'll need to select believable evidence—information that supports and clarifies your big idea. Such evidence can take the form of:

- Descriptions of benefits your product or idea provides.
- Statistics and related objective facts.
- Quotes or testimonials (perhaps from others who have tried your solution).
- Product samples.
- Answers to possible objections about your product or idea.

You probably have limited time, so be sure your support material is powerful and succinct, but also be prepared to back it up in detail if asked.

4 **Close with a call for** *action.* An action close makes the difference between a nice, informative message and one that gets results.

The action close seeks to do two things:

1   Persuades your listeners to do something specific.
2   Summarizes the benefit they can expect from taking this action. This becomes the conclusion of the message.

An action close tell listeners what to do and makes it as easy as possible for them to comply.

The action close should tell your listeners exactly what to do. It should also make it easy for them to comply. The tone of the action step should be assumptive—it should imply that you assume they will do what you ask. You should be moving from the conditional phrasing, such as "If you do it," that you used at the beginning of your message, to the more definitive, "Here's how you do it." Assume that your audience has understood and agrees with your reasoning. They now simply need to be nudged a bit to obtain the benefits you promise.

The following are examples of action closes:

- Go to our website today, while you're thinking about it—and I'll send you a free examination copy of the Executive Planner. You'll be surprised how much time this modern management tool will save you. The impact on your productivity will be substantial!
- Authorize two additional employees to work on the taskforce, and I will pay to send them to the software training classes out of my

departmental budget. The classes start in two weeks, so I need your approval right away.

■ Get a DVD describing the specific benefits of [product, service, or idea] by signing the sheet I am passing around.

We close this discussion of the ANSA pattern with one more example. Assume you do not have time to develop a complete introduction and conclusion. Your down-the-hall speech might go something like this:

(Attention) Jackson, we are very close to losing major money on the Maloney project.

(Need) The process is taking too much time because the staff is underqualified with a slow learning curve.

(Solution) If we hire a consultant now, we can speed up the process. The cost of the consultant is 50 percent less than the cost of delivering this project late. I have identified the appropriate consultant, and she is available on Monday.

(Action) With your approval, I'll make the arrangements, and we'll be back on track by the end of next week.

Remember: grab attention, establish the need, offer your solution, and request action. One last step: stop talking! Give your target audience time to say "Yes." Then go to work.

Organize the Longer Message

The ideas for selecting and organizing information presented in this chapter will help you develop effective messages. You can readily apply these to virtually any communication medium, including emails, memos, conversations, or brief presentations. But what about longer business communications such as major reports or multi-part presentations? The answer is that the same principles of selecting and organizing information apply to the long, complex presentation.

Occasionally, a longer briefing will call for the use of several of these patterns of arrangement. The bad-news portion may, for example, be followed by a persuasive appeal using ANSA. Or a STARR pattern can be used within a longer report to explain some actions you took.

Having these patterns at the front of your mind when preparing any message can be invaluable.

Performance Checklist

After completing this chapter, you should be better able to apply some principles for selecting and organizing information for your message. Specifically, you should now understand that:

- You must be clear about your specific goal—your big idea: what do you want your reader or listener to *do*, *think*, or *feel* as a result of getting this message?
- The big idea of your message will seek to fulfill one of three basic purposes: inform, persuade, or give bad news.
- If you have no significant time restraints, traditional organizational patterns include a well-developed introduction (attention-grabber, agenda, purpose, benefit) and conclusion (summary, action, final statement).
- The traditional bad-news message often uses a pattern of arrangement which includes these steps: buffer, transition, reasoning, refusal or bad news, alternative, and optimistic close.
- Persuasive business messages seek to get readers or listeners to *do* something they normally would not do without some prodding. They awaken people's emotions and often use an indirect approach.
- If you must convey a message quickly due to limited time with your audience, use "quick-and-dirty" patterns of arrangement rather than just winging it.
- The STARR pattern gives logical structure to explanations and informative messages.
- The ANSA pattern of arrangement is an often-helpful persuasive tool. ANSA stands for "attention," "need," "solution," and "action."
- For long messages, break the overall message into smaller units, applying an appropriate organizational pattern to each section.
- Never end a presentation with a Q&A. Doing so risks losing control of the message and runs the risk of contradicting or deflating your message with an off-topic question.
- Wrap any presentation with a final statement that reiterates your big idea.

What Do You Know?

Activity 4.1: Persuading a Speaker

Prepare an outline of a persuasive message asking a local business leader to speak to your student group or professional organization. Write down the ideas you would use to persuade this person in a format that would be useful if you called him or her on the telephone. Assume that the person will need some persuading because you cannot pay for a speaker. Give special thought to potential motivators that would cause the receiver to consider accepting your invitation. Anticipate objections and address them.

Activity 4.2: Preparing a Current Event Informative Presentation

Prepare a brief oral presentation to fulfill the following situation:

Topic. A local current event. Identify a current business event that has an impact on you or your community as reported in a local publication. (Check your local newspaper or its online version.)

You, the speaker. You are a consumer or a community member who is being affected by the event in some way.

Your audience. Business people (organizational leaders) like yourself and their families.

Objective. To inform your audience of three things:

1 The summary of the article describing the event.
2 How the company's actions will or have affected your audience(s).
3 What they (your audience) should do as a result of this event.

Time. Three minutes, maximum.
Dress. Business casual.
Preparation. Fill out and turn in an Outline Worksheet (shown below).

OUTLINE Worksheet

Introduction

- **Attention-grabber.** Based on what I know about my primary audience, what will get their attention (and also relate to topic and situation)?

  _____

- **Purpose.** As a result of this message, what do I want my audience *to do*?

  _____

- Are there any reasons I should be *indirect* with the purpose of this message (including cultural considerations)? If so, how should I temper my expressed goals?

  _____

- **Agenda.** How am I going to accomplish my objectives; that is, what is my *agenda* for delivering the message?

  _____

- **Benefit for audience.** What's in it for them, *specifically* and *personally*?

  _____

Conclusion

- **Summary.** Exactly what do I want my audience *to remember* (the essence of my main points)?

  _____

  _____

- **Specific action.** Exactly what do I want my audience *to do*?

  _____

  _____

- **Strong final statement.** What is the *last thought* I want to leave with them?

  _____

  _____

Body

Choose from these common patterns:
1 Chronological order.
2 Problem–solution.
3 Topical or spatial.
4 Cause-and-effect.
5 Bad news: buffer, transition, bad news, reasons (or reasons first, for a more indirect approach), alternatives, positive close.

- Point 1: _____
  Support material (such as statistics or examples):

  _____

- Point 2: _____
  Support material: _____

  _____

- Point 3: _____
  Support material: _____

  _____

- Point 4: _____
  Support material: _____

  _____

STARR and ANSA Worksheets

STARR Worksheet

First

Who is my target audience?

What do I know about this audience?

Is there anything else really important that affects this message?

The STARR pattern can work for many situations when you have very little time to make your case with your target audience. Use the first four steps for a progress report. Add the final step (recommendations) when you have the opportunity.

1   **SITUATION. Exactly what is the situation or issue at hand?**
     (Briefly define the situation for your audience, who may not know as much about it as you do.)

2   **TASK. What is (or was) my particular job or responsibility?**
     (Be specific about what you did or are doing on this particular issue or process.)

3   **ACTION. What did I do (or what are we doing)?**
     (Clearly explain the process, step-by-step.)

4   **RESULTS. What did I (or we) accomplish?**
     (Tell exactly what happened as a result of your actions. Remind your audience "what's in it for them"—why your results benefit whatever their goals are.)

5   **RECOMMENDATIONS. How can I (we) apply what I learned?**

     (Review what you learned; suggest how that knowledge and experience might benefit your audience or the company's goals.)

ANSA Worksheet

First

Who is my target audience?

_____

_____

What do I know about this audience?

_____

_____

Is there anything else really important that affects this message?

_____

_____

The ANSA pattern can work for almost any persuasive message. ANSA is a four-step sequence, but sometimes the middle two steps are presented in a different order (the solution coming before the need development). Sometimes, when the need is obvious, more emphasis is placed on getting attention and then presenting your solution.

1 **ATTENTION. What can I say that will get my audience's attention?**
(Try a statement of the topic, reference to the occasion, a startling statistic, a rhetorical question, a quotation, a definition, or a story.)

2 **NEED. How can I explain that this is a personal problem for my audience?**
(Expose a problem your audience can identify with; help them identify a personal need.)

3 **SOLUTION. What can I say to convince my audience that I have a solution to the problem?**
(Explain to them how to satisfy that need; select believable evidence—information that supports and clarifies your proposal.)

4 **ACTION. How can I clearly ask for action that will get results?**
(Ask for something specific; tell them what's in it for them; tell them exactly what to do.)

Reinforce With These Review Questions

1 Traditional, formal presentations (time permitting) should have three major parts. What are these? (1) _____,
(2) _____, and (3) _____.

2 True/False—An effective introduction should grab attention, provide an agenda, and suggest listener benefit.

3 True/False—Ending a presentation with a question-and-answer session is a good tactic.

4 Positive, routine, or informative messages should use a(n) _____ pattern of arrangement.

5 What does the acronym STARR stand for?
   S = _____,
   T = _____,
   A = _____,
   R = _____,
   R = _____.

6 True/False—Linking features to benefits means telling listeners "what this means to you."

7 What does the acronym ANSA stand for?
   A = _____,
   N = _____,
   S = _____,
   A = _____.

8 True/False—The bad-news message pattern puts the bad news after a buffer and then either before or after the reasoning.

9 True/False—One especially effective way to defuse a refusal message is to offer the listener an alternative.

10 Selecting and organizing the content of a message should always be done in light of your _____ analysis.

Mini-Case Study: Charlie's Short-Notice Presentation

As he walked into the office, Charlie's boss called out: "Hey, Charlie, I need you to come into the meeting with Division and give them a progress report on the company's new branching strategy." (The retail division has launched an aggressive expansion with new branches opening almost monthly.) "We are meeting in half-an-hour. Can you be ready to go?"

Meeting in half an hour?!, thought Charlie. *How can I possibly put together a sensible presentation that soon?* But that's not what Charlie said. Instead, he said, "Sure. I'll be ready."

Immediately, Charlie started running the Straight Talk Model through his mind. He realized that he knows a lot about the context—he's been working with these people for years and has a pretty good fix on what they want to know. He also realizes that the media–source–timing issues have been pre-determined—he is to deliver the information via a presentation to the Division Heads at 10 a.m. But what about Step 3? How can he best select and organize the information?

Twenty minutes later, Charlie was ready. He had put together a good introduction (attention-getter, agenda, and listener-benefit statement) and then used a chronological pattern of arrangement to describe the progress on building the new branches. He covered the oldest branch's results first and then progressed up to the newest branches under construction. He invited questions but ended with a final statement that reiterated that the strategy is working well and on schedule.

After the initial panic of being hit with the task of presenting on short notice, he was surprised and pleased to see that he really was ready and could display confidence—with a little help from the Straight Talk Model.

Questions

1 What kind of an introduction would you use for such a progress report? Be as specific as possible. (Can you think of an interesting story about expanding the number of branches?)

2 Do you agree with the chronological pattern of arrangement? What other alternative(s) might make sense?

3 What kinds of questions or possible resistance might the speaker antici-pate from this audience? How can he or she prepare for contrarian or skeptical comments?

five

Enhance Your Message with Powerful Support Material

Visual aids can make you appear more confident, more professional, and more of an expert. They can add color, humor, and images that you could never convey in words.

(Tony Alessandra, *Communicating at Work*)

Support Materials for Stronger Messages

The "stickiness" of a communicated message—how well the audience remembers—depends on how interesting, memorable, and effective the speaker is. While some people just seem to have a knack for getting and holding the attention of their listeners, anyone can learn the techniques for doing this. We can develop our own tool kit of tactics that greatly improve our likelihood of getting across to our listeners.

Performance Competencies

When you have completed this chapter, you should be able to:

- Understand the importance of enhancing your message.
- Recognize multiple options for enhancing your message.
- Appreciate the potential impact of appropriate examples and stories.
- Identify the functions that visuals fulfill for listeners and for speakers.
- Describe the most commonly used visual formats and understand the use of each.

- Identify six consistency elements to apply to visuals.
- Avoid over-complicating your visuals and overwhelming your message.
- Explain at least seven ways to make the most of projected visuals in oral presentations.
- Evaluate feedback on your visuals in order to continually improve your design and delivery.

The Way It Is … Dan Gives a Briefing

Dan Steenburg's boss asked him to give a ten-minute briefing on his department's activities at the weekly management meeting. When it was time to speak, he produced hard copies of his materials and fumbled in his pocket for the jump drive that contained the presentation. As everyone waited (not patiently, we should add), he loaded his presentation into the conference room computer and searched for the right file. Finally, he was ready, but the batteries were dead on the remote mouse, and he had not brought his own, so he had to ask someone to change his slides.

When his slides were finally projected on the screen, each one contained ten-to-fifteen lines of information per page. Some included charts and graphs, but many were just text and numbers. None had any pictures. The type was so small that the people in the front had to squint to read it, so he told his audience, "You probably can't read this, but …" several times during the presentation. He then read what was on the visuals word-for-word.

His supervisor kept asking the same questions: "What are you trying to show here?" and "What exactly does this mean?" and "Can you give me an example?" She was obviously confused and disappointed with Dan's presentation.

If Dan is lucky, his visual aids and the way he uses them are not significantly worse than what is expected in his organization. Hopefully (for him), everybody does data-dump slides. If that's the case, all he's accomplished is to look average in front of his management. But if Dan's company has come into the twenty-first century and expects well-prepared visuals, used skillfully, his professional image just took a dive.

An increasingly important part of message delivery is the use of stories/examples and visual aids. Almost any oral communication can be enhanced with the use of some form of support. Today's generation is the most visual in history. We have all been subject to far more visual stimulation than people who lived before the ubiquitous presence of television, movies, videogames, and computer graphics. In short, people expect to *see* something in addition to receiving audio messages.

Similarly, today's audiences expect some elements of entertainment in messages they receive. Think about people you regard as effective communicators and we are willing to bet they use stories.

First: Use Stories and Examples

We have all heard stories since we were little children. We bet you can still remember stories your parents or siblings told you when you were a tiny tyke. What is it about stories that make them stick in our memory?

Chip and Dan Heath's excellent book, *Made to Stick*,[1] explores the question of why some ideas succeed while others fail, and concludes that much of the success has to do with how well the ideas are communicated. Stories, they argue, are one of the most powerful instruments for achieving message "stickiness."

While being an audience for a story may seem like a passive role—we are just sitting back and listening—this passivity may be like the proverbial floating swan who, below the surface, is paddling like crazy. In other words, our minds are actively engaged. "When we read books, we have the sensation of being drawn into the author's world. When friends tell us stories, we instinctively empathize. When we watch movies, we identify with the protagonists."[2]

The Power of Stories (Especially to Grab Attention)

Some of the most effective communicators start their speeches, briefings, and even meetings by launching immediately into a story. Hyrum Smith, co-founder of FranklinCovey, the training and consulting firm, modeled this behavior dramatically. Smith would often start a speech by launching into a story. No "Good morning." No "It's good to be with you today" or other such comments. He'd simply start telling a story.

One such story told of a crew on a 1978 United Airlines DC-8 that experienced an in-flight emergency. The landing gear appeared to be malfunctioning, risking collapse upon landing. As the vividly-told story evolves, we learn that the captain insists on burning off fuel long after his fellow crew members caution him that they don't have enough to make it to the airport.

The flight crashes just short of the runway, killing ten people, although the cockpit crew survives. Later legal action against the captain challenges his decision to "ignore the collective wisdom" of the other crew members, resulting in the catastrophe. Smith then simply asks about the "collective wisdom" we may be ignoring.

The story is told with compelling detail and the imagery sticks with the audience. An important theme of his message is introduced, all in an engaging manner using a story that sticks in the mind.

The power of stories lies in their ability to trigger mental images that stick in the mind. Stories may be the single most powerful way of enhancing message content.

Example is a first cousin to the story. Typically, examples amplify on a point but are less robust than a story. A message making a point about how certain sales behaviors (say, getting customers to test drive the product) result in a better close ratio may enhance this point by describing several sales people who apply the behaviors and have had demonstrable improvement in their ability to close sales. The example: "Tara increased by 30 percent the number of hands on demos her customers participated in. Her close ratio rose from 12 percent to 27 percent."

Stating a key idea (collective wisdom is important, or get customers into a test drive) with no further support is rarely effective. It is human nature for people to ask "Why?" or "How?" to almost any assertion. Few are willing to take a directive without questioning it to some extent.

Spinning Tales and Leadership[3]

It should be no surprise that when it comes to leadership, movie mogul Peter Guber's thoughts turn quickly to storytelling. After all, storytelling is the business in which Guber emerged as a leader. But he also makes a powerful argument for the use of stories as tools for leadership.

At a recent Wharton Leadership Conference, Guber noted that the best way to communicate with and motivate employees is to tell them a story—to repackage an enterprise's vision, goals, and challenges into a narrative that audiences can understand, embrace, and share.

Uncertainty makes for a complicated business environment, but leaders can help employees embrace the goals mandated in that environment, Guber suggested, adding that the tool to do so is available to all. "Narrative bonds information to an emotional experience," he said. There is no need to be in the movie business to tell effective stories. Everyone is "a factory of old stories. So when you want your tribe, your group, your human resources people, your executives, your customers, your shareholders to do something, you have to remember you've already got something playing on the record machine in your head."

> He doesn't suggest conjuring up random anecdotes. Rather, the goal should be to form narrative out of a situation at hand, and make others feel like characters in the drama. It's about giving others a story to imagine and tell others as they embark on a project.

Use Visual Displays to Enhance Message Comprehension

Why use visuals? People you communicate with today were raised with much visual stimulation: television, movies, videogames, and computer graphics, to name a few types. About 60 percent of people prefer to receive information visually (as compared to hearing or feeling). They are not accustomed to processing words alone—they want to see something presented graphically. In addition, studies of listener comprehension over the years have repeatedly come to the same conclusion: visuals help receivers get the message. Studies confirm that audiences remember up to twice the information when they see it in addition to hearing it. In fact, the Kodak Corporation estimates that any given audience remembers 20 percent of what they hear and 80 percent of what they see. (Of course, Kodak *is* in the visuals business.) The case for using visuals is solid. Any oral presentation (and most documents) will benefit from visual displays of information.

The case for using some form of visuals is solid.

Visuals Help Both the Speaker and the Listeners

Visuals are vital to you as a communicator because they help fulfill at least five important functions. Visuals help *speakers* to:

- Develop the content of their message.
- Organize ideas and create continuity of thought.
- Strengthen the impact of their message.
- Clarify important concepts or associations.
- Provide attention-holding variety.

In addition, visuals help speakers to stay on track since they serve as notes. A quick glance at a slide is often all a speaker needs to keep his or her message on track.

Visuals help *listeners* to:

- Clarify and digest abstract ideas and relationships.
- Retain information.
- Avoid boredom, daydreaming, confusion, and apathy.

To make the most of these functions, you, as a communicator, should look at visuals as an integral part of your presentations, not as afterthoughts. Plan your visuals as you draft your message. Also, keep in mind that visuals are not just appropriate for formal presentations but may be very useful in other forms of oral communication such as interviews, meetings, and even conversations. You are not, of course, limited to the use of slides—sometimes simple printed visuals or pictures are useful, especially in one-to-one communication.

Visuals may be appropriate for a variety of communication situations, not just presentations or speeches.

Empirical Support for the Use of Visuals?

Two studies (3M/Wharton School and the University of Minnesota/3M) concluded that there are three areas in particular where the use of visuals can improve presentations.

1 **To improve communication effectiveness.** Visuals add another sensory channel to the oral communication process. Visuals utilize right-brain visual and spatial processing to complement the left-brain processing used in listening. Synergism between left- and right-brain processes creates better "whole-picture" communication. People have been communicating visually since early history.

2 **To improve audience's perceptions of the presenter.** Presenters using visuals are perceived as significantly more prepared, professional, persuasive, credible, and interesting. Also, presenters using slides are perceived as "more professional" than those using overhead transparencies. Those using animated movements and transitions as with presentation packages like PowerPoint™ are regarded as very professional.

3 **To improve the speaker's confidence.** Visualization encourages better organization and planning, which boosts a speaker's confidence. Poor presenters using good visuals can be as effective as good presenters not using visuals. "A typical presenter using presentation support has nothing to lose and can be as effective as a better presenter using no visuals. The better a presenter is, however, the more one needs to use high-quality visual support."

In addition, the use of visuals results in improved efficiencies. Groups reached faster decisions (12 percent improvement with use of visuals), spent less time in meetings (average 18 minutes with visuals, versus 26 minutes without visuals), and saw a highly significant improvement in audience action.

The University of Minnesota/3M study showed the following improvements when visuals are used:

- The audience's likelihood to take action improved 43 percent.
- The perceptions of the presenter were 11 percent higher.
- Information retention, comprehension, attention, and agreement improved by 10, 8.5, 6.5, and 5.5 percent respectively.[4]

Visual Aids: What are the Options?

The term "visuals" is used broadly to describe anything other than the communicator's voice that (hopefully) enhances the message. Occasionally "visuals" are not technically visual, such as when using sound clips or even music. But most of the time they are something the audience (or listener) looks at. Here are quick looks at the most commonly used visuals.

Computer-Projected Slides (Usually PowerPoint™)

The most ubiquitous form of visual in today's business world is the Power-Point slide. This Microsoft software has revolutionized the use of projected visuals. It is not uncommon to hear widespread grumbling about PPT slides. Most complaints are based on the *misuse* of PowerPoint, however, not the fact that it is being used too widely (although there is some legitimacy to the over-use concern, as well. We have heard anecdotes of business audiences applauding when a speaker said he was not going to show any slides!)

Projectors may face technology failure. (It happens more often than you might think.) As a precaution, it is best to print off the slides onto paper in case of total equipment failure. Also, have an extra bulb for the projector. If you intend to use a laptop and projector, you should set up early and become very familiar with the software as delays/errors, clips that don't play, or other glitches will make your presentation look bad. Dan, in our opening example, should have gotten to the conference room early to set up.

Flipcharts

These large sheets of blank paper are used to write down key points during a presentation or idea-generating meeting. They can be pre-prepared or used as a more interactive device. If you pre-prepare flipcharts, they function as low-tech slides. To create the sense of progression, some trainers write key points as they speak. If you do not have good handwriting or artistic skills, this would not be an effective option. Use flipcharts only in situations where all audience members can easily see them—that is, they are not more than a few feet away.

Overhead Transparency Projectors

Yes, you might still find one or two of these, but they signify "old" and "out of date." The one significant advantage that this approach has had over PPT is that the speaker can use a special pen to write on the slide and project the image onto a white board/screen. In this sense, it can function like a flip-chart. (Computer software now allows you to write on slides as well.) However, most organizations don't even have these around anymore.

Sounds and Video Clips

These can be useful (or fun), but the most common problem with clips is that they don't work! Technology gremlins seem to pop up way too often. Always make sure that you have checked the equipment on which you will be playing the sounds or clips and check the volume. If you are playing the recording in a large room, you will need to experiment with the volume so that everyone in your audience can hear. Practice playing each recording. You shoot your credibility in the foot if your audience has to wait while you to cue up the track.

Props

The word "prop" derives from the word "property," a theater term for the portable items that actors carry in their hands. For the purposes of presentations, these are everyday objects that can be used as visual aids to enhance your speech. To ensure that the audience can see the objects, you should use big objects or be prepared to pass them around your audience.

Two caveats, however:

1 Someone may like your prop so much that you won't get it back, so don't use anything too valuable.
2 Props can be distracting. Members of your audience will watch them being passed around and will look down when they are holding them, so know that you need to allow time for that diversion.

Motivational speakers sometimes use props to suggest a theme. Zig Ziglar used to perform with an old-fashioned water pump. He'd pump the handle as he spoke about the importance of "priming the pump" to get oneself motivated. Another speaker used large cylindrical cans that he would move around the stage as he talked about all that we "can" do.

Sketches/Role Play/Simulations

These are small presentations that simulate a point or part of your presentation. These are used more in training sessions, but can be put to good use in other forms of communication as well. For example, inviting a meeting attendee to describe how he or she would close a sale (role played) might be an appropriate application.

The risks associated with this "visual":

1   You may embarrass or make a participant feel uncomfortable.
2   You may get a badly performed role play that will undermine your message.

Handouts

Printed handouts of key information or data are common in presentations or meetings. Workbooks (a form of handout) are used in most training sessions. The key to effectiveness is to not let the handout distract your listeners. If the handout is more interesting than you, you will lose their attention.

Some speakers like to offer handouts of their slide deck so the audience can make notes and have a record of the presentation. You have at least three options here:

1   **Full-page slides.** Speakers who have too much information on their slides in the first place usually select this option so that their audience can see all the little numbers. We discourage this option.
2   **Three-to-a-page.** This is the choice for speakers who want their audiences to take lots of notes and who have limited information in a large font on their slides. We *like* this option.
3   **Notes pages.** In PPT, the top half of the page is the slide on the screen, and the bottom half contain any additional information you say or want to leave behind. We like this option, too, because the focus remains on the speaker during the presentation and on the support material later, when the audience looks back to review.

Another Look: Tufte's War on PPT

Princeton Professor Edward Rolf Tufte has earned some measure of fame for his criticism of PowerPoint visuals. He has spent decades studying "information design and visual literacy" which deal with the visual communication of information. He coined the term "chartjunk" to refer to the useless, non-informative, or information-obscuring elements of quantitative information displays he says appear too often on PPT slides. He also speaks of "data–ink ratio" to argue against including non-informative decoration in visual displays of quantitative information, and says that all ink not used to convey and display data should be eliminated.[5]

Tufte also says that decorations can help editorialize about the substance of the graphic. But, he cautions, it's wrong to distort the data measures in order to make an editorial comment or fit a decorative scheme.

Tufte criticizes the way Microsoft PowerPoint is *typically* used, arguing, among other things, that:

- It is used to guide and reassure a presenter, rather than to enlighten the audience (we are not sure this has to be an either–or, but that is his argument).
- It has unhelpfully simplistic tables and charts, resulting from the low-resolution of computer displays.
- It forces a linear progression of information on the audience (whereas, if you distributed handouts, readers could browse and relate items at their leisure).
- It uses poor typography and chart layout, from presenters who are poor designers and who use poorly designed templates and default settings.
- It supports simplistic thinking, from ideas being squashed into bulleted lists.

Finally, Tufte argues that the most effective way of presenting information in a technical setting, such as an academic seminar or a meeting of industry experts, is by distributing a brief written report which can be read by all participants in the first five-to-ten minutes of the meeting. Tufte believes that this is the most efficient method of transferring knowledge from the presenter to the audience. The rest of the meeting is then devoted to discussion and debate.

Although your authors do not agree with all of Tufte's concerns (he focuses most of his work on technical or academic presentations), his point of view sparks interesting debate.

Use Individual Visuals for Major Points

Plan each visual so that it drives home a single point. The quickest way to lose the effectiveness of a visual aid is to over-complicate it or try to convey too much information. Keep them simple and concise. Never display a chart or graph that your audience cannot comprehend in 20 seconds or less. You can accomplish this by sticking to one key point and removing any superfluous materials. Dan, in our opening story, violated this rule by showing unreadable, "busy" data.

Too much information defeats the purpose of visuals.

Be sure to know exactly when to present your illustration so it coincides with your message. Reveal the chart, graph, or illustration only when you are ready to reinforce a particular point. Showing one thing while talking about another will distract or confuse your listeners. This sounds like a simple point, but we have seen many cases where the visual and spoken messages are out of sync.

Use an Appropriate Type and Overall Design Concept

Use visuals that are appropriate in terms of type and overall design concept. To select the appropriate type of visual aids, pay attention to the expectations about visual aids in your industry, organization, or company. Carefully observe what other, successful people are doing with visuals, then meet or exceed those expectations. Of course, you can often find bad examples, but look at what the best speakers are doing and emulate—or exceed—that behavior.

Knowing the "appropriate" design concept involves reviewing the first step of the Straight Talk Model—defining your context. You should do so by analyzing the situation, your audience, and your purpose. Use the details you gathered to make your basic choices for templates, colors, fonts, clip art styles or pictures, charts, and, especially, words. We will discuss each of these elements later in this chapter.

Apply Common Visual Formats

Several tried-and-true formats work well for business visuals. Among these are word charts, pie charts, line charts, and bar charts. Additionally, reports and presentations often require discussion of processes or organizational hierarchy, which suggests the use of tables, flow charts, and organizational charts. (*USA Today* and other publications do a great job with the visual display of information. Look carefully at these to get creative ideas for your own graphics.)

Word Charts

A word chart states key ideas concisely and directly. It is probably your simplest visual and certainly the one people most often use in oral presentations. In preparing word charts, economy of language is crucial. The sample chart illustrated in Figure 5.1 shows you some rules for making word charts. Note that the five lines of body copy are parallel and that the template is dark with light lettering for clear contrast. (The cat is optional, but we rather like our yawning cat.) Figure 5.2 shows a light background with dark lettering.

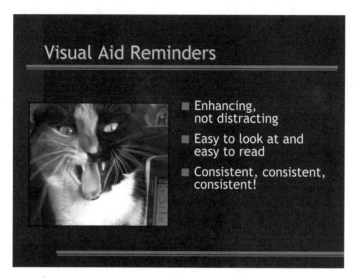

FIGURE 5.1 An Example of a Word Chart with Dark Background

Do Your Homework

- Find an interesting job description
- List the specific duties and requirements
- Determine needed education/ experience
- Evaluate how you fit
- Plan a positive strategy

FIGURE 5.2 An Example of a Word Chart with a Light Background

The most common mistake in the use of word charts is too many words. You should not post every word you plan to say, and you need not use complete sentences. As you draft your word charts, be a ruthless editor: cut out any words you can delete while maintaining the meaning you want to convey.

Word Charts With Graphics

Often, word charts are made more interesting with the addition of clip art or graphics. Figure 5.3 shows the relationship between three elements. Figure 5.4 shows the addition of art (in this case an illustration, but it could be clip art, cartoons, etc.) to add viewer interest to a word chart slide.

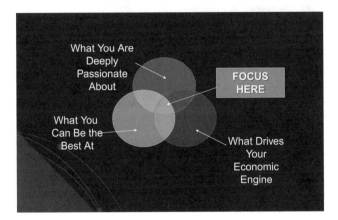

FIGURE 5.3 An Example of a Word Chart with Graphic

FIGURE 5.4 An Example of a Word Chart with Art

Pie Charts

A pie chart is a simple, circular illustration that is divided into segments to show part-to-whole comparison. It can effectively show only a few broad divisions (since a pie can only be sliced into a limited number of pieces). When creating pie charts, cut segments of the "pie" accurately, beginning at the top and moving clockwise for each new segment. Label each "slice," showing what it illustrates and the percentage it represents. Use large, clear lettering for the chart.

Graphics software packages like Excel™ or PowerPoint™ will automatically slice the pie correctly for you. You can also select a three-dimensional design, as shown in Figure 5.5.

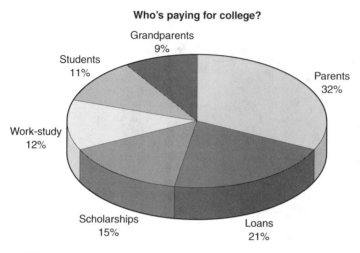

FIGURE 5.5 An Example of a Pie Chart

Line Charts

A line chart is a "trendy" way to show a continuous picture of trends or changes over time. It can also show simple comparisons of trends by color-coding different lines. An example of a multiple line chart is shown in Figure 5.6. Be sure to use dramatically different line types and colors so that distinctions are clear.

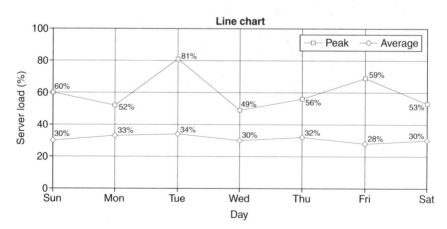

FIGURE 5.6 An Example of a Line Chart

Bar Charts

A bar chart compares one item with others. The most common types of bar charts are:

- Vertical bar charts, which are especially effective if you want to illustrate "height" and compare accomplishments, such as nearness to a goal or dollars of profit.
- Horizontal bar charts, which illustrate and compare distances over time.
- Segmented bar charts, which clearly visualize how different parts contribute to a whole over time.
- Grouped bar charts, which dramatically compare groups in specific times or areas, as shown in Figure 5.7.

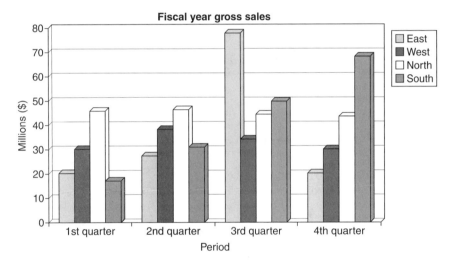

FIGURE 5.7 An Example of a Bar Chart

Area Chart

Area charts show comparative data in a slightly different way. The sample below (Figure 5.8) shows relative sales in three different stores over a course of time.

Gantt Charts and Organizational Charts

Gantt charts (so named for their inventor, an early management theorist) and organizational charts usually require significant detail, so we recommend them for oral presentation visuals only when they can be made very simple. Flow charts show step-by-step progression of processes or procedures to simplify the receiver's understanding. They are particularly helpful in giving instructions or explaining the solution to a problem.

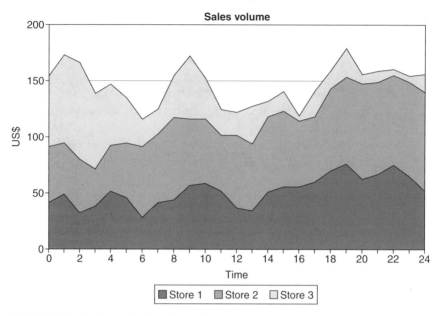

FIGURE 5.8 An Example of an Area Chart

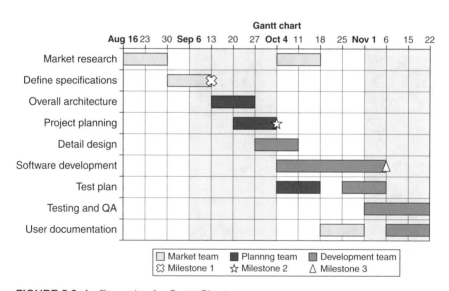

FIGURE 5.9 An Example of a Gantt Chart

Organizational charts illustrate the structure of a company, such as who works for whom and how many departments are in each division. Since many companies are very complex, organizational charts are useful to both internal and external audiences. They show lines of authority (chain of command) and job responsibilities. Software packages often have templates for building organizational charts.

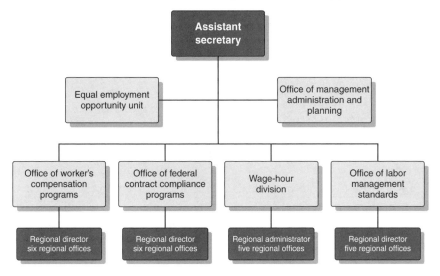

FIGURE 5.10 An Example of an Organization Chart

The Use of Photos in Slides

Photographs can add interest to slides and are widely used. Communicators should, however, be aware of possible legal ramifications.[6] When presentations are directed to internal audiences in an organization or to small groups, you are unlikely to risk legal action (with a few exceptions we'll describe below). Bear in mind, however, that when photos are used for public presentations, advertising, or widely-distributed showing, people in the pictures and the photographer may be entitled to credit and/or compensation for their work.

If you do not want to solicit permission or pay for a photo, you have several options. First, check online for materials that are copyright free—photos that are "in the public domain." A second option is to take your own photos. Finally, you may want to purchase individual photos (or sets of similar photos) from the producer. Any limits to their use will be spelled out in a purchase agreement, but generally if you pay for a CD with related pictures, you are granted almost unlimited use of them. If you elect to use pictures captured off the Web, keep in mind some guidelines described below.

The most common problem you will run into is a photo with people in it. If you are using their images for editorial purposes (somewhere in a limited-exposure presentation), it's usually okay to use them without permission. If you are using photos with people in them for advertising, you need their permission. People have a right to profit, and to exclude someone else from profiting, from their photograph or likeness.

In using images of people, be careful not to:[7]

- Defame the person in the image through captions or narration.
- Portray them in a false light.
- Libel them or slander them with falsehoods.
- Injure their reputation.
- Subject them to hatred or contempt.
- Hold them up to ridicule.
- Distort their image by cropping or altering.

In all of these cases, an individual can sue for monetary losses and mental anguish. If you have even the slightest concern about damaging a person, courtesy dictates that you show them the picture you plan to use, to be sure they are comfortable with it. If the photo will be widely shown or distributed, ask the person to sign a release form okaying its use.

Check Visuals for Design Consistency

Your visuals should be consistent in terms of background, font, structure, capitalization, spacing, and illustrations. In the next few sections, we will look at each of these areas of consistency.

Maintain design consistency in visuals or you will distract your audience.

Background (Templates)

A template is a consistent design background for your visual materials such as slides. In selecting a template, choose only one and then stick with it for the entire presentation. Do not mix different templates, since this will cause your message to look inconsistent and unprofessional. Keep in mind also that the more illustrations you plan to use, the simpler your template should be.

When deciding upon a template, choose a style that symbolizes your message and shows respect for your target audience. For example, avoid overly "cute" templates (say, one with balloons or children's drawings) if you are doing a serious business presentation. If the context of your message is somber, select a conservative style. If your purpose is motivational, upbeat, or entertaining, consider a template with a border of stars, flags, cartoon characters, or other icons associated with the topic of the talk. Be creative, but be certain that your overall design is suitable for the occasion, your audience, and your purpose.

When choosing color, keep in mind that high contrast between background and text provides excellent visibility in a lighted room. The traditional standard is a dark background with white or yellow text. You are not restricted to this combination, but remember that cool, dark colors (such as blue) appear to move away from the audience and warm, light colors (such as yellow) appear to move toward the audience. You might try colors that complement your company logo or that symbolize your message. Finally, consider colors that might be particularly appropriate for the country or culture of your audience. Most important, however, is that you have contrast so that your audience can easily read your slides.

Fonts

Your fonts (also called typefaces) should be consistent in terms of size and type throughout your presentation's visuals. All titles should be the same size and the same font from slide to slide, as should all body copy. (If the font is larger on one visual and smaller on the next, your audience will feel like the screen is moving toward and away from them, which is disconcerting.) However, the fonts for title and body copy may be different from each other.

Two basic types of fonts are serif fonts (in which the letters sit on small "platforms") and sans serif fonts (with no "platforms"). Serif fonts are traditional, and some experts consider them easier to read. Sans serif fonts look contemporary and may be more dramatic. Examples of some common serif and sans serif fonts are shown in Figure 5.11.

Box below gives examples of different serif and sans serif fonts that are typeset in the particular fonts described

Examples of Serif Fonts	Examples of Sans Serif Fonts
Bookman Old Style, **Bold** and *Italic*	Arial, **Bold** and *Italic*
Garamond, **Bold** and *Italic*	Univers, **Bold** and *Italic*
Times New Roman, **Bold** and *Italic*	Comic sans, **Bold** and *Italic*

FIGURE 5.11 Examples of Serif and Sans Serif Fonts

For slides used in oral presentations, we suggest a minimum size of 28 point for body copy and a minimum size of 36 point for titles in most standard fonts with a clear difference between the two. Title fonts may be bolded, italicized, or significantly larger. Avoid using underlining because it will look like a hyperlink.

What Are "Points?"

The term "points" refers to a sizing method for measuring typefaces. The term comes from the traditional printing industry, where 1 point equals 1/72 of an inch. This was a measure of how much "lead" to place in the molds used in old-fashioned printing presses. This form of measuring type sizes has carried over, although most printing presses no longer use lead type.

Figure 5.12 shows some font sizes.

Box below describes different point sizes please typeset in that particular size

Insufficient size contrast	Effective contrast
Title (24 pt)	Title (36 pt)
Bullet points (18 pt)	Bullet points (24 pt)
Title (24 pt)	Title (36 pt)
Bullet points (18 pt)	Bullet points (24 pt)

FIGURE 5.12 Font Sizes

Avoid the temptation to use many different fonts or many different sizes. You may mix a sans serif font for your titles with a serif font for body copy (or vice versa), but be certain they look sufficiently different from each other. Don't select similar fonts for titles and word chart copy; make them either exactly alike or very different to create sufficient contrast. You might add an additional display font occasionally for a special effect, but be careful. (Display fonts are such things as Maximus, Century, Bauhaus93, Auriol, and dozens of other artsy designs. Use those rarely.)

Generally avoid unusual or excessively decorative fonts.

Too much variety in fonts creates a "busy" look that can be distracting. Be aware, also, that when producing PowerPoint™ slides, some fonts do not always show up as you expect. Some computers may distort a font that looks fine on another machine. Stick with the common, traditional fonts or, if you elect to use more unusual ones, be sure to check what they look like when projected—*before* your presentation (a good idea anyway). Remember that the fonts you choose will make an impression on your audience, just like the templates and colors you use.

Structure

Bullet points or enumeration on visuals are a good way to break up the text and to provide information that is easy to digest. *Bullet points* refer to listed items that are preceded by a bullet (■) or small symbol. *Enumeration* refers to such a list when each item is numbered (or lettered). Use enumeration when a list is sequential (e.g., step 1, step 2, etc., or (a), (b), etc.), or when you may need to refer back to the list of items.

When using bullets or enumeration on visuals, the points should be "parallel"—the grammar should be the same. If your first point begins with a verb, each succeeding one should also begin with a verb. Similarly, if you start with a noun, adjective, gerund (a word ending in –ing), or adverb, start every point with the same word form. For example, notice the parallel construction in the following sets of points:

■ Analyze the environment, Consider the options, Select information. (*Each clause begins with a verb*)
■ Cost of doing business, Return on investment, Comparison with competition. (*Each phrase begins with a noun*)
■ Overall goal, Specific purpose, Hidden agenda. (*Each phrase begins with an adjective*)
■ Deciding on our mission, Communicating the goals, Encouraging participation. (*Each phrase begins with a gerund*)

Making each point parallel makes the message clearer for your audience and conveys your professionalism.

Parallelism means starting each bullet point with a similar word form (noun, verb, gerund, etc.)

Capitalization

Use capital letters sparingly in visuals. You may print your titles in all capital letters, but for the most part, a mixture of uppercase and lowercase letters is more natural and easier to read. All-caps feels like yelling to some listeners. Capitalize only proper nouns (names) and the first letter of the first word in each bullet point of body copy, as you see in the figures used in this chapter so far. Don't capitalize the first letter of each word because then everything will look like a title.

Spacing

Your titles or headings should begin on the same spot on each visual (such as centered, flush left, or flush right). Also, start your body copy on the same line on each visual. The space between your bullets should be consistent as well. Avoid the urge to spread bullets out if you only have two or three. Use that extra space for a picture or other graphic, instead. If you don't have an appropriate illustration, "white space" (the portion of the visual with nothing on it) is perfectly fine and is preferable to spacing that varies. Imagine reading a book that is single-spaced on one page and triple-spaced on the next!

Use consistent white space on all slides.

The space between bullets should be about one-and-a-half times the size of the bullet font. So, if your bullet is 36 point (about a half-inch), the space between items should be about three-quarters of an inch. This is not an exact rule, of course. But be consistent with your spacing, even when you have only a few bullet points.

PowerPoint's™ Consistency Features

If you are using PowerPoint™, you can check for consistency in spacing, type style, sizing, and bulleting by looking at your work on the "Slide Sorter." Spacing standards can be set up using the "Slide Master" function. By taking time to get familiar with your software, it can save you a great deal of time in the long run.

Illustrations

"Clip art" is an assortment of pictures, cartoons, illustrations, and icons (symbols) available in computer graphic programs. The term comes from the old days when graphic designers would physically cut and paste pieces of art onto documents or layouts. Clip art helps to illustrate your points and break up your documents. It can even help your audience to focus on the words on your slides if you choose illustrations that "point." However, be careful with clip art because it can become too "cute" very quickly.

Figure 15.3 shows some examples of clip art available in your PPT program.

Your graphics should be similar in size and type throughout your presentation. Since their purpose is to enhance your message, not distract from it, be sure the illustrations match the message. For example, don't mix cartoon-character clip art with realistic-looking photo art. Clip art available online through Microsoft is organized by family resemblance, making it easy for you to keep the pictures consistent. If you choose photographs, try to use them throughout your presentation. Mixing art types, like mixing too many fonts and sizes, looks haphazard. Consistency looks more professional.

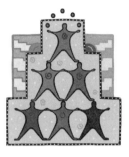  

FIGURE 5.13 Examples of Clip Art

Where, exactly, can we get art for our computer-projected visuals? This is easy. You may first check Microsoft for its downloadable clip art. (In Microsoft Word, you can get into this by clicking "Insert" and "Picture," and then "Clip art." Then type in what picture you want and follow the prompts. Other word-processing software may vary.) Another approach is to use a search engine such as Google.com and search for "images." Type in descriptions of what you want pictures of and you will get clip art, photos, etc. Then simply right-click your mouse on the images you want and save them to your computer. Be aware that the resolution (color and clarity) of the pictures may vary considerably, so check them before pasting into your slides.

Love–Hate Relationship with PowerPoint

The love–hate relationship regarding PowerPoint is nothing new. In addition to Edward Tufte (cited on page 115), another critic of PPT, Peter Norvig, asks us to "imagine a world with almost no pronouns or punctuation. A world where any complex thought must be broken into seven-word chunks, with colorful blobs between them." Then he reminds us that we don't have to imagine it. It is a present-day reality of a PowerPoint presentation. (To see a hilarious example of how Abraham Lincoln's Gettysburg address would have appeared in Power-Point format, visit www.norvig.com/Gettysburg.)

Regardless of which side of the discussion holds more credibility for you, one cannot argue that presenting to someone is primarily one-way communication. And that's rarely a very effective method in most situations. Often, PowerPoint creates an obstacle to an honest, shirtsleeve conversation. It can inhibit give and take of discussion and debate.

"While PowerPoint didn't invent one-way communication, it certainly perfected it!" says Abhay Padgaonkar, writing in *Marketing Profs* online newsletter.[8]

Avoid the Misuse of Visuals

Although we are obviously enthusiastic about the value of good visuals, a few cautions are in order. Visuals can be misused when they:

- **Are too complicated.** Probably the single most important thing to remember about visuals is to keep them simple and concise. Simple design lingers in the mind of the receiver very effectively. Your receiver should be able to look at a visual and "get it" within a few seconds.

- **Overwhelm the message.** Remember that the visual presentation of information is a way of *supporting* the speaker and his or her message; it is not the message itself. Your presentation will be primarily spoken words; the visuals support and reinforce your words, but do not replace them.

When Less is More

One of our regular clients, a former Navy pilot in business development with a defense contractor, was preparing a briefing for a Navy rear admiral. The purpose of the presentation was to explain the capabilities of a new airplane. The draft version of the slide show contained too may charts with too many numbers and words.

We decided to try a slide with only an illustration of the airplane on its mission, which was communicating with a variety of satellites, ships, and other airplanes. It looked much more interesting than words and numbers, so we created another scenario on a second slide. My client, who was an excellent and knowledgeable speaker, would simply show the pictures and explain the scenarios. He liked the idea but was not sure how this non-traditional concept of presentation—neither words nor numbers on the slide—would be received.

On the day of the briefing, the admiral listened passively as our client presented his scenarios—one by one. No response (and our client was questioning the radical decision to omit all the little numbers). After the last one, the admiral interrupted with "Wait!" My client thought he must have made a mistake with his creative approach until the Admiral asked, "Do you have another scenario of another mission?" He had been engaged and wanted more.

This one incident had more impact on the preparation of presentations at that company than hours of training could have. Success is particularly powerful in changing traditional behavior.

One further point: we strongly recommend *not* using a laser pointer with your visuals for two major reasons. First, it is extremely difficult to get the red spot to stand still and your audience's eyes will be distracted all over the screen. Second, if your visuals are well-designed and focus on one major point, you should have no need to point to certain parts of the slide.

Deliver Your Visual Aids with Confidence and Style

The following are some suggestions for boosting your effectiveness with visuals when delivering an oral presentation:

- **Leave the lights on while you show slides.** Well-prepared slides can be seen with normal projection equipment if the lights in the room are on or slightly dimmed. By keeping the room lighted, you avoid the problem of losing listeners who tend to doze off in the darkness. You also maintain eye contact with them more effectively and you'll be able to see and talk with them. Remember, you as the speaker should be the center of attention, not the visuals.

- **Use a remote mouse that allows you to change the slide without physically touching the projector.** Running back and forth to the keyboard distracts your audience. Also, change your own slides rather than saying "next" to someone at the computer.

- **Avoid turning away from your audience and talking to the image on the screen.** Set up your laptop with its screen facing you, so you don't need to look at the projected images. Glance at the visual but maintain eye contact with your audience.

- **Keep your slides to a reasonable number.** Don't overload your audience, and don't expect the slide show to be a substitute for a good presentation.

- **Minimize the number of transition types you use with presentation software.** PowerPoint™ and similar software allow you to do a variety of actions when switching from one slide to the next. Screen changes include a simulated curtain coming down and slides dissolving from one to the next. Some novice users want to try every bell and whistle and gimmick in the software; however, such gimmickry is distracting. If your audience is more curious about what your next slide change will look like than what your next idea will be, you're in trouble. Stick with quick transitions.

- **Check your visuals out in advance.** Computer and projector differences can cause visuals to look different. Be sure the projector is working—technology problems are the number-one source of presentation failures and can be huge stress producers. Be as well-prepared as possible for such problems. Arrive early enough to test equipment. Store your slides on several storage devices (on disc or a USB drive). Check out the videotape or DVD player, slide projector, and computer hookup. Make sure your DVD is cued up to the right place before you begin. Don't rewind or advance a videotape while your audience waits. Know your equipment, and use it smoothly.

Be prepared to use visuals efficiently. Don't make your audience wait while you cue up the clip.

Get Feedback on Your Visuals

Just as in other forms of communication, your learning process for using visuals does not stop with the actual delivery of your message. Step 5 of the Straight Talk Model reminds us of the importance of evaluating feedback for ongoing improvement. In visuals, as in any other form of communication, the reactions of your audiences can be valuable.

While you are designing your visuals, solicit feedback from trusted colleagues. Often, another person will see gaps, missing data, confusing layout, or other problems that you miss. Ask them to react to the template or the colors. Use open-ended questions and listen carefully to their responses. Be sure to have someone proofread your visuals. Typos, misspellings, or missing words can quickly undermine the effectiveness of your visuals—and your credibility.

Get feedback on your visuals. Audiences will inevitable note something you missed, such as typos or other distractions.

During the delivery of an oral presentation, note your listeners' reactions to the visuals. If they seem to be squinting at them, they are probably too hard to read. If they scratch their heads or seem to take a long time to read them, they may be too confusing or busy. If they don't get your cartoon, drop it from future presentations.

Be willing to give others your feedback about their visuals as well. If the graphics are good and helpful, let them know; if not, suggest why they were not helpful. Share the guidelines in this chapter with your associates and you will all produce better visuals for better communication.

Performance Checklist

After completing this chapter, you should be better able to apply some principles for selecting and organizing information for your message. Specifically, you should now understand that:

- Message content will be enhanced with the use of appropriate stories and examples. These help engage the audience and can lead to better retention.
- Visuals used in oral presentations will help speakers develop, clarify, and enhance their messages, and will help listeners understand and remember.
- Your analysis of the situation, audiences, and objectives with your audiences must be considered as you plan the appropriate visuals for your talk.
- Common visual formats include word charts, pie charts, line charts, bar charts, tables, flow charts, organizational charts, and props or models.
- Consistency elements for your visuals include background (template), fonts (typefaces), structure, capitalization, spacing, and illustrations.
- Over-complicating is the most common mistake with visuals. Don't allow your visuals to overwhelm your message—and don't read them word-for-word.
- Checking out the technology and your presentation visuals *before* your presentation is a must. Surprises are never fun!
- You can get feedback about your visuals from your peers and from the responses of your audience. Your visuals should clarify and enhance your message.

What Do You Know?

Activity 5.1: Preparing a Bar Chart

Using the hypothetical information given below, prepare a bar chart showing the top-ten occupations in ascending order by percentage of growth. Use a presentation software package such as PowerPoint™ and select the style of bar chart that best expresses your message.

According to one survey by the US Department of Labor, the ten most rapidly growing occupations are as follows. The number following each reflects the percent of growth in employment between 2000 and 2010.

Employment interviewers	66.6
Computer programmers	73.6
Paralegal personnel	132.4
Tax preparers	64.5
Office machine and cash register servicers	80.8
Computer systems analysts	107.8
Food preparation and service workers, fast-food restaurants	68.8
Data-processing machine mechanics	147.6
Computer operators	87.9
Aero-astronautic engineers	70.4

Activity 5.2: Recognizing Design Mistakes

Based on what you have learned in this chapter, can you identify the design issues that should be corrected in the slide in Figure 5.14? The audience is advertising representatives and the presentation is about time-management. The speaker is highly enthusiastic and funny, and the purpose is to motivate.

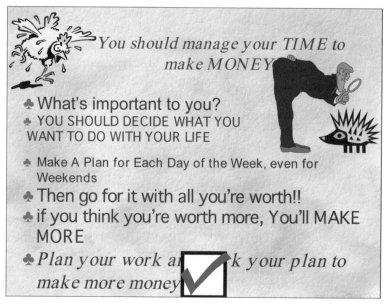

FIGURE 5.14 A Poorly Designed Slide

Activity 5.3: Selling a New Taxi Service

Using Poweroint™ or similar software, prepare between four and seven visuals you could use to deliver a briefing to sell corporate clients on the use of Century Sedans in Denver. Be prepared to explain what you did in each visual. Be sure to apply the ideas discussed in this chapter. Here is the story Century is trying to get across:

> The company is betting that corporate customers who visit Denver will support an upscale taxi service. Century Sedans launched its company with a fleet of 11 new Cadillac Fleetwoods shortly after Denver's new airport was opened in the mid-1990s. Since then, they have systematically replaced the Fleetwoods with Escalades, Cadillac's luxury SUVs.
>
> "We are not a limo company," said Dana Capaletti, Century's sales director. "We have upscale taxis, charge flat rates, and offer impeccable service without the ostentation of the limo." The company studied the market in Denver and identified a niche to serve customers who wanted

a luxury car service that was dependable and available by reservation up to six months in advance. The fact that the SUVs can go well through snow is another need customers identified.

Capaletti says that a major share of its business is done with customers who fly into Denver International Airport and then go to major corporate offices in the metro area. Each vehicle is driven by a chauffeur in a black suit, and is equipped with such conveniences as wireless Internet connections, refreshments, and special reading lights.

Customers are charged a flat-rate cost of $60, which is quoted when the reservation is made and can be paid for by credit card, a feature some cab services still do not offer. The flat rate is for the service of the sedan; up to four persons may ride at no additional cost. "We only charge for pickup and delivery. If we get slowed down by traffic or a snowstorm, that is our loss," Capaletti says.

Comparable costs for services from DIA (airport) to downtown via Yellow Cab averages $40 to $48, depending on traffic and weather conditions.

Optimistic about the future of Century's service, Capaletti said the company is adding more Escalades to its fleet each month. No vehicle remains in the fleet longer than three years, and each is inspected weekly. Capaletti also said each vehicle carries $1 million in liability insurance.

Activity 5.4: Preparing Visual Aids for a Presentation

Select a business-related problem from a current magazine or newspaper. Describe the problem or dilemma and several potential solutions. Prepare a computer-generated slide show (using PowerPoint™ or similar software) for your presentation. Create one good slide for each of the following:

1 Attention-grabber
2 Agenda/purpose
3 Benefit to the audience
4 Point #1
5 Support for point #1
6 Point #2
7 Support for point #2
8 Point #3
9 Support for point #3
10 Summary
11 Q&A
12 Action step
13 Strong final statement (visualized)

Reinforce With These Review Questions

1 True/False—Stories and examples tend to engage audiences better than straight factual statements.

2 Name three things visuals can help listeners do:
   (1) _____,
   (2) _____, and
   (3) _____.

3 True/False—Each visual should reinforce one major point.

4 True/False—Pie charts should only be used when presenting to someone in the food industry.

5 A consistent design background for a slide presentation is called a _____.

6 Three types of fonts are:
   (1) _____,
   (2) _____, and
   (3) _____.

7 True/False—The most common mistake with word charts is using too many words.

8 True/False—Clip art used should be from the same "family" if possible, for consistency.

9 Name three other forms of visuals beside slides:
   (1) _____,
   (2) _____, and
   (3) _____.

10 True/False—Turn toward the visual when talking about it. This will direct your audience's attention to the right place.

Mini-Case Study: Dan Gets Some "Advice"

Let's look back at our opening story of Dan Steenburg and his presentation visuals. In his case, the visuals complicated the communication rather than complementing it. If he worked for a typical, progressive company today, he would lose credibility because of the lack of professionalism in delivering his message.

After the presentation, Dan's boss, Mia, took him aside and gave him some coaching. "Look, Dan, you had some good ideas to share, but your visuals didn't help you at all. People expect decent visuals—specifically slides—with presentations. Your work reflected poorly on you."

Mia, who is known for being direct with her subordinates, went on. "Also, the way you selected and organized your information, then how you designed your deck, violates many of the rules of effective communication. You tried to show too much information, crowded into visuals that are hard to read. Telling the audience 'You probably can't read this …' does not excuse poor-quality visuals. You further compounded the problem by making us wait and by obviously not being familiar with the technology."

Dan wanted to crawl into a hole by now, but Mia continued: "I'm sorry if this is embarrassing to you, but I'd rather embarrass you than run the risk that you will again embarrass the department in front of executives or customers. We're a pretty sophisticated company, and you need to upgrade your approach. Slides should accompany almost any formal presentation. Being unaware of this or being incapable of producing acceptable visuals will be a significant disadvantage to you and your career here."

Dan left the office shortly after and headed to the nearest bar.

Questions

1   Was Msia unduly harsh? Was her advice and correction merited?
2   Would Mia's perspective be accurate at a company where you work? Why or why not?

six

Deliver Your Message with Confidence and Impact

There are four things people you communicate with won't forgive you for: not being prepared, comfortable, committed, and interesting.

(Roger Ailes, *You Are the Message*)

Delivering Your Messages

Many people experience some anxiety when speaking before others. In public speaking, this anxiety is often quite significant. But even in less-formal situations such as giving a briefing or leading a meeting—or even participating in an interview—anxiety can play a significant part in inhibiting effectiveness.

Communicators who fail to consider the delivery part of their communication efforts run the risk of having their carefully planned messages fall flat.

This chapter discusses the steps necessary to deliver your message content in ways that maximize its impact on your audience.

Performance Competencies

When you have completed this chapter, you should be able to:

- Polish your delivery using appropriate verbal, non-verbal, and platform-management skills.
- Speak clearly and expressively, pay attention to timing, avoid distracting vocal patterns, and minimize verbalized pauses.

- Manage notes and visual aids comfortably, and handle audience questions succinctly.
- Maintain eye contact, dress professionally, exhibit physical control, and project enthusiasm.
- Express confidence through an understanding of your material and your audience's needs.
- Appreciate the importance of being yourself and continuing to improve your delivery skills.

The Way It Is ... Communicating on the New Job

Brenda Flores was both excited and anxious about her management position with a high-tech multi-national corporation. As an engineer, Brenda had contributed to the design and development of several important, successful products. And now, her division had undergone a major re-organization at the very top level that had resulted in the appointment of a new vice-president.

Brenda had heard that the new VP was just one indication of a new corporate focus on her division, and she expected that there would be a larger budget and more opportunities for upward mobility. That was the exciting part.

Brenda had also heard that this new VP placed a high priority not only on smart people with good solutions, but also on those who could engage an audience and present their ideas with professional style. He expected his team to "step up and speak up."

Brenda was comfortable in small meetings with other engineers, but she never had to actually stand up and present there. She did well making a point in a limited time, but she always depended on notes and numbers. And even though she thought of herself as Senior Manager material, she realized she didn't sound as confident or look as "put together" as the people in the level ahead of her. The thought of having to "give a speech" or even to speak up in a meeting in front of her new boss pretty much terrified her. The more she thought about it, the more she questioned her ability to move ahead.

Everybody worries a bit about communicating in front of others. People want others to think well of them; they care about how effective they are being and sincerely want others to get their messages. They want to participate in group decisions and offer suggestions and ideas. And employers want people who do exactly those kinds of things. A company's most valuable people are those who communicate well.

This chapter discusses the fourth step in the Straight Talk Model: delivering your message. Specifically in this chapter, we will concentrate on five key factors necessary to deliver effective oral messages:

- Polishing your verbal delivery skills.
- Developing your platform-management skills.
- Polishing your non-verbal delivery skills.
- Showing confidence and enthusiasm.
- Rehearsing and editing.
- Managing anxiety and expressing confidence.
- Being yourself and becoming your better self.

The Widespread Use of Oral Communication in the Workplace

Oral communication in business is widespread and often takes the form of presentations. When you plan, prepare, and create a message to deliver to others, you make a presentation. Presentations vary in their degree of formality, but all are purposeful communication aimed at achieving a specific result. These are not speeches, although a speech can be one form of presentation. We are using the term to denote something broader. The following are some examples of presentations common in businesses:

- Alan Harris explains service department bills to his auto-repair customers. He communicates what work was done, why it was done, and how much it cost. Alan makes presentations.
- Heidi Astin sells upscale automobiles at a mid-size Porsche dealership. She greets customers, provides technical information, encourages test drives, advises on financing options, and handles all facets of these big-ticket sales. Heidi makes presentations.
- Michelle Harker serves as a facilities manager overseeing nine buildings for a rapidly expanding regional bank, She reports regularly to the bank's executive committee describing progress on new construction, remodeling, and maintenance issues. She shares her expertise and recommends the best office options for the company's needs. Michelle makes presentations.
- Carol Tanaka is searching for a new job, one that makes the most of her recently completed MBA. She has interviews almost every day and works hard to sell her talents and skills to prospective employers. Carol makes presentations.
- Carl Steinburg is having a performance appraisal with his boss today. He feels good about his work accomplishments and hopes to be considered for a promotion. Carl will make a presentation.
- Eric Jessop represents his company in community-service efforts that teach young people how to avoid drugs, alcohol, and relationship problems. Eric makes presentations.

- Marin Pickard has a highly responsible position in business development for an aircraft manufacturer. She represents both the company and its products to influential clients across the globe. Marin makes presentations.
- Charles Dunwoody is a Human Resources Manager who participates in decision-making meetings involving personnel issues from staffing to the results of employee surveys. Charles makes presentations.

"Hold it a second," you may be saying. "It's beginning to sound like *everything* people do is some form of a presentation." Well, that's about right. We all spend a large portion of our lives making presentations—offering information, persuading, or giving bad news to others. That is the reality of the work world.

Most communication activities can be viewed as "making presentations."

Polish Your Verbal Delivery Skills

Your specific audiences and the culture of your business will help shape the decisions you make about your communication style over the course of your career. As you speak and observe the reactions to your speaking, you will learn appropriate responses and make adjustments that become your personalized style. Some generic guidelines for success—some tricks and some common mistakes to avoid—can also be helpful in polishing your delivery skills.

Your verbal skills go beyond the words you choose. They also include the way you use your voice—pronunciation, articulation, volume, and pitch—and the dramatic aspects—emphasis, pace, and timing. In other words, verbal skills include how you use words to speak clearly and expressively. In the following sections we will look at ways in which you can improve your verbal skills.

Message delivery goes beyond the words of the message.

Speak Clearly

Concentrate on improving your pronunciation, articulation, volume, and pitch so that your audience can easily and comfortably hear and understand your words. Pronounce words correctly. Replace just one "pitcher" for "picture," and you will lose credibility with your audience. Articulate your words. Say all the letters in all the syllables of every word. Don't relax into "lemme" for "let me" or "gonna" for "going to."

Adjust the volume of your voice to your audience. Don't speak so loudly that you sound like an orator—like an old-fashioned pitchman on a soapbox. But don't speak so softly that you sound insecure or lacking in enthusiasm either. One myth is that if you speak quietly, an audience will lean in to hear you. The truth is that if you speak too softly, your audience is likely to go to sleep. Instead, simply direct your talk toward the people farthest from you. This focus will help you increase your volume.

Use variation in volume as well as in other vocal qualities such as pitch and rate of speech. Sameness becomes monotonous; variation attracts and holds people's attention and interest. Psychologists say that no one can pay attention to an unchanging stimulus for very long. We can't watch grass grow or paint dry. It's just too boring. Unfortunately, speakers who insist on using never-changing vocal patterns sound just about as boring.

Vocal variation (of pitch, rate, and volume) helps hold listener attention.

Speaking at a Lower Pitch

In many cultures, adults sound more credible when they speak using a lower pitch. To find the lowest pitch that is comfortable for you, try this: lie flat on your back and relax. Breathe from your diaphragm without moving your shoulders (this is easier to learn while lying down than while standing up). Then read out loud. The pitch you hear is your natural pitch. Try to maintain the same sound when you are standing up by simply relaxing and breathing from your diaphragm. Do not, however, maintain this pitch monotonously. The idea is to speak naturally, just a little lower, and with more resonance.

Speak Expressively

Work to perfect your emphasis and pace so that your audience can easily understand the meaning of your words. When you outline your presentations and practice your delivery, determine which words are the most important and then underline or highlight those words in your notes. Which words you emphasize can change the meaning of your sentences. Think of the different inflections you could give the question, "What do you mean by that?"

- *What* do you mean by that?
- What *do* you mean by that?
- What do *you* mean by that?
- What do you *mean* by that?
- What do you mean by *that?*

You can hear how different emphasis changes the sentence's implications and meaning. Be sensitive to implications of various inflections. The above examples can sound inquisitive or accusatory, depending on the emphasis. Perhaps your listeners will hear these "hidden meanings."

Let's try one more example. Put the emphasis on a different word in this simple statement:

- *I* think Maryanne can do that (but no one else thinks so).
- I *think* Maryanne can do that (maybe she can).
- I think *Maryanne* can do that (she could, but no one else can).
- I think Maryanne *can* do that (she could but may not want to).
- I think Maryanne can do *that* (she can't do much else, but that she can do).

Emphasis on a different word can change the implied message of even a simple statement.

Many speakers get feedback that indicates that they talk too fast; some talk too slowly. But trying to slow down quick-speak may seem awkward, as can trying to speed up a deliberative, slower pace.

If you tend to speak quickly (some cultures encourage this), consider this. A better alternative may be to identify material that is new, difficult, unusual, or particularly important for the audience and focus on presenting that information at a slower pace. Then return to your comfortable, normal, faster pace. Again, you may want to highlight this important information on your outline.

The challenge of speaking too slowly is that people listen faster than you can deliver the message. Their minds go ahead of you and may jump to unintended conclusions. It can be difficult to listen to 120 spoken words a minute when your brain is thinking at 500 wpm. You simply have too much "free time" to let the mind wander.

Speaking too slowly can be just as distracting as speaking too fast—perhaps more so.

Pay Attention to Timing

One of the most dramatic effects a speaker can learn to use is timing. The pause can be a powerful emphasis tool. There are many places a pause can enhance your presentation:

- After you walk to the front of the room but before you begin speaking.
- Before you make an important point ("This is the bottom line:" [pause]).
- After you make an important point ("Our profits would be in the millions [pause] if we …").

- When you ask a question (pausing may feel awkward; however, most speakers don't wait long enough).
- As a transition between main points ("That sums up the problem." [pause] "We are looking at several solutions.").
- After your final statement and before "Thank you."

The rate of speech can either help or hinder the listener. Go slowly enough to get the ideas across, but not so slow that listeners "fill in the blanks" or wander off.

Speaking with an Accent

Do you think that you have an accent that distracts your audience and diminishes the perception of your credibility? Well, everyone has an accent! We all have a vocal signature. If you are from a geographical location that is unique to your workgroup, you might sound different from them. Or, if the language you are using is not your native tongue, you will sound different from native speakers.

Typically, your accent or even your sentence structure and vocabulary, which might be different, are not the problem. Audiences are open to such variations in today's global business environment. A mild accent can be charming—*unless* your audience has trouble understanding you. Then we recommend one basic tactic: *articulate all of the syllables in all of your words*. Focusing on articulation will also slow you down and give your audience time to become accustomed to your rhythm. Soon, your accent will be one reason why you are unique and engaging—and it will no longer be a distraction.

Avoid Distracting Vocal Patterns

Some speakers get into voice patterns that undermine their professionalism. Speakers who let the end of sentences trail off into a soft mumble are one such example. Another distracting vocal pattern is what is called "up-speak." Here the speaker raises intonation at the end of a statement, making it sound like a question. Say the following sentences aloud using up-speak—raising intonation on the italicized word—and you'll hear how this can undermine a message.

- She's very good at everything she *does*. (The listener will ask: "Is she?")
- The management is concerned about the *costs*. (The listener will ask: "Are they?")
- My name is John *Mansfield*. (The listener will ask: "Are you sure?")

Notice how up-speak creates a note of uncertainty in what is spoken. Unfortunately, some people habitually use up-speak without noticing how it can undermine their assertiveness and make them consistently sound tentative.

Up-speak creates a sense of uncertainty and can undermine your credibility. You will sound less confident when your statements sound like questions.

Minimize Verbalized Pauses

Few things can drive an audience crazy like the liberal use of verbalized fillers, such as "ah," "um," "uh," and (a popular favorite) "ya know." Some intelligent and apparently rational men and women salt their every utterance with these expressions until their listeners want to scream at them, *ya know?*

The human talker abhors a vacuum. When the detested monster, silence, raises its ugly head, some beat it to death with "ah," "uh," "um," or "ya know." Do yourself a favor: ask someone you trust to point out when you are drifting into this habit. Commit yourself to listening for and eliminating your own filler words. Rid yourself of the fear of silence.

Filler Word Use[1]

Why do some people fill the air with non-words and sounds? For some, it is a sign of nervousness; they fear silence and experience speaker anxiety. Recent research at Columbia University suggests another reason. Columbia psychologists speculated that speakers fill pauses when searching for the next word. To investigate this idea, they counted the use of filler words used by lecturers in biology, chemistry, and mathematics, where the subject matter uses scientific definitions that limit the variety of word choices available to the speaker. They then compared the number of filler words used by teachers in English, art history, and philosophy, where the subject matter is less well-defined and more open to word choices.

Twenty science lecturers used an average of 1.39 uh's a minute, compared with 4.85 uh's a minute by 13 humanities teachers. Their conclusion: subject matter and breadth of vocabulary may determine use of filler words more than habit or anxiety.

Whatever the reason, the cure for filler words is preparation. You reduce nervousness and pre-select the right ways to say ideas through preparation and practice.

Develop Your Platform-Management Skills

As a speaker, one of your tasks is to manage the communication process. Two aspects of platform management include the careful use of notes and visual aids and the handling of audience interaction, especially question-and-answer (Q&A) opportunities. Work to achieve professionalism in these tasks, which we will discuss in the following sections. (Again, we note that your "platform" may not be a formal speech, but these principles apply to all oral-communication situations.)

Use Your Notes Carefully

If possible, avoid using notes altogether when delivering your message—just use your visuals. Well-prepared visual aids provide a useful set of notes for your presentation. You should be familiar enough with your topic to rely almost entirely on the outline on your visual aids. If you are using a laptop computer, simply turn the screen toward yourself and you will have your "notes" right there.

However, you may need additional notes when:

- Your material is new or too complex to show using just visual aids.
- Visual aids are not appropriate, such as when you are introducing someone or giving a luncheon speech.
- You need to emphasize certain, specific words or concepts, and precise wording is imperative.

In such cases, we suggest writing key words or phrases on note cards that you can carry easily and unobtrusively. If you use note cards, be sure to write only key words (the fewer the better!) in large letters on the cards. Also use cards that are at least 5 × 8; don't try to hide them from your audience.

Note cards are rarely necessary when you use visual aids.

As we have said, the biggest preparation mistake a speaker can make is to write a presentation word-for-word. If you write it, chances are you will read it. Reading a manuscript, no matter how well-written, will negate the positive effects of all your other work on your presentation. You will appear unprepared and unprofessional, and you will severely diminish your chances for success. The only exceptions to this may be in high-level negotiations or when presenting a carefully worded public announcement where a misstatement could create legal difficulties. Dignitaries in delicate negotiation situations may read a prepared speech, too. But such situations are rare in workplace communication.

Corporate executives often have so many speaking engagements that they employ trusted assistants or professional speechwriters to prepare their remarks. Sometimes, this is acceptable. However, it is never okay to read every word. Even the most script-dependent speaker can learn and then just say the first sentence and the last one. No-one needs to read, "Good morning and welcome to Big Corp" or "Thank you so much for coming, and please enjoy your tour of our facility."

If you choose to use handouts, determine if you want the audience to follow along with you as you speak, or if your handouts are for later reference. If the handouts cover additional material or follow a different order than your presentation, distribute them afterwards.

Manage Your Visual Aids

Your objective with visual aids is to convince your audience that you are the one in control. Your visual aids should not appear to be managing you (like the dog who "walks" the owner). First, be sure your slides look right on the screen and confirm that any embedded sound or video will play. Then, learn to work your equipment. Know, for example, how to move back to your previous slide. Use a remote mouse yourself (thus avoiding the dreaded, "Next slide, please"). If you need a flipchart, check for fresh markers.

Manage your use of visual aids. They can be a source of distraction rather than a help in getting your message across.

When you are presenting, focus on your audience, not on your visual aids. Avoid facing the screen, either reading the slides or talking to them (both look very unprofessional). You may turn and gesture toward the screen to draw your audience's attention to a bullet point or illustration, but immediately turn your face and body back toward your audience. Or, better yet, have your slides displayed on a laptop facing you.

If you can, and if the room allows, stand to the audience's left of your visual aids so their focus is first on you and then on your visual aids. Almost every culture reads from left to right, and after we blink or look down, we automatically look to the left first. Remember, you are most important; your visual aids are just that—aids to support you and your message.

Handle Questions Constructively

You should consider two platform-management issues regarding questions: when to take them and how to answer them. Planning the "when" part makes the "how" part easier. We will discuss these issues in the following sections.

When to Answer Questions

Some speakers feel that they lose control of the situation when the Q&A section starts, so they avoid it as long as possible, in hopes that time will run out. We advise a different strategy. First, tell your audience when you are going to take questions during your presentation. If you are comfortable with interruptions, encourage them, but be aware that you are likely to be interrupted with a question about something that you are planning to cover later in the presentation. When that happens, you either have to jump ahead in your organization (not the best solution) or tell the questioner that you will address the material soon.

Most speakers are better off announcing that they will take questions at the end of each section or at the end of their presentation. This avoids the problem of having the presentation organization thrown off, and gives you the opportunity to answer most of the questions that would have come up.

Second, decide exactly when you will ask for questions at the end. You have two choices: before your summary or after your summary. Either time is fine, based on your personal preference and style. However, do not wait until after your final statement to ask for questions. If you do, you run the risk that the last question asked will be the one that is awkward for you to answer, and that will then be your final impression on your audience. Instead, tell your audience something like this: "I'll take one last question, and then I have a final thought to leave with you."

If you take questions after your summary, you might want to briefly summarize again, perhaps enhancing that summary with issues you addressed in your Q&A. But always leave the audience with a strong, carefully rehearsed final word. (See discussion of this in Chapter 4.)

Always keep control of your final statement. Don't end on a Q&A.

How to Answer Questions

Entire books have been written on strategies for answering questions. The basic plan, however, is comprised of three simple steps:

1   Answer the question directly.
2   Offer one piece of support or elaboration.
3   Stop.

Avoid the most common mistake that speakers make when answering questions: they go on and on. Make your point and stop talking. Less is more. If the questioner needs more information, he or she will ask for it. So memorize the three steps: answer, support, stop.

Don't try to bluff. If you don't know the answer to a question, say so. It's perfectly fine—actually, it's preferred—to just say, "I don't know." Then follow up with a comment about finding the answer and getting back to the person who asked the question—if you really intend to do so.

Of course, sometimes you will have to respond to a question that requires more than the "answer, support, stop" plan. Try these tactics:

- Just answer the question directly.
- Rephrase the question ("What I understand that you are asking me is …").
- Use the bad-news organizational pattern.
- Defer to someone else ("Joe is the expert …").
- Steer the question with a bridge ("What's most important is …").

However you choose to answer your questions, just remember to plan the material for afterwards. Your audience will remember your final words.

The most common mistake in dealing with listener questions is to rattle on rather than answering the question efficiently.

Polish Your Non-verbal Delivery Skills

Your non-verbal skills include how you look and how you move. Obviously, you should take your cues from your target audience and your organization, but some fundamental non-verbal abilities are essential. Among these are eye contact, professional appearance, physical control, and enthusiasm, which we will discuss in the following sections.

Establish and Maintain Eye Contact

In business situations in Western cultures, we expect speakers to look at us when delivering a message. Speakers who do not look us in the eye are regarded as insecure or untrustworthy. When addressing groups, the best way to maintain eye contact is to look at one individual for a few seconds and then move on to another person. Don't just scan over the audience— really *look* at individuals. Try to get to everyone in the room, and be aware of tendencies to look too much at some people and not enough at others. (Some speakers tend to look to one side of a room more than another. Avoid this tendency.)

Look directly at each member of your audience.

Develop and Display a Professional Image

Appearance, dress, and grooming communicate powerful messages. Your audience will make some assumptions about you and your message based on how you look. If you aren't sure how to dress for a particular presentation, you are better off being dressed too formally than too informally. Success experts encourage people to dress as if they were at the next level in the organization. If your next promotion is to Director level, then dress like a Director. You can often enhance your credibility by dressing just a bit sharper than the audience expects.

Avoid wearing something that may be distracting.

Don't wear anything that is distracting. In business contexts, men should avoid ties with odd patterns or belt buckles with unusual designs. If you are short, stout, or tend to gesture broadly, you should not wear a double-breasted jacket that makes you look wider and constricts arm movement. Women should not wear things that move or make noise (such as dangling earrings or charm bracelets). They should generally avoid bright nail polish or unusual make-up colors that distract their audience. If you ever find yourself tugging at anything, then you know what to fix next time. (For example, if your hair falls in your face, either cut it or fasten it back.)

Many excellent books and magazine articles can provide dress and grooming tips. Stay current with what is acceptable for the business environment in which you work. But the simplest rule of thumb is to avoid dress or grooming that may distract your listeners from your message.

Professional Image Matters All the Time

As part of the reorganization of a major business unit, senior management was considering the future of one relatively small facility. The General Manager (GM) and his management team at the facility spent several weeks preparing a selection of options and detailing support material. One option was to close the facility altogether; another was to relocate. A less financially attractive, but more personnel-attractive, option was to remain open as a Center for Excellence. Complicating the issue was the fact that the ultimate decision would be made by a new senior vice-president (SVP) who had only visited the site one time and who knew very few of the people involved.

On the day of the decision-making meeting, the facility's GM was completely prepared. He was also dressed in his best suit and had practiced his presentation using the technology in the SVP's conference room. In addition, the GM brought a secret weapon: his entire management team. They, too, were completely prepared and dressed in their best business suits. Sitting in a line at the wall of the conference room, they presented an impressive professional image.

The SVP was apparently influenced. He decided to keep the facility and its people. Did the united force of the team's professional image make an impression? We'll never know for sure, but we do know that it surely didn't hurt.

Exhibit Physical Control

Your sense of personal dynamism or self-confidence comes across via body language such as gestures, posture, and mannerisms. Gestures can be useful to punctuate the message. For example, a pause with a shift in body position can be the non-verbal equivalent of a new paragraph or line of reasoning. Your body movements should be comfortable and natural, yet purposeful.

Make body movements purposeful, not random.

Gesture Spontaneously and Naturally

Everyone has different tendencies to use or avoid gestures. For some, it feels uncomfortable to point or raise hands in exclamation. For others, it may appear that if you tied their hands, they'd be speechless.

The most effective hand gestures are in what is called the "honor zone." This is the area between your waist and shoulders and is where people expect to see gestures. Common mistakes people make with gestures include:

- Failing to use enough gestures.
- Repeating the same gesture to the point where it becomes monotonous, distracting, or annoying.
- Contriving hand movements that look artificial or overly dramatic.
- Choosing gestures that cannot be seen clearly. (A hand motion hidden from audience view by a podium is of no value. Stay in the "honor zone.")
- Leaving their hands in the wrong place for too long.

Keep gestures in the "honor zone" between waist and shoulders.

Your audience should believe that everything you are doing with your face, your hands, your feet, and the space around you is purposeful, yet not forced.

The rules for where you should put your hands have relaxed somewhat. Speech teachers used to have clear lists of "do" and "don't" positions. Now, for example, it may be acceptable to put a hand in your pocket in some speaking environments—but not at the moment when you are making your most serious point. The following are some hand movements you should still avoid:

- Crossing your arms (this may convey defensiveness) or putting your hands on your hips (this can look angry or aggressive).
- Placing your hands in front of you in the "fig leaf" position (especially for male speakers).
- Hooking your fingers together at your ribcage in the "opera singer" pose.
- Gripping the podium (the "white knuckle" syndrome) or clasping your hands behind your back (for more than a moment or two).

Use Appropriate Body Movement

Body movement is another important way to bring life to a presentation. Pausing between key points and physically moving to another place in the room helps your listeners know that you have completed one point and are now ready to address another. This is the non-verbal equivalent of a new paragraph. Such pauses and movement help your listeners follow your logical development. If you cannot freely move around, you may still use the pause with a shift in position or a change in the direction you're looking to indicate the same things. Whenever possible, avoid the speaker-behind-the-podium format. If you need a microphone, a cordless, clip-on microphone is best for freedom of movement.

Smile

Start your presentation with a smile. It relaxes both you and your audience. Look for other appropriate places in your speech when a smile would be appropriate, as well. The rest of the time, use facial expressions to enhance the emotions you are communicating with your message.

A smile is often the best non-verbal expression. It reassures your audience.

We once worked with a very charming corporate executive who was often interviewed by the media. He was always very focused, and his answers were always succinct and articulate. However, when he concentrated, he tended to draw his eyebrows together—his "thinking" face. The resulting expression looked like anger or defensiveness. To develop his skills, he videotaped his performance, and he was shocked at how stern and intense he looked. He learned to dial back the intensity by replacing the "thinking" expression by slightly raising his eyebrows instead of drawing them together. This one change made a dramatic difference in both his interviews and in his inter-personal interactions.

Keep Your Weight on Both Feet

Again, this sounds obvious, but speakers tend to forget that the audience can see their feet. They will cross them, bounce, and rock back and forth, all of which can be terribly distracting. If you concentrate on keeping the weight on the balls of your feet, you will be balanced and ready to move when you want to. Be careful to avoid "dancing"—where you shift the weight from side to side.

Use Physical Space Wisely

The space around you when you speak is yours, so use it to enhance your presentation. The rule about moving around is: walk, or stand still. When you are standing still, stand *completely* still. Do not dance with your feet, your knees, or your shoulders. When you walk, do it for a reason. As we men-tioned earlier, changing your position in the room can show a natural break or emphasize a point in the content of your talk. It can also re-attract the audience's attention, allow them to adjust their own physical positions, and give them chance to think about what you are saying.

Use a shift of body position to show a shift in ideas. This can be like a new paragraph in a written message.

Show Enthusiasm and Confidence

Enthusiasm is your most important delivery skill. Audiences and readers will forgive many things, but if you don't seem to care, neither will they.

Assuming you are well-prepared, you should be comfortable expressing enthusiasm about your material. It's okay to let your audience know that you are excited about your topic. And, of course, you focused on your audi-ence's concerns when you selected your specific information, which automa-tically expresses your enthusiasm for them.

You should also be comfortable expressing enthusiasm about yourself. Show confidence—not cockiness. Believe in yourself—who you are and what you have to offer—what you know and what you are worth. Know that your contributions are right on target because you are experienced and prepared. Then (literally, if you are speaking), you can stand up straight, hold your head up high, and face your audiences head on.

Your audience will forgive many things, but if you don't care, neither will they.

Have Confidence in Your Ideas

If you have completed your preparation, including thoroughly analyzing your audience and selecting material based on the needs of that audience, you should have confidence in your point of view. The time you invest in the first four steps of the Straight Talk Model always pays off. Avoid the temptation to skip a step. Develop the habit of being thorough and professional in developing your messages. A little extra effort and thought can pay huge dividends in your professionalism.

A little extra preparation and attention to detail can have a dramatic impact on your confidence and communication effectiveness.

Rehearse and Edit

Nothing builds confidence like being well-prepared, even to the point of being over-prepared—totally comfortable with your grasp of the subject matter. And nothing improves the likelihood of speaking success like thorough preparation of the content and delivery of the presentation as well as practice in handling anticipated questions that may arise.

When preparing, put special emphasis on the opening remarks and the conclusion. If you've practiced your opening repeatedly and it goes well, you'll gain confidence for the rest of the presentation. If it doesn't sound so good during your rehearsal, edit it to make it better.

The best way to practice is to work on one section at a time, such as the introduction or the transition from your introduction to your first main point. As we mentioned earlier, don't write your talk word-for-word. If you memorize it, you will sound like you are reciting to the audience rather than having a conversation with them. Instead, practice each section until you are comfortable and fluent. Even if it comes out a little different during the actual presentation, it will still sound natural and spontaneous.

Prepare opening and closing remarks most carefully.

You should also time the presentation to make sure it fits the time allotment or is simply not too long. Audiences are almost always pleasantly surprised when a speech is shorter than expected; they are almost always disappointed when it runs too long.

If possible, videotape your practice. We highly recommend this for important, formal presentations, especially if you are inexperienced. If video is not available, the second best place to work is in front of a large mirror so you can see your non-verbal behavior while you are going over the words. In either case, you can see and hear what works and what you want to improve. Do not practice with *only* an audio-tape recorder. An audio recording without the enhancement of your non-verbal skills is not sufficient feedback.

Self-Consciousness Can Become Self-Destructiveness

Over-concern with mechanics once you've reached the point of giving the presentation can only distract and create anxiety. The following is some good advice we have paraphrased from speech experts:

Self-consciousness tends to be self-destructive. If you are overly worried about the way you look, you often overcompensate, and this draws attention to yourself that would not ordinarily be centered on you. It's when you are trying to walk nonchalantly that you walk stiffly or affectedly. It is when you are trying to smile naturally (say "cheese") that your smile tends to look artificial. If you are caught up in conversation or telling a story and the conversation or the story causes you to smile, you are usually unaware of the smile itself, and it is at that point that the smile is, and appears, most natural. So, when you are speaking and get caught up in the message—when you are interested in communicating the ideas to the listeners—you are not usually uncomfortable or noticeably concerned with how you look or how you sound. It's the idea that is at center stage, not the self. Simple remedies: be listener-centered; be message-centered; do not be self-centered.[2]

Manage Anxiety

Relax! Easier said than done, you may say. However, if you are well-prepared and rehearsed, you should be able to relax to a degree where anxiety should not be a problem. You may still feel that brief flush of nervousness just as you are being introduced or beginning your presentation, but it will soon leave because you are prepared. Such nervousness is perfectly natural and is rarely visible to your listeners.

Remember that "stage fright" is normal; it's your body's adrenaline kicking in, which provides extra energy. In fact, speakers who say that they are not nervous at all may face a greater challenge, since an audience might perceive their relaxed attitude as a lack of enthusiasm, or, worse yet, a lack of respect for them.

"Stage fright" is normal and can be useful. It keeps you mentally alert.

Overcome Anxiety Symptoms

Everyone's nerves show in a different place. Here are some tricks for common nervous reactions:

- **Racing heart.** If you have time before your presentation, plan a workout or a run. If your time is limited, find some way to get your heart rate up with some form of exercise like sit-ups, push-ups, squats, or a quick walk to burn off excess energy and take advantage of the extra oxygen.
- **Dry mouth.** Chew your tongue. We know this sounds disgusting, but chewing your tongue creates saliva and helps dry mouth. Don't do it where people can see you—you'll look like a cow.
- **High or weak voice.** Try exercises to improve your voice. Such exercises can make your voice sound stronger or lower-pitched.

Exercises for Voice Improvement

Try the following simple exercises to build better vocal tone and a stronger-sounding voice:

1   As you are waiting to speak, concentrate on deep breathing. Your lowest natural pitch is supported by good breath-control from your diaphragm. If you are familiar with "yoga breathing," use that (see point 3 below).
2   Concentrate on moving your belt buckle in and out when you inhale and exhale. Don't move your shoulders when you breathe deeply. This heaving motion tightens the muscles around the throat and makes a tight-voice problem worse.
3   Borrow a relaxation strategy from yoga: inhale on four counts, hold for four counts, then exhale for four counts.

- **Shaky hands.** While you are waiting to speak (and while no one is looking), make hard fists and then stretch out your hands several times to increase blood flow and control. However, if you still have the shakes, don't show the audience! Avoid holding up your hands until you get involved with your presentation and calm down.
- **General insecurity.** Stand (or sit) up straight. This is our best all-purpose solution. Nothing conveys personal confidence better than good posture. The extra benefits are that you look more attractive and you can

breathe better. Lift your chest, pull your shoulders back and down, and raise your head. Face your audience squarely with your body and look them in the eyes. Smile. You're ready to go.

Keep in mind that, although many of the tips in this chapter seem to refer to presentational speaking (giving speeches or briefings), they also apply in less "formal" communication situations such as interviews or meeting management.

When Stage Fright Feels Debilitating[3]

Excessive speaking anxiety isn't just found in inexperienced people. One established and otherwise successful business person wrote to one of your authors (Sherron) with this problem:

I am so terrified of giving presentations that I might turn down a better paying job, just because I will be expected to speak in front of groups! I am confident and successful one-on-one and in meetings, but the thought of everyone looking at me standing up there in the spotlight makes me physically sick. How can I get past this fear?

The response from the experienced communication coach went like this:

You are not alone!

The most important thing to remember about presentation anxiety ("stage fright") is this: if you don't have it, you've been dead for several days!

Stage fright is a positive mental and physiological response that creates extra adrenalin. That's a good thing because it fuels your physical energy and your intellectual enthusiasm. Everyone's "speaker nerves" show up differently. For example, even after all my years of presenting, I have insomnia the night before a major event, and I always fret so much about the technology letting me down that I take my presentation on my laptop, on a CD, on a USB drive, and in hardcopy. In your case, the thought of everyone looking at you triggers your presentation anxiety.

First of all, it sounds like you are doing everything right in terms of preparation. If you are confident and successful one-on-one and in meetings, then you obviously are focused and organized with appropriate material to inform or persuade your target audience. Good for you! I usually advise speakers to be certain that they are the primary focus for the audience and that their visual aids are the secondary focus. Visual aids are, after all, "aids"—there to make the presentation clearer for the audience but not to distract.

At the same time, a rule about stage fright is to not let it show. For example, a speaker whose hands shake should not hold them up for the audience to see. Therefore, in your case, to avoid showing your audience that you are nervous, make your visual aids the primary focus of your presentation during the first few minutes until you have your nerves under control.

I would suggest a double attention-grabber—both on the screen and in handouts that you distribute immediately before you begin speaking. If you put something in your audiences' hands, they will look down at it (and not at you). For those who read quickly and look up, have something on the screen that is dramatic, thus once again taking the focus away from you.

Then, as you move through your presentation, be sure that either your slides and handouts are identical or that your handouts supplement the slides with additional detail, so your audience will continue to have something to look at other than you.

I do not suggest what some speakers choose to do: stand in the dark and use bright slides. Your audience wants to see who is talking rather than just listening to a unidentified voice in the void. But don't worry—they will indeed be looking at your handouts and slides until you are comfortable enough to command their attention.

Appearing nervous is better than appearing dead. Your audience will forgive many things about your delivery skills (while you are working to improve them), but they will never forgive you if you aren't enthusiastic, if you don't appear to care. So learn to use that stage fright to your advantage. Dale Carnegie said it best: "Train your butterflies to fly in formation."

Also remember that, as you improve, it's perfectly okay to use little tricks and to bend the "rules." The end result will be an even more confident and successful speaker: you!

Be Yourself and Become Your Better Self

Some people who are perfectly comfortable communicating one-on-one believe that they must become someone different when they address a group. They may have seen effective speakers and try to mimic their excellent platform skills. Such emulation can be valuable as you learn delivery techniques from other people, but you should not try to become someone else. Allow your personality to be reflected in all your communication. In brief, be comfortable as yourself. You are as good as anyone, and, because you have prepared your topic, you are likely to be perceived by your audience as the expert on that topic.

Your audience will generally perceive you as the expert on your topic.

Being yourself does not mean that you should disregard the corporate culture of the organization where you are speaking or the social cultures of your audience. You may need to adapt your style. If in doubt, for example, about your casual, energetic style with an unfamiliar audience—particularly an international audience or one made up of individuals considerably older or higher in status than you are—don't try to change your style. Instead, temper your exuberance and try to be a bit more formal in your delivery. As your audience becomes comfortable with you and you build your credibility with your excellent material, you can share your personality with them.

Know that Your Audience Wants You to Succeed

Your audience doesn't want your presentation to fail. When people have taken the time to hear what you have to say, they don't want to feel their time has been wasted. Even listeners who strongly disagree with you—what we call "hostile listeners"—want you to explain yourself clearly if for no other reason than that they can then attempt to shoot down your ideas.

Your audience wants you to succeed!

A poor presentation can be just as embarrassing and uncomfortable for the audience as it is for the speaker. Think of times that you've seen people do a poor job of expressing an idea. What has your reaction been? You probably felt some embarrassment for those persons and may have found yourself trying to rephrase their ideas for them. Remember that no one is out to get you. Just as you want speakers to succeed, your listeners want you to succeed.

Know That You and Your Audience Need Each Other

Every presentation begins with the listener needing something. By coming to your presentation (or interview, briefing) or inviting you to talk, listeners are expressing a need for information, friendship, help, approval, clarification—maybe even inspiration. They hope that something you say will improve their lives.

You as a presenter have needs, too. Probably the strongest need is for approval. Only your listeners can give you this. They can give you such approval in many forms, from a simple vote (a raising of hands) to a signature on a document (a sales agreement) to an outburst of applause or a hearty thank you. Without some indication of approval, response, endorsement, confirmation—*something!*—you'll feel lost at sea, adrift, seeking a signal. This can be tough on the ego. (*No* response is in many ways worse than outright rejection.)

No response from our listeners is the most uncomfortable outcome we can experience.

Since listeners need what you have to offer—information, suggestions, instructions, a welcome, or entertainment—and you need what they offer—approval, appreciation, or applause—work together to create a circle of rapport. A good presenter is like a swan—calm and serene on the surface and paddling like crazy underneath. Remember these pointers, and you can look and sound confident about your message content, your organization, yourself, and about handling unforeseen objections or other surprises.

Remember Feedback and Constant Improvement

Getting feedback is a critical part of the Straight Talk Model and is the key to becoming your better self. Keep in mind that improvement of delivery skills is a life-long project, and the guidelines we have discussed in this chapter are just ways to get you moving in the right direction. We'll discuss more about soliciting and receiving feedback in Chapter 9.

Continue to polish your verbal and non-verbal skills and to develop a style that meets your audience's expectations consistent with the corporate culture. Speak clearly and expressively. Dress professionally. Exhibit control with appropriate facial expressions, hand gestures, and body movement. Prove that you know your material by thoroughly rehearsing in advance. Be comfortable with your notes and your visual aids. Be prepared to answer questions. Express confidence in your material, based on your preparation. Display confidence in yourself through your professionalism and enthusiasm. Most importantly, be yourself. You are who the audience came to see. You are the most important part of your message, and your unique personality is your most valuable platform skill.

As Brenda in our opening story discovered, oral communication skills are very much at the core of many jobs. She was doing fine in her interview for the job but suddenly found herself outside her comfort zone when realizing that she'd be required to present professionally to her new vice-president. This need not be the case.

Once you gain control over your anxiety, you, like Brenda, have the opportunity to dazzle your audience with good verbal and non-verbal skills, platform management, and a projection of confidence that is the hallmark of professionalism. By applying each step of the Straight Talk Model, you can achieve considerable success in delivering oral messages with confidence and impact.

Performance Checklist

After completing this chapter, you should be better able to apply some principles for selecting and organizing information for your message. Specifically, you should now understand that:

- Delivering effective oral messages depends on your ability to polish your verbal and non-verbal delivery skills, develop your platform-management skills, show confidence and enthusiasm, rehearse and edit, manage anxiety and express confidence to be yourself and become your better self.

- Polishing your verbal delivery skills includes speaking clearly and expressively, paying attention to timing, avoiding distracting vocal patterns, and minimizing verbalized pauses.

- Polishing your platform-management skills includes using notes and visuals effectively and handling audience questions constructively.

- Words that you emphasize can change the meaning of your sentences; listen carefully to avoid unintended hidden meanings.

- Polishing your non-verbal delivery skills includes maintaining eye contact, displaying a professional image, and exhibiting physical control.

- Expressing confidence and enthusiasm is accomplished by practicing your material, being idea-conscious, and knowing that you and your audience meet needs for each other.

- Being yourself and becoming your better self are functions of a sensitivity to the speaking context (especially the culture) and of feedback you can apply to improve.

What Do You Know?

Activity 6.1: Taking a Self-Inventory

Oral communication skills and attitudes improve through evaluation—by others and by you. This self-inventory identifies your starting point. It will be useful to you only to the degree to which you are totally honest in your answers. You need not show this to others. Use it as an honest look within yourself. You may want to re-take it after you have applied the skills discussed in this book to develop your communication skills further.

The following checklist shows how you see yourself as an oral communicator. Read each statement and circle "yes" or "no." After answering "yes" or "no," review each answer and circle the (+) or (−) to indicate how you feel about your answer. A plus means you are satisfied; a minus means you wish you could have answered otherwise.

Answer honestly based upon how you actually feel or act, not how you wish you would.

1 Before I enter into an important communication event, I often think carefully about the context, audiences, culture, and my objectives.
yes no (+) (–)

2 I often have great ideas I'd like to share with other people.
yes no (+) (–)

3 I enjoy trying to explain my ideas to others.
yes no (+) (–)

4 I often get the conversation going among my friends and even with people I don't know.
yes no (+) (–)

5 When I stand up to speak in any group, I feel excited (but not overly anxious).
yes no (+) (–)

6 Before trying to influence others, I make it a point to be certain that I know as much as possible about my audience(s).
yes no (+) (–)

7 I am good at persuading others to my views.
yes no (+) (–)

8 I am comfortable and efficient in preparing visual aids (PowerPoint™ slides, etc.).
yes no (+) (–)

9 I communicate my feelings and ideas well and therefore have influence in my job and social settings.
yes no (+) (–)

10 I like to teach groups of people new things.
yes no (+) (–)

11 I enjoy planning ways to simplify and present ideas so others will understand them.
yes no (+) (–)

12 When communicating, I consider audience feelings and attitudes to be at least as important as facts and ideas.
yes no (+) (–)

13 In comparison with my colleagues or associates, I think I speak more clearly and carefully than they do.
yes no (+) (–)

14 I have a good vocabulary and can phrase ideas well.
yes no (+) (–)

15 My physical delivery (use of hands, posture, expressiveness) is one of my strongest communication skills.
yes no (+) (–)

16 My voice has good variation, is pleasant, and conveys enthusiasm well.
yes no (+) (−)

17 I am eager to hear helpful criticism from others after I speak.
yes no (+) (−)

18 Improving my oral communication skills is one of my highest priorities.
yes no (+) (−)

19 I have the basic qualities needed to be an excellent oral communicator.
yes no (+) (−)

20 I speak clearly and pronounce words correctly.
yes no (+) (−)

21 People seem to enjoy what I say; I hold their interest.
yes no (+) (−)

22 I use humor and story-telling effectively.
yes no (+) (−)

23 I handle audience questions very well.
yes no (+) (−)

24 I feel that I am getting better and better in my communication skills.
yes no (+) (−)

25 After a communication experience, I review what I should have done differently to create a positive outcome.
yes no (+) (−)

Now, review your self-inventory. For each item where you circled a minus sign (indicating that you don't feel good about your answer), write a goal for personal improvement. Your goal should be specific and clear. For example, if you write a goal for statement 4, you might say, "I will start conversations with one person I don't know each day this week." For statement 16, you might say, "I will work for greater vocal variation to hold listener interest." For statement 22, you might say, "I will practice incorporating more stories in my presentations and conversations."

Write your goals in the spaces below. If you have more than five areas to work on, put them in order of importance. Then write your top five goals here:

Goal 1: _____
Goal 2: _____
Goal 3: _____
Goal 4: _____
Goal 5: _____

For each goal you have set above, sketch out an action plan and timeline for its accomplishment. Be specific about the activities needed to achieve the goal. Where will you get the knowledge you need? How will you gain the experiences needed for growth? Be specific about what you will do.

Activity 6.2: Evaluating a Successful Speaker

Attend a live speech or view one on TV or video. (The speaker may be someone you know personally, a business or political leader, a member of the clergy, a television show host, or anyone who makes a living doing oral presentations.) Take notes during the presentation. Look for applications (or misapplications) of the ideas in this chapter. Then write a brief description of the speaker, commenting on this person's delivery style. Suggest ways he or she could improve.

Activity 6.3: Preparing a Team Presentation

1   As a team, select a company that is internationally known and that is currently managing multiple challenges. (Some examples: the airline industry, pharmaceutical regulation issues, corporate ethics scandals, product recalls, employee discrimination suits, etc.)

2   Assume that you are a communication consulting team and your job is to advise the company or organization on how best to handle the communication aspects of their challenges.

3   Working in a team, develop a presentation to persuade your target audience to take a specific course of action.

4   Prepare computer-projected visual aids for your presentation.

5   Practice your presentation based on the information in this chapter.

6   Before you present, be prepared to tell the class about your target audience so they can role-play and ask you questions as if they were that audience.

7   Keep the presentation to ten minutes plus a question-and-answer session. Remember to close with your final statement; don't let the Q&A be the final thing your audience hears.

Activity 6.4: Preparing a "How-To" Presentation

Prepare a four-to-six-minute "how-to" presentation. To get double benefit from this presentation, select a topic that teaches how to improve speaking effectiveness. Some examples are:

▪   How to use gestures for greater communication effectiveness.
▪   How to use vocal variation.
▪   How to reduce speaker anxiety.
▪   How to dress for a business presentation for your organization.
▪   How to create and use humor in a presentation.
▪   How to create an effective introduction (or conclusion).
▪   How to handle questions and answers after a presentation.

You are not limited to the topics listed above, but your presentation must be communication-related. Apply the ideas discussed in this chapter. Practice in front of a mirror.

Activity 6.5: Selling a Product

Develop and deliver an effective five-minute sales pitch. Select a product or service that would be appropriate to sell to a person who is just completing graduate school and is beginning a new business career. This should be a real product (or service) and should sell for not more than $300.

	Good	Needs Work
PRESENTATION EVALUATION		
SPEAKER:		
TOPIC:		
SPEAKER'S TARGET AUDIENCE:		
EVALUATOR:		
Directions for the speaker: evaluate yourself on each point before you present. Directions for evaluator: evaluate the speaker on each point.		

	Good	Needs Work
CONTENT		
Uses relevant material for audience's knowledge level		
Acknowledges audience's wants and concerns		
Has sufficient depth in support material		
Uses interesting examples for audience and situation		
Uses appropriate visual aids (if appropriate)		
ORGANIZATION		
Grabs audience's attention		
States clear agenda		
Includes benefit in introduction		
Follows clear organizational plan		
Summarizes essence of main points		
Asks for clear action in conclusion		
Closes with strong final statement		
DELIVERY		
Moves comfortably and gestures naturally		
Looks at each member of the audience		
Speaks conversationally and enthusiastically (vocal variation)		
Handles visual aids effectively		

Overall comments:

Finally, what is the likelihood that you would buy this product, hire this person, or support this proposal? Why, or why not?

FIGURE 6.1 Presentation Evaluation Worksheet

Apply a persuasive pattern of arrangement (as discussed in Chapter 4) and be prepared to explain why you structured the presentation as you did. If possible, videotape your delivery and review it with a colleague or your boss. Ask for concrete feedback. (Invite your evaluator to use the form in Figure 6.1. Also fill out a self-critique based on your viewing of your tape.)

Reinforce With These Review Questions

1 True/False—Verbalized pauses or "filler words" are helpful in that they keep the flow of information constant.

2 True/False—"Up-speak" makes statements sound like questions, thus undermining the perception of speaker confidence.

3 In addition to verbal skills, communicators should be aware of their _____ and _____ skills as well.

4 True/False—Speaking expressively involves putting the emphasis on the right words in a sentence.

5 When using visual aids in a presentation, maintain your focus on your _____.

6 The three steps to answering questions (and avoiding rambling) are:
(1) _____,
(2) _____, and
(3) _____.

7 True/False—When speaking to a group, scanning over the whole audience is a good way to build eye contact.

8 Nothing reduces anxiety like being well _____.

9 True/False—Being idea-conscious can help overcome being self-conscious.

10 True/False—You are the most important part of your message and your unique personality is your most valuable platform skill.

Mini-Case Study

When Andrew walked into the conference room, all he could think was, "I feel like a donkey in the Kentucky Derby. I shouldn't be here talking to these big-shot, successful people. I'm going to look and sound like a total idiot."

Andrew is the Facilities Manager for Ajax Credit Union. His job is to be certain that the buildings and facilities for the company's 12 branch offices are kept in tip-top condition. It's a complex and demanding job for which Andrew earned a degree from the local State College. But somehow, Andrew, despite his considerable expertise in all aspects of building planning and maintenance, still feels like, as he puts it, "a glorified janitor."

Now the Board of Directors has asked him to come to their monthly meeting and talk about the remodeling of several branches. He knows what to tell them and feels that he will be able to answer any questions, but he is still, well, freaked out by the thought of standing up and delivering his message.

Questions

1   If Andrew came to you and expressed these fears, what would you tell him?
2   Describe three specific ways Andrew could best prepare for his presentation.
3   What, if anything, would you advise Andrew to avoid?

seven

Contribute to Effective Meetings

Meetings, of course, do serve a purpose. Consider this: Our national economy is based on a 35- to 45-hour workweek. Without meetings, this figure would dwindle to a few hours at the most. Our whole system, as we know it, would collapse.

(Stephen Baker, *I Hate Meetings*)

Communicating in Meetings

Meetings, conferences, and other forms of group discussion constitute a significant portion of business people's workday. Most companies value the many benefits of group communication. When done effectively, participative management—the involvement of people in organizational decisions—can produce better decisions and higher levels of employee engagement.

The major downside of meetings is, of course, their high cost. Bringing groups together (and away from other productive work) can result in countless hours of labor costs. Good communication processes—on the part of leaders and participants—can mitigate these cost expenditures and provide other benefits to organization. This chapter looks at the pros and cons of meetings, describes how to apply the Straight Talk Model, and teaches some simple tactics for maximizing meeting effectiveness.

Performance Competencies

When you have completed this chapter, you should be able to:

- Apply the Straight Talk Model to your role as a participant in meetings and group decision-making.
- Analyze the context in terms of situation, audiences, and goals with those audiences in meetings.
- Consider the advantages and disadvantages of meetings when selecting communication media options.
- Know how to invite the appropriate mix and number of people to a meeting.
- Use brainstorming, criteria-setting, and the nominal group process (NGP) to help the group select and process information and achieve viable solutions.
- Recognize and deal with individual dominance and "groupthink" to make better group decisions.
- Describe the rules of effective meeting participation.

The Way It Is ... The High Cost of Fruitless Meetings[1]

Shawn Hughes was delighted to get a job at Moose Lips Corporation, a mid-size manufacturer of camping and recreational gear in the Pacific Northwest. When his supervisor saw that Shawn had studied business communication, she asked him to look at the problems the company was having with their meetings. Shawn's first step was to gather some background information about previous meetings from the company president, Matt Bayless.

Matt had built Moose Lips from a one-person operation to a substantial company. Despite rapid financial growth, Matt was worried about increasing production costs and competitor activity. He didn't see any specific problem, but he was uneasy about the future. Then he had an idea: "We'll have a big meeting and get some new ideas."

Matt sent a memo to all employees "inviting" them to an all-day retreat at the Homesteader Conference Center about 20 miles out of town. The agenda was set: all employees would get together to "share their ideas" on how to retain market share and "any other topics relevant to the success of the business." The entire company would close down all day Friday while the employees met.

A few days before the big meeting, word filtered back to Matt that a number of the Moose Lips employees were complaining about having to spend a whole day at Homesteader. They were feeling pressure to keep up with their work and were coming up on the busiest time of the year. Besides, no one clearly understood what they were supposed to accomplish at the meeting.

Matt was upset by the grumbling. He sent another memo explaining that, while there would be no decision-making at this meeting, the opportunity to "share input" was very important, and he expected everyone to be there.

The big day came, and 115 people showed up. In the opening session, Matt said he was concerned about the company's market share and production costs. He explained that the morning would be spent in 12-member "buzz groups" dealing with "market share issues." Each group would report back to the whole assembly just before lunch. The afternoon would follow the same format but would deal with "production cost issues."

The groups were assigned randomly, and everyone from Matt down to the lowest-level employee participated. By five o'clock when the meeting broke up, it was clear that most people were frustrated by the process. No one could clearly describe what had been accomplished. And the cost to the company went far beyond the rental cost of the facilities and the catered coffee breaks and lunch. The cost included well over 1,000 personnel hours.

Shawn took careful notes while Matt admitted that the meeting was a disaster. "And a lot of other meetings are almost as bad," he told Shawn. Incidentally, Matt implemented none of the suggestions from the retreat.

Meetings are a fact of life in every organization. Unfortunately, many meetings are not productive. Nevertheless, group communication can be valuable if those participating learn when and how to make the most of meetings. This chapter discusses that challenge from two points of view. First, we will consider how you, when called upon to a lead a meeting, can maximize results. Second, we will discuss ways you can be a productive participant in meetings.

Apply the Straight Talk Model When You Lead a Meeting

The first decision a leader must make is whether to have the meeting in the first place. This decision will be largely influenced by the first step in the Straight Talk Model, in which you define the communication context.

Define the Context from a Leader's Perspective

To define the context of a meeting from a leader's perspective, you must take into account the meeting's situation, audiences, and objectives with each audience, which we will discuss in the following sections.

Define the Meeting's Situation
The leader's first task is to assess the situation that calls for a meeting. What happened—exactly—that made you think, "Let's have a meeting on this?" For example, a sudden drop in sales of a particular product or a sharp increase in customer complaints may pose problems that need to be

addressed. Another example may be a conflict between employees who need to work together. While employees may see such conflicts as merely good-natured competition, the leader may see the situation as damaging to the organization.

Of course, not all meetings are reactions to problems. Some seek to assess current strategies, explore opportunities, or plot future directions. Things get complicated when several situations conflict or confuse each other. Seek to target the most significant situational need. Sometimes the meeting needs to "put out first" before addressing other issues. What is the most significant situational factor?

Consider the Organizational Culture
The typical use (or overuse or misuse) of meetings becomes an aspect of the corporate culture. To what extent are the common values of the company supportive of group decision-making? Some organizational cultures place a high value on collective input for many, if not most, decisions. Other cultures defer more to formal leadership and use meetings more as information-dissemination tools or, occasionally, to attempt to gain buy-in via some level of participation. Any variation of these cultural aspects may be perfectly appropriate for the particular organization, but communicators who go into meetings unaware of such cultural expectations risk failure.

Define the Meeting's Audiences
The decision to hold a meeting is often driven by the vested interest of certain people. In the sales or customer-service problems mentioned above, sales managers would be likely to have a major interest. The example of departmental conflict would be something company supervisors would want to address. Future planning generally involves most or all functional areas to be represented.

If the situation requires that only two or three people make a decision, a face-to-face conversation or a conference call may be preferable to a formal meeting. If the situation involves the interests of more than a few people, and a meeting looks like the best way to resolve the issues, the leader must next decide who should be invited to attend. People invited to a meeting should meet these criteria:

Invite the right people—those with interest and knowledge.

---

1   **They have some expertise about the issue being discussed.** When people in the group don't know enough to deal with the problem (like when all the employees of Moose Lips were asked to work on complex productivity issues), the solution will reflect pooled ignorance. The group process simply won't help.

2   **They have some involvement or vested interest in the outcome of the discussion.** Make sure that departments or people who will be affected by the solution are represented in its discussion. If such key people are excluded from the decision-making process, they are unlikely to be committed to implementing a solution—even a good one.

3   **They are reasonably skilled in the group decision-making process.** Invite people who express themselves well and who appreciate that differences of opinion can be useful. Avoid narrow-minded, inflexible, or dogmatic people.

4   **They share the overall values of the organization.** If participants are antagonistic or in disagreement with the company's goals, it makes no sense to have them participate in decisions affecting those goals.

5   **They hold similar organizational rank or level.** Top executives in a company may inhibit free discussion from lower-level workers or supervisors.

Be sure, too, to invite the right *number* of people. Groups should have enough people to represent a variety of opinions, but not so many that the process bogs down. Ideally, for problem-solving, groups of four-to-twelve participants work best. Many fast-moving companies prefer action teams of four or five members for most situations.

Typically, groups of four to 12 people are best.

Define the Objectives of Your Meeting
The most important question to ask yourself before a meeting is this: "As a result of this meeting, exactly what do I want to occur?" If you haven't already done so, this question will remind you to think about where your audience is on your Persuasive Continuum we have discussed elsewhere. Do participants have little or no knowledge of the problem, so you need to provide detail and discussion on a particular troubling situation? Or do they already have all the background, the current facts, and the pros and cons of all the options, so all you need to do with this meeting is generate the final decision?

Although participants may be encouraged to focus on the topic dictated by the situation, meetings seldom have just one goal. Both leaders and participants will have other secondary or unspoken objectives, even when the task seems clear. These subsidiary objectives, or "hidden agenda" items, real though they may be, are implied but never stated. As long as such hidden agenda do not take away from the effectiveness of the group, leaders should not worry about these sub-objectives. If the ulterior motives of some people deter the group from accomplishing its work, leaders should talk with participants candidly (in private) and solicit their cooperation in putting the group's needs above their own.

Self-Evaluation: a Meeting-Evaluation Checklist

Consider a typical meeting you have recently attended (at work, in a club, at school, or in a church or civic organization). Compare your meeting to the following characteristics of an effective meeting. Check those statements that applied to the meeting you attended or led.

1 The appropriate and necessary participants were invited.
2 An agenda was prepared prior to the meeting.
3 Meeting participants had an opportunity to contribute to the agenda.
4 Advance notice of meeting time and place was provided to those invited.
5 The meeting's facilities were comfortable and adequate for the number of participants.
6 The meeting began on time.
7 The meeting had a scheduled ending time.
8 The use of time was monitored throughout the meeting.
9 Everyone had an opportunity to present his or her point of view.
10 Participants listened attentively to each other.
11 There were periodic summaries as the meeting progressed.
12 No one person or sub-group dominated the discussion.
13 Everyone had a voice in decisions made at the meeting.
14 The decision process used was appropriate for the size of the group.
15 When used, audiovisual equipment was in good working condition and did not detract from the meeting.
16 The meeting ended with a summary of accomplishments and specific action steps.
17 The meeting was evaluated by participants.
18 People carried out any action agreed to during the meeting.
19 A summary memo or minutes of the meeting was provided to each participant following the meeting.
20 The meeting leader followed up with participants on action agreed to during the meeting.

Score the meeting's effectiveness
Number of Statements Checked × 5 = Meeting Score

A score of 80 or more indicates a high-quality meeting. A score below 60 suggests that your organization has many opportunities to improve the quality of its meetings.

Consider Your Media, Source, and Timing Options as a Leader

Group decision-making can be a very expensive medium. As illustrated in our opening story, people-costs can add up quickly, especially when too many people are involved or the meeting is poorly managed. To determine whether a meeting makes sense for a particular communication situation, the leader should consider the advantages and disadvantages of meetings as a medium. When the disadvantages outweigh the advantages, *do not have a meeting.* Use another medium instead.

Who should run the meeting and when should it be held? The "boss" need not always be the meeting leader. Sometimes, he or she should delegate meeting management to another person—one who, for example, has the strongest need, most experience, or a passion for the topic or situation. For example, if the organization is considering a new product, a manager in product development—a person well aware of the challenges and opportunities associated with the proposed product—might be the best person to lead a group discussion. If a meeting leader has a vested interest (that may be less advantageous to the group) or has already decided his or her position on a topic, it may be time to invite a more objective person to lead.

Take into account the purpose of the meeting. If you are discussing initial options, you might not need a senior executive. If you are making the final decision, then you might.

Timing factors to keep in mind include potential work conflicts (e.g., scheduling an extensive meeting when end-of-month reports are due), possible worker fatigue (e.g., scheduling an unusually early morning or late evening meeting), or outside factors (e.g., near a major holiday or other significant event). A participant scheduled to leave for a business trip (or a vacation) the next day is not likely to be fully checked in to a meeting this afternoon. Empathize.

Determine the Advantages of Meetings-as-a-Medium

An obvious advantage of group decision-making is that a variety of points of view can be brought to bear on the problem. This can be useful if the group has developed ways of processing the ideas that come up. To be successful, the group must develop ways of:

- *Sharing ideas* so participants can build upon one another's insights.
- *Resolving differences* among group members which, if left unattended, would lead to excessive conflict and prevent eventual agreement.
- *Drawing out* useful information from all participants while toning down those who tend to dominate.

When groups succeed at doing these things, synergy and high commitment can result. Synergy is a frequent outcome of the combined efforts of people. For example, synergy happens when three workers who can each produce 200 gizmos per hour when working alone increase their combined output to 800 gizmos per hour when working together. In problem-solving meetings, synergy happens when the group's solution or output is greater than the sum of the input from all the participants individually.

> **Synergy**
>
> Synergy is sometimes described as a $1 + 1 = 3$ (or more) phenomenon. This is where people working together create alternatives that are genuinely better than solutions individuals could ever come up with on their own.

The likelihood that synergy will result from a meeting is largely determined by the nature of the problem and by the way the group processes information and builds consensus. Studies show that groups are better at solving problems that require the making of relative rather than absolute judgments. That is, groups can better solve problems for which there are many potential solutions. Problems having only one correct answer can often be better solved by a motivated individual—or, in some cases, by a computer.

Groups tend to work better at making *relative* judgments rather than *absolute* judgments.

The group process can be more successful than people working alone when the problem is complex, has many parts, or requires that a number of steps be followed. Groups also seem better at dealing with controversial or emotionally charged problems. A problem is emotionally charged when people have taken strong moral or ethical points of view and cannot feel good about a compromise or another viewpoint. Their strong feelings make them less flexible.

Groups can often make better decisions about emotional or controversial problems than individuals.

Another critical advantage of group decision-making is that participants are likely to feel a stronger commitment—or, at least, less resistance—to a group solution they've helped design. This finding has been consistently supported by group dynamics research. Similarly, when those participating are commissioned to execute the decision, they will do so more faithfully because they understand how the decision was reached. This level of commitment is tough to achieve when someone else makes the decision without consulting others.

Perhaps the strongest advantage of group decisions is less resistance to its implementation once decided.

Groups Versus Teams

Organizations place a lot of emphasis on working in teams. Do work *teams* differ from *groups*? Organizational behavior experts do see a distinction: a work *group* interacts and shares information primarily to make decisions and to help one another perform within each member's area of responsibility. Groups create no positive synergy that would result in a performance level higher than the sum of the individual efforts. *Teams*, however, generate positive synergy through coordinated effort. The sum of the team's output is something greater than the sum of the individual inputs. The implication for workplace communication is that teams require meetings and group interaction, while work groups could use other media, such as giving instructions to individuals.

Determine the Disadvantages of Meetings-as-a-Medium
When leaders opt for group problem-solving, they knowingly relinquish some control over the decision process—they give the group some power that was theirs. Although giving up control can result in more useful decisions, the final decision may not be what the leader would like to see happen. When leaders give power to a group, they must be willing to accept the group's decision. If the group's work is overturned by a leader who wanted a different result, the entire process is a sham, and people may not be willing to participate in the future. The leader's credibility will be damaged as well.

Leaders who arbitrarily overrule a group's decision hurt their credibility and undermine future participation.

Unfortunately, some leaders use meetings as a way to pass responsibility to others *instead* of having to make a difficult or painful decision. They use meetings as a substitute for action. Consciously or subconsciously, they hope that by "talking it out," they can avoid the unpleasant necessity of acting. Such buck-passing quickly becomes obvious to people.

Another disadvantage of group decision-making is, as we mentioned earlier, that meetings cost much time and money. A group decision takes more time than a leader's decision, and the costs of such time can really add up. If it takes a 12-member committee three hours to make a decision, and the average committee member's salary is $40,000 a year, the decision costs about $720. And this estimate includes only direct labor costs. (Note: a salary of $40k/year is approximately $20 per hour. You can rather quickly do the math by multiplying those numbers. Benefits and other payroll costs can quickly double these figures, of course.)

Direct salaries of meeting participants are only a portion of the real costs. Ripple effects of damaged productivity or increased employee and customer frustration should also be considered.

You also need to consider the ripples of psychological costs to the individual and the organization, which can be staggering. For example, subordinates may do monotonous busywork while awaiting direction from their boss in conference. Customers may be annoyed that they cannot talk with someone tied up in a meeting. The meeting-participants' work piles up, so that they are faced with a stack of phone messages, a pile of papers in the in-basket, and half-a-dozen people who just have to talk about some pressing matter when the meeting ends.

The leaders who work most effectively, it seems to me, never say "I." And that's not because they have trained themselves not to say "I." They don't think "I." They think "we;" they think "team." They understand their job to be to make the team function. They accept responsibility and don't sidestep it, but "we" gets the credit…. This is what creates trust, what enables you to get the task done. (Peter Drucker, management guru)

Help the Group Select and Organize its Information

Groups work with two types of information: that brought by the individual participants and that generated during discussion. Leaders can get the process of selecting and organizing information off to a good start by assigning advance preparation and by using a written agenda.

Assign Advance Preparation

The meeting's objectives should not be a mystery. If people are invited to work together, they should know what the meeting is about and what kinds of information and/or ideas they may need to gather and bring with them. Examples of needed data might be sales results, personnel records, copies of competitors' publications, or creative ideas being used by other companies. Effective leaders get people thinking on the right wavelength even before the meeting begins.

Assign preparation before the meeting to increase effectiveness.

Distribute an Agenda
Give each participant a written agenda (or a draft agenda) in advance of the meeting. Include the following elements in your written agenda:

- Items to be handled (presented in proper sequence). Be sure to distinguish between *informational items* (requiring minimal discussion) and *discussion items* (where participants will be actively involved in information-sharing and problem-solving).
- The starting time and anticipated ending time.
- Time for scheduled breaks (if any).
- The name of the person responsible for leading the discussion of each agenda item.

The meeting's leader should not be bashful about enforcing time limits. It is not unusual for participants to fall in love with the sound of their own voices. Be tactful but firm about moving the meeting along. Some leaders use a timer to signal (in an impersonal, mechanical way) when to move on.

Start with an Introduction
Just like in the beginning of a presentation when you engage your audience, share your agenda and purpose, and explain why the message is important, your meeting should also have a complete introduction. Take the time to be sure that everyone is focused on the right material and in the right frame of mind.

Meetings Need Attention-Grabbers, Too

Atmosphere in the room was tense. People spoke quietly, if at all. The future of a product was at stake, and careers were at risk. The speaker was already standing, remote mouse in hand. His entire management team sat at rigid attention in a line against the wall. It seemed that everyone in the division had managed to squeeze into the conference room to hear the presentation and learn the verdict.

The executive vice-president who had called the meeting—known by all as a military history buff—looked around at the large number of people, and exclaimed, "452!" Then, with a little mock surprise at the stunned look on the faces in the room, he asked, "Don't you know what

452 is?" Heads shook. "It's the largest number of people ever carried on a C-130—during the evacuation of Saigon in 1975. When I walked into this room and saw all of you here, all I could think of was '452'!" He smiled. And with that smile, everyone in the room relaxed and focused on the task at hand. The EVP had accomplished two things with his opening comments: he had grabbed everyone's attention, but, more importantly, he had established the tone that he wanted for his meeting.

While every good communicator thinks about an introduction in a presentation, many forget to use one in a meeting. In doing so, we may miss an opportunity to gain attention, set the tone, and prepare the participants for the messages exchanged. Take the time to develop an introduction.

Apply Systematic Idea Processing
Leaders need to direct their meetings to systematically generate and process information. Three approaches to doing this are brainstorming, criteria-setting, and the nominal group process.

BRAINSTORMING
The term "brainstorming" is often used loosely to describe the process of presenting creative ideas in a free-flowing environment. Actually, the term refers to a specific process, requiring adherence to clear rules. Be sure everyone is on board to the specific rules before using this process. This may require reminding people and, occasionally, pointing out when they are violating the rules.

The short list of rules for effective brainstorming are:

1   Participants must withhold criticism (verbal or non-verbal) of any ideas.
2   The group must avoid judging any idea as being too "wild."
3   The *quantity* of ideas generated is most important.
4   Participants should seize opportunities to "hitchhike" on or add to ideas suggested by others.

Rules for authentic brainstorming are easy to state but often difficult to follow.

Obeying these rules can be challenging. Brainstorming requires an open climate where participants can toss out highly creative ideas without being subject to criticism. As such, it is a process for producing *tentative* ideas that can later be refined to solve specific problems. Once the group has generated ideas, the next step is to see whether these ideas are viable for solving the problem or dealing with the issue the group is focusing on.

Eight Rules To Brilliant Brainstorming[2]

1 USE BRAINSTORMING TO COMBINE AND EXTEND IDEAS, NOT JUST HARVEST THEM

Andrew Hargadon's *How Breakthroughs Happen* shows that creativity occurs when people find ways to build on existing ideas. The power of group brainstorming comes from creating a safe place where people with different ideas can share, blend, and expand their diverse knowledge. If your goal is just to collect the creative ideas that are out there, group brainstorms are a waste of time. You may as well stick to a Web-based system for collecting ideas. Even an old-fashioned employee suggestion box is good enough for this limited task.

2 DON'T BOTHER IF PEOPLE LIVE IN FEAR

Groups bring out the best and the worst in people. If people believe they will be teased, paid less, demoted, fired, or otherwise humiliated, group brainstorming is a bad idea. If your company fires 10 percent of its employees every year, people might be too afraid of saying something dumb to brainstorm effectively.

3 DO INDIVIDUAL BRAINSTORMING BEFORE AND AFTER GROUP SESSIONS

Alex F. Osborn's 1950s classic, *Applied Imagination*, which popularized brainstorming, gave sound advice: creativity comes from a blend of individual and collective "ideation." This means building in time for people to think and learn about the topic before the group brainstorm, as well as time to reflect about what happened after the meetings. When I studied the IDEO team as they developed a new hair-cutting device, engineer Roby Stancel told me that he prepared for the session by going to a local hardware store to look at all kinds of cutting machines—lawn mowers, hedge clippers, and weed whackers—to inspire him before the group session.

4 BRAINSTORMING SESSIONS ARE WORTHLESS UNLESS IDEAS LEAD TO ACTION

Brainstorming is just one of many techniques that make a company creative. It is of little value if it's not combined with observing consumers, talking to experts, or building prototype products and experiences that provide an outlet for the ideas generated. I've worked with "creative" companies that are great at coming up with ideas, but never implement them. I once studied a team that spent a year brainstorming and arguing about a simple product without producing a single prototype, even though a good engineer could have built one in an hour. The project was finally killed when a competitor came out with a similar product.

5 BRAINSTORMING REQUIRES SKILL AND EXPERIENCE BOTH TO DO—AND ESPECIALLY—TO FACILITATE

Not everyone can walk into a room and lead a productive brainstorming session. It is not a job for amateurs. In all the places I've seen brainstorming used effectively—Hewlett-Packard, SAP's Design Services Team, the Hasso Plattner Institute of Design at Stanford University, the Institute for the Future, frog design, and IDEO—brainstorming is treated as a skill that takes months or years to master. Facilitating a session is a leadership skill that takes even longer to develop.

6 A GOOD BRAINSTORMING SESSION IS COMPETITIVE— IN THE RIGHT WAY

In the best brainstorms, people compete to get everyone else to contribute, to make everyone feel like part of the group, and to treat everyone as collaborators toward a common goal. The worst thing a manager can do is set up the session as an "I win, you lose" game, in which ideas are explicitly rated, ranked, and rewarded. A Stanford grad student once told me about a team leader at his former company who started giving bonuses to people who generated the best ideas in brainstorms. The resulting fear and dysfunction drastically reduced the number of ideas generated by what had once been a creative and cooperative group.

7 BRAINSTORMING SESSIONS CAN BE USED FOR MORE THAN JUST GENERATING IDEAS

Brainstorms are places to listen, learn, and educate. At IDEO, they support the company's culture and work practices. Project teams use brainstorms to get input from people with diverse skills throughout the company. Knowledge is spread about new industries and technologies. Newcomers and veterans learn about who knows what. The explicit goal of a group brainstorm is to generate ideas. But the other benefits of routinely gathering rotating groups of people from around an organization to talk about ideas might ultimately be more important for supporting creative work.

8 FOLLOW THE RULES, OR DON'T CALL IT A BRAINSTORM

This is true even if you hold only occasional brainstorms and even if your work doesn't require constant creativity. The worst brainstorms happen when the term is used loosely and the rules aren't followed at all. Perhaps the biggest mistake that leaders make is failing to keep their mouths shut. I once went to a meeting that started with the boss saying: "Let's brainstorm." He followed this pronouncement with 30 minutes of his own rambling thoughts, without a single idea coming from the room. Now, that's productivity loss!

CRITERIA-SETTING

The process of setting decision criteria is used to answer the question, "Exactly what would the ideal solution to the problem look like?" or "What specific standards or measurements (such as cost, time, availability, and so forth) must be met to make this an optimal solution?" The criteria spell out a picture of such an optimum or ideal answer—in detail. For example, if a company selling consumer electronic products were dealing with a problem of deciding what new products or services to offer for sale on their website, they might establish criteria like these:

The ideal product/service would:

- Appeal to our typical family-oriented customer.
- Be of exceptional quality or rugged durability.
- Sell for less than $500.
- Be unique and not available in other stores.
- Produce profit margins of at least 30 percent.

Once the criteria are clearly stated (and posted somewhere for quick reference), the group can compare each product or service idea against the criteria to narrow the field and move toward a decision. Taking time to specify criteria of an ideal solution is an important step in the group process.

Clarify and post agreed-upon criteria before discussing possible solutions.

THE NOMINAL GROUP PROCESS

Both brainstorming and criteria-setting are effective techniques for identifying potential problem-solving ideas. Once these potential solutions are generated, however, groups must process the data and determine which can best meet the group's objectives. The group can condense input into the best possible solution by listing and ranking ideas as a group, by voting on proposals, or by using the nominal group process (NGP).

NGP can boil down possible solutions to identify the best options.

The NGP is an idea-processing approach that combines individual work with the group process. (That's why it is called "nominal"—participants also work alone.) Rather than having group members immediately speak up with their points of view (a process that may *commit* them to that view since they've voiced it "publicly"), the NGP allows participants to write down ideas privately. Following a clear definition of the problem or issues, group members spend 10 to 20 minutes writing out their ideas about possible solutions. Then, each participant provides one idea from his or her list, and a facilitator writes the idea on a flipchart in full view of the group. Ideas are not discussed at this point, although people may clarify or explain the concept. This round-robin listing of ideas continues until the members have no further ideas. Then a silent vote is taken where participants rank-order the ideas.

The steps of the process, once again, are:

1 Individuals write solution ideas working alone.
2 The group moderator records ideas from each person, one at a time, usually on flipcharts.
3 Participants clarify ideas if necessary.
4 Participants silently vote to rank ideas (a final solution may require several votes).

Wrap it Up With a Complete Conclusion

The end of your meeting should include the same points that you find in a traditionally organized presentation: summary, action step, and final statement. This is your opportunity to review your major decisions and confirm necessary actions along with the people responsible for those actions. At the very end of your meeting, try to loop back to the reason that you met in the first place, and close with your appreciation of everyone's attention and work.

Monitor the Delivery of Information in the Group

The next step in the Straight Talk Model is delivery of the message. In the group process, the message is forming as we go, so "delivery" takes a different form. The leader must constantly *monitor* the flow of ideas in a group. The two most common problems to avoid are individual dominance and "groupthink."

Message "delivery" in group situations involves monitoring the flow of ideas as the "message" evolves.

Avoid Individual Dominance

In many groups, certain individuals (or small subgroups) quickly dominate a discussion by virtue of their personality, organizational position, or personal status. These people may range from being particularly charming (and thus disproportionately influential because everybody likes them) to being highly autocratic, stubborn, or just loud. The problem is compounded when status differences are involved. A vice-president working in a small group with low-ranking personnel will have more influence, even if he knows less about the topic. In our opening story, Matt Bayless, the president of Moose Lips, should not have placed himself in one of the buzz groups. He would naturally dominate the group because he's the boss. A leader should also take care to handle conflict directly. If participants disagree, it is up to the leader to ensure that each person gets his or her say.

Be sensitive to status and rank differences since these may impede the free flow of ideas.

Avoid Groupthink

The term "groupthink" describes a condition of like-mindedness that can arise in groups that are particularly cohesive. Under groupthink, people in the group will exert pressure against any dissenting viewpoints. Such thinking deters creativity and fresh approaches to problems or issues. While cohesiveness is normally a desirable condition in groups, it can be carried so far that it becomes counterproductive. This is especially likely when the group has high enthusiasm and where members' desire for consensus or harmony becomes stronger than their desire for the best possible decision. Under such conditions, critical thinking and the independent and objective analysis of ideas become less important than keeping everyone in the group happy and friendly.

Symptoms of Groupthink

Some monumentally poor decisions can arise when everyone in a group thinks alike and the group culture pressures people toward conformity and cohesiveness. The following are key symptoms of groupthink.

1   An overemphasis on team play, unanimity, and getting along harmoniously.

2   A "shared stereotype" view that competitors or those in opposition to the group are inept, incompetent, and incapable of doing anything to thwart the group's efforts.

3   Self-censorship by group members; individuals are suppressed to avoid rocking the boat.

4   Rationalization to comfort one another and reduce any doubts regarding the group's agreed-upon plan.

5   Self-appointed "mind-guards" who function to prevent anyone from undermining the group's apparent unanimity and "protect" the group from information that differs from their beliefs.

6   Direct pressure on those who express disagreement.

7   An expression of self-righteousness that leads members to believe their actions are moral or ethical, thus letting them disregard objections to their behavior.

8   A strong feeling of esprit de corps, faith in the wisdom of the group, and a tendency to take risks.

Each of these symptoms of groupthink damages realistic thinking and effective decisions. A combination of several or all of these can be devastating to group effectiveness.

Avoid the Risky Shift Phenomenon

One subset of groupthink is the risky shift, meaning the condition under which the group is willing to take a more extreme position than any of its members would be likely to accept. This is the corporate equivalent of the lynch-mob mentality. People as a group accept a decision or course of action they would never consider if they had to be personally responsible for the outcome. Don't let the collective nature of the group allow people to hide—or deflect responsibility.

In summary, then, the major communication concerns about "delivery" of messages in meetings are reducing individual dominance and groupthink. The message of a meeting evolves as the group works. Straight Talk communicators facilitate that evolution.

Evaluate Feedback and Following Up After the Meeting

The last step in the Straight Talk Model reminds us to evaluate feedback for continued success. Meeting follow-up largely determines whether the time spent was worthwhile or not. Leaders can help to ensure that meetings are successful by following up on assignments, reviewing meeting minutes or notes, and sharing feedback.

Feedback on meeting effectiveness is as important as feedback on a speech. Use it to become a better communicator.

Follow Up Promptly on Assignments

Know what follow-up is expected of each group member and review this information at the end of the meeting. Make notes of what people agreed to do. Then follow up to be certain that the work is completed. Don't let group decisions drop through the cracks. If you do, people will see the time spent on the meeting as a waste.

Review the Minutes

Good meetings usually include minutes, a written record of major ideas, solutions, and actions agreed upon by the participants. Typically, the leader asks one person to take the minutes and distribute them for group members to review later. Be certain that these minutes are accurate and complete. Hard copy or email versions are the most common form.

Give, Solicit, and Receive Feedback

Write a note, send an email, or call the group members to provide feedback. Tell them what you liked about the process or suggest ideas on how they and the group might be more effective. Be tactful and constructive. Similarly, compliment participants who have made good contributions. Let them know that you respect their communication skills and enjoy working with them. This can help build future rapport, making your next group meeting more comfortable. If you disagree with group members, reassure them that you respect their opinion or still value them as friends or colleagues but have a different point of view. Respect differences.

Reinforce effective meeting participation to build future participation.

Test Solutions

The ultimate feedback about a solution, of course, is whether it works or not. Do follow-up systematic observation to gather data that will tell you whether the decision produced the desired results. If not, re-open discussion of the problem and try again. No individual or group makes the perfect decision every time. Group problem-solving, like all forms of communication, requires constant monitoring and continuous improvement. To accomplish this, remember that feedback is your friend.

Apply the Straight Talk Model When You Participate in Meetings

So far we have discussed leadership of meetings. Let's now put the shoe on the other foot to consider your roles as a participant in determining the success of a meeting. Attention to the Straight Talk Model will improve your effectiveness when participating in meetings or group problem-solving, which we will discuss in the following sections.

Define the Context as a Participant

Just as when you lead a meeting, the first step in applying the Straight Talk Model to communication when you participate in meetings is to define the context. The context of the meeting is defined by the situation, the audiences, and objectives with those audiences.

Define the Meeting's Situation

Understanding the situation includes limiting or focusing upon the meeting's central issues, evaluating the external climate, and evaluating corporate culture. To the extent possible, clarify the purpose for the meeting. Ask the person who called the meeting what the meeting is about. Then, think about the external climate and corporate culture as it relates to the situation. For example, if the meeting is going to deal with a sharp drop in sales, learn what you can about current market factors that may be causing this decline. Search publications or the Web about the product and competitors.

Ask for clarification about the meeting's situation before attending.

Define the Meeting's Audiences

Find out who else will be attending the meeting so that you can plan ways to meet their needs and expectations. The other participants are the primary audience for your meeting. (But don't forget the hidden audience or the decision-maker who may not be present in the meeting.) Then take some time to view the situation through the eyes of the other participants. Could the drop in sales be a result of high turnover of service people? Are the manufacturing people feeling a lot of pressure to meet demand? How are these people likely to react in the meeting?

Define the Objectives With Each Audience

Next, think carefully about what you want to accomplish with each of these audiences. Hopefully, you will want to work to solve the problem, but you will also face opportunities to make an impression on other people who may be useful to you in your career. Plan your objectives with each audience.

Once you have a clearer picture of the context of the meeting and have researched the meeting's topic, make notes of ideas you may want to offer. Having these ideas already thought through will help you present them more clearly. However, don't come to the meeting determined to sell your idea. Plan to first listen to the give and take of others.

Avoid coming to a meeting with a inflexible point of view.

Selling Versus Participating

As a participant, avoid the temptation to force or intimidate people into accepting your preconceived ideas. Selling your point of view, while supposedly being open to participation, is one kind of a hidden agenda. It implies that you really just want the group to *think* they are participating. Don't try to manipulate the group into ratifying an idea you have already decided upon. Be prepared to share your thoughts, but use the group process to generate and test other ideas as well.

As you define your objectives with each audience, be aware of hidden agenda—yours and theirs. For individual participants, the hidden agenda may include such things as:

- Getting some "exposure" (that is, to favorably impress others).
- Providing a status arena in which they can assert their power or ability.

- Filling some perceived quota for going to meetings.
- Having an opportunity to socialize with others.
- Providing a chance to assert dominance of one group or department over another (or a chance to break that dominance).
- Working on communication skills.
- Diffusing decision responsibility so that one person won't have to take all the heat if a decision fails.
- Getting away from unpleasant work duties.

Understanding these unspoken objectives can help you recognize people's motives and better understand their participation.

Consider Your Media, Source, and Timing Options as a Participant

Communication media options for participants in a meeting are somewhat limited. You, as a participant, will normally be limited to oral media with possible use of visuals. Meanwhile, timing can be important in meetings. Be careful to present your ideas when the group is ready to deal with them. Don't jump the gun and offer your solution before there has been appropriate discussion or before the issues have been clearly delineated. This can be a real temptation when your preparation has unearthed a great solution. Hold back until the group is ready to consider solutions before offering your input.

You may also have options about the source of your input ideas. Perhaps the flow of ideas in the meeting can work best if you invite someone else to present your idea. A statement like, "Janice and I were talking about some possible sales incentives the other day. Jan, why don't you tell them what you suggested to me." If the group receives these ideas well, you'll boost Janice's credibility (and probably solidify an ally).

Sometimes another person can better present your ideas.

Select and Organize Information as You Prepare for a Meeting

To understand how you can best select and organize your thoughts for a meeting, you should be aware of the different types of meetings. Companies use meetings for two general reasons:

- **To inform (advise, update).** Informative meetings use primarily one-way communication from leader to participants. As such, the participant's job in an informative meeting is to listen and assimilate the information. In many cases, an informative meeting is really a presentation to a group with some question-and-answer interaction. Reaching group consensus is not a top priority.

Prepare for such meetings by being ready, willing to digest the information. Attend the meeting with the intention of asking appropriate questions, if the meeting leader requests questions. A good question sends the message that you are both listening and also have the ability to apply the information you hear.

- **To make decisions (solve problems, set goals).** Decision-making meetings involve much more give-and-take. They succeed or fail in large part based on the climate created. If a climate of openness and free expression is created, the likelihood of success improves. In decision-making meetings, you will combine the ideas and information you bring to the meeting with those of other participants. Through discussion, these ideas are refined and combined with other participants' information, resulting in group-generated information. Ideally, the group's ideas, generated through group discussion, will be greater than the sum of the individual inputs (synergy will occur).

  Prepare for such meetings by doing whatever research you can on the topic and certainly by completing any advance assignments. You might also bring your material on a USB drive or in multiple hardcopies to share. Attend the meeting with the clear intention to contribute all of what you have prepared, as necessary, but keep an open mind to assimilate other information you might hear. Know that the person who does not speak up appears to simply have nothing to say.

As we mentioned previously (see pp. 179–182), two common ways of producing group-generated information are through brainstorming and criteria-setting. The leader should use these only after the group has clearly defined the purpose and objectives of the meeting. Although you may not be formally leading the meeting, you might suggest a process for moving the meeting along.

Deliver Your Ideas by Participating Actively

Your effectiveness in meetings will call upon the entire range of communication techniques and skills discussed in this book. Your participation affords opportunities for listening actively, delivering mini-presentations, and participating within the rules or guidelines that make meetings effective.

The group's success often arises from the participant's feelings about being at the meeting. Be open-minded and optimistic that the meeting will accomplish its goals. Arrive at the meeting a few minutes early. Be fresh and organized. Greet others cheerfully and contribute to a friendly, positive climate.

Your behaviors (verbal and non-verbal) will impact on the meeting's climate.

Listen Actively

In meetings, it is especially important to use retention listening—the kind of listening that helps you remember and use information being offered by others. To do this, it is important to concentrate on the group member who is speaking. Force yourself to keep your mind on that person and avoid doing other things like daydreaming or doodling. Don't even think about checking email on your Blackberry.

About Those Phones

Sometimes people forget that the rules about keeping time apply to meetings. We had an experience in a meeting where a speaker had 30 minutes on the agenda to present background for a decision-making discussion. After 40 minutes, he was still droning on, explaining what most of the audience knew already. Heads were down; almost everyone was reading email on Blackberries in their laps. At 50 minutes, Blackberries appeared on the table. At about an hour, attendees were holding their Blackberries up in front of their faces, as if to block out the speaker. He missed it all and spoke for an hour and 15 minutes. Unfortunately, no one heard him after that first 30 minutes.

Do your best to find areas of interest between the group member who is speaking and yourself. Focus on what you can get out of what the person is saying. Listen for central themes rather than for isolated facts. For example, you may find that many of the arguments from one person are focused on costs, while another person may talk more about creativity. Too often, listeners get hopelessly lost because they focus on unimportant facts and details and miss the speaker's main point. Ask questions when you don't understand a topic.

Perhaps the best advice is to listen as if you will be required to report the content of a message to someone within eight hours. Take notes of what others are saying. Don't try to get their ideas word-for-word, but jot down key points. The simple process of writing key ideas as you hear them helps you retain information. Learn ways to do this efficiently.

Deliver Effective Mini-Presentations

Present your ideas in clear, organized ways with support for your key ideas. Use delivery techniques that convey enthusiasm and sincerity. In particular, speak clearly and expressively. Avoid rambling. Instead, contribute your ideas directly and concisely. Remember to focus on specific benefits for your listeners. Pay attention to timing so that you do not monopolize the meeting or present an idea before the group is ready to deal with it. Use visuals if appropriate. For example, feel free to sketch out a concept you are trying to explain if that would help people understand.

Deliver your ideas freely. That's why you were invited to the meeting. Similarly, listen to other participants. Consider their ideas carefully. Add your thinking by hitchhiking on the ideas of others. That is how groups can make better decisions than individuals.

Participate Within the Rules

Many meetings fall apart because people are unwilling to play by the rules. Participants may jump ahead to present their solution ideas before the problem has been clarified or other ideas have been collected. They may fail to support the climate of openness by putting down other people's ideas. Avoid those behaviors. Instead, apply the following ideas for participating within the rules of group communication:

- Help the leader stay focused on the topic; avoid going off on a tangent with unrelated talk.
- Avoid getting into side conversations, dominating the discussion, interrupting the meeting, or getting overly emotional.
- Be open and supportive of the ideas of others. Ask clarifying questions in non-threatening ways. Express approval when appropriate.
- Help the leader control the meeting. If arguments break out, try to clarify both points of view objectively. If the group wanders off the topic, suggest that they re-focus on the key question.
- If the group selects brainstorming or criteria-setting, stick to the guidelines. If the group wants to define certain decision criteria, don't jump ahead to proposing a solution before the criteria are clearly established.
- Pay attention. Make notes.
- Remember that much of your value to the organization comes from your ideas and contributions to the group. Give them the benefit of your experience and point of view.

Evaluate Feedback for Your Continued Success

Improvement in communication skills is based on realistically evaluating feedback from others. As we discussed in Chapter 1, giving, soliciting, and receiving feedback are important to your growth as a communicator. The key is to determine when your communication is working and when it is not, so that you can modify the areas that are less effective.

In meetings, pay special attention to non-verbal messages from other participants that may indicate that you are dominating the conversation, talking about things that are unrelated to the group's focus, or failing to draw in other people. If non-verbal cues indicate that you may be doing these things, simply ask the group, "Am I going down the wrong road here?" or "Have I been talking too much?" People will respect your openness and willingness to accept feedback. In addition, be willing to offer feedback to others and to the leader about the meeting. If you are tactful, everyone will benefit from your thoughtful suggestions.

Be sensitive to input about your participation. Ask if you are contributing effectively.

And finally, be willing to evaluate your own participation with the Credibility Checklist. As you look back on the meeting, did you show concern for others? Did you share your expertise? Did you support your suggestions with examples of success? Did you contribute with confidence? You will only continue to improve if you can recognize both your strengths and the areas where you should focus in the future.

The Straight Talk Model Applied to Moose Lips

Let's revisit the meeting at Moose Lips Corporation described at the beginning of the chapter. As you think about the Straight Talk Model, consider the context. The president, Matt Bayless, had built the company from a tiny one-man show to a 100-member-plus company. As a company grows, the complexity of communicating increases. While leaders of small organizations can sit down and chat about ideas, things get more complicated (the context changes) when more employees participate. Each employee brings his or her agenda to a discussion, and, while multiple inputs can be useful, processing these ideas can be a challenge.

At the heart of Moose Lips' problem is the inappropriate choice of medium (Step 2 in the Straight Talk Model). A large-scale meeting involving all employees simply doesn't work. The discussion topics themselves are vaguely worded with no clear objectives, and the participants don't have appropriate background information to address the topics. The typical outcome in such a situation is pooled ignorance rather than useful ideas. Matt further damages the likelihood of a successful meeting by participating as an equal with the group. His formal power as president of the company will undoubtedly stifle discussion or cause participants in his buzz group to work toward a hidden agenda of impressing the boss.

Performance Checklist

After completing this chapter, you should be better able to apply some principles for selecting and organizing information for your message. Specifically, you should now understand that:

- The first decision leaders must make is whether to have a meeting in the first place. To do so, they should consider the situation in light of the advantages and disadvantages of meetings as a media option.
- Synergy is a major objective of problem-solving meetings. Groups achieve this by working effectively and avoiding the pitfalls of the group process.
- Inviting the right people and keeping the number workable will enhance the likelihood of success of a meeting.
- An effective agenda can streamline a meeting by helping participants prepare in advance.
- Meetings, like presentations, are more successful with complete introductions and conclusions.
- Leaders help their groups select and process information by using techniques such as brainstorming, criteria-setting, and the nominal group process (NPG).
- Brainstorming and criteria-setting are two ways to generate useful information from meeting participants.
- You can be an effective meeting participant by using retention listening techniques, by offering clear, direct mini-presentations, and by participating within the rules or guidelines that make meetings effective.
- Individual dominance and "groupthink" can damage a meeting and result in poor group decisions.
- Risky shift is a subset of groupthink whereby groups make excessively risky decisions.
- Ask for feedback on your meeting participation and evaluate yourself with the Credibility Checklist.

What Do You Know?

Activity 7.1: Knowing the Advantages and Disadvantages of Meetings

Summarize in your own words the two major advantages of meetings:

1 _____

2 _____

Summarize in your own words the two major disadvantages of meetings:

1 _____

2 _____

Now, summarize in your own words the ways in which meetings can lead to poor decisions.

1 _____

2 _____

3 _____

4 _____

Activity 7.2: Brainstorming

Working in groups of five-to-seven people, practice the process of brainstorming. Select one of the problems below and, carefully applying the rules of brainstorming discussed in this chapter, generate as many ideas as possible for solving the problem. Encourage creativity and innovation. Be especially careful to avoid judging ideas. Record all ideas on a chalkboard or flipchart. From your brainstorming process, identify five ideas that have the best potential for solving the problem or achieving the goal.

Use one of these topics (or select your own problem):

- Developing a creative advertising program (or viral campaign) for _____ (a product or service).
- Living on an extremely limited income (determine a dollar figure).
- Restructuring your department or company.
- Launching a campaign to overcome a competitor's advantages.
- Getting people to use mass transit/one-dollar coins/valet parking/online courses (or similar topics).

Activity 7.3: Using the Nominal Group Process

Apply the nominal group process to the problem dealt with in Activity 7.2. After brainstorming, dedicate a fixed amount of time to working individually to list and prioritize the best ideas. Then go through the process of recording and narrowing the ideas as described in this chapter. Select as a group the best alternative(s) based on NGP input.

Activity 7.4: Rating Yourself as a Meeting Participant

Since meeting participation can be an important part of many careers, take a few moments to review your attitudes toward meetings. Answer "Yes" or

"No" to each of the following questions based on how you tend to react to and participate in meetings. Be honest.

1 Do you enjoy most meetings?
2 Do you understand the specific purpose of the meetings you attend?
3 Do you understand your roles in meetings you attend?
4 Do you hold back on judging the ideas of other people until they have finished explaining?
5 Do you complete your "homework," such as looking up information or studying proposals, before meetings?
6 Do you arrive at meetings a few minutes before schedule?
7 Do you engage in side conversations while the meeting is in progress?
8 Do you look for excuses to leave meetings for reasons such as non-emergency telephone calls?
9 Do you ask clarifying questions when you are not sure about something?
10 Do you use both support and retention listening techniques?
11 Do you actively participate in discussions when you have something worthwhile to contribute?
12 Do you suggest ways to stay on the subject or move the group process along toward a conclusion?
13 Following meetings, do you follow up with agreed-upon action?
14 Do you contribute to improving meetings by giving feedback to the people who conduct them either by a note, phone call, or visit?
15 Do you evaluate your own contribution to meetings in terms of how well you expressed your concern, expertise, power/success, and confidence?

Except for questions 7 and 8, a "Yes" response is preferred. If you answered "No" to these and "Yes" to questions 4, 7, and 8, your contribution to meetings is less than it could be. Your career progress may depend on your developing different attitudes and skills with regard to meetings.

Reinforce With These Review Questions

1 People invited to a meeting should: (a) have some expertise on the topic, (b) have a vested interest in the outcome, (c) have decision-making skills, (d) share the organization's values, (e) all the above.

2 True/False—It is best to invite participants who have strong preconceived opinions about solutions to the problem.

3 The three advantages of meetings are: (1) _____, (2) _____, and (3) _____.

4 True/False—A group and a team are the same thing. Both create synergy.

5 True/False—When using "brainstorming," the group must create a culture that is open to all kinds of ideas, even very unconventional ones.

6 True/False—The nominal group process is an idea-processing approach that combines individual work and the group process.

7 The two most common ways that the free flow of ideas is inhibited is when groups face (1) _____ or (2) _____.

8 True/False—Groupthink arises when everyone in the group thinks alike and the group culture pressures people toward conformity.

9 True/False—As a participant in a meeting you should listen actively and be prepared to deliver mini-presentations.

10 True/False—When seeking feedback as a meeting participant you should pay attention to non-verbal cues as well as spoken comments.

Mini-Case Study: Andreas Hates Meetings

"In the entire five months I have worked at this company I have yet to attend a meeting that seemed to accomplish anything. We have meetings every Tuesday because, well, we have always had meetings every Tuesday!" Andreas was venting a bit to a friend at the coffee shop. "We gather together—usually a few minutes late—and nobody seems to know why we are here. The Department Manager passes out a sheet of paper he calls an agenda, but it simply lists a few announcements. Then he reads this to us!" Andreas shook his head as he stirred his coffee.

"He could send us all a memo and we'd save a lot of time. Of course, the people who have been with the company do seem to get a perverse kick out of kidding each other and talking about office gossip. Maybe there is some social value in meeting, but I'll be darned if I can see any other reason for wasting so much time every week. These blab sessions are getting annoying, especially since I always have some real work waiting back at my desk."

Questions

1 Based on the ideas in this chapter, what seems to be the main problems with the meetings Andreas is attending?

2 As a leader, what would you do to improve the quality of meetings? If you were Andreas, what options might you have to improve the communication and his satisfaction?

3 What does Andreas' description say about media selection in his company?

eight

Participate in Effective Conversations and Interviews

Questions have the power to turn confusion into clarity, resistance into acceptance, division into consensus, and the frustration of not knowing what to say into the satisfaction of having said it.

(Sam Deep and Lyle Sussman, *What to Ask When You Don't Know What to Say*)

Improving One-to-One Communication

Communicating with individuals one at a time is likely to be an expensive medium, so making the most of it certainly makes sense. We use it (appropriately) when sharing complex messages, dealing with potentially emotional content, and when simply building relationships.

Despite its relative informality, application of the Straight Talk Model still applies nicely. This chapter focuses on sending and receiving messages in conversation and its more structured cousin, the interview. Since listening plays an especially important role, we will elaborate on some key listening principles as well.

Professional Competencies

When you have completed this chapter, you should be able to:

- Recognize how conversations and interviews can be highly effective ways to gather ideas, build relationships, and solve problems.
- Understand and apply principles of active listening.
- Describe the relevance of three elements of the listening process.

- Apply the five-step Straight Talk Model in conversations and in interviews—as an interviewer or interviewee.
- Apply basic conversation skills, including: (1) having things to talk about (being well-read and informed), (2) finding your conversation partner's interests, (3) practicing conversation starters, sustainers, and closers, and (4) being willing to take time for conversation.
- Display greater confidence, increased professionalism, create healthier relationships, and project intelligence in interviews and conversations.
- Describe and produce examples of four types of questions commonly used in interviewing.
- Recognize the three key ingredients of the successful interview: (1) a clear purpose for having the interview, (2) ample opportunities for interaction between participants, and (3) effective listening.
- Apply the STARR pattern of arrangement to interview questions.
- Appreciate the importance of preparation and practice before interviewing.

The Way It Is ... Luca Gets Tongue Tied

Luca was attending his first company conference. The whole office staff was at the hotel training room, and the morning session had just ended. For the first three hours, he had listened to reports given by various leaders in the company. The new product introduced was particularly interesting. Even to a new employee like Luca, the company's future looked rosy.

At lunchtime, the employees went to the room next door where tables for six were set for the meal. Luca didn't know many company people and wasn't sure where to sit. After stalling a few minutes, he selected an empty chair at one of the tables. It wasn't until after he'd sat down that he discovered that one of the company vice-presidents was also seated at his table. "Oh, no," Luca thought. "What am I going to talk about with this guy? I'm sure I'll make some stupid remarks—after all, I haven't been speaking English all my life. Maybe I should move to another table."

But it was too late. John Bannister, the VP of Marketing, warmly introduced himself to Luca. He knew Luca was new with the company and cheerfully welcomed him aboard. Then the conversation went something like this:

MR. BANNISTER: "So what do you think of the company so far?"
LUCA: "It's fine."
MR. BANNISTER: "Are you originally from around here?"
LUCA: "No."
MR. BANNISTER: "Then what brings you to the city?"
LUCA: "My girlfriend."
MR. BANNISTER: "Oh, what does she do?"
LUCA: "She's looking for work. She wants to be a model, or maybe an actress."
MR. BANNISTER: "I see."
LUCA: "Yes, sir."

Can you feel the tension between Luca and Mr. Bannister? In all likelihood, the lunch conversation will now turn to others at the table. Luca's lack of conversational skills may prove to be a serious problem for his career and his relationships. As importantly, Bannister's attempt at conversation didn't go so well either. Imagine if this same level of interaction had occurred in a more formal interview situation.

Effective interviewing is conversation that is *planned* and has specific *purposes*. Although we often associate interviewing with the job-seeking process, it has many other, equally important, functions in business communication. Interviews actually take many forms, ranging from informal conversations to highly structured interrogations. This chapter looks at a broad range of conversation and interview skills needed in the business world. We will use the term "interview" throughout, but the principles apply to less-formal one-to-one conversations, as well. The advantages to learning such skills include:

- Greater confidence and comfort with people.
- Increased professionalism and image.
- More-healthy relationships with others.
- Greater ability to display your intelligence and good judgment.

The Straight Talk Model has direct application to conversations and interviews, as we will discuss. Hopefully you will not experience communication flops like Luca did. But could you be missing opportunities in your everyday one-to-one interactions?

Recognize the Characteristics of Conversations and Interviews

Conversations and interviews are one-to-one communications that allow immediate two-way sharing of information. Interviews are a form of conversation, and, like good conversations, all participants in the interview will give and get information, and all will hopefully think they have benefited in some respect from the exchange. But there are some differences between conversations and interviews, as well.

One-to-one communication allows easy two-way sharing of ideas.

Unlike casual conversations, interviews have a purpose other than, or in addition to, affording the participants enjoyment. In truly productive interviews, both parties share a sense of purpose. In addition, interviews have time limits, and participants should bring their remarks to a close at or before the set time.

Both conversations and interviews can be highly effective ways to gather ideas, build relationships, and solve problems. In many situations, no medium is as effective as the interview. For example, when sensitive or highly personal information is being shared, the interview provides for opportunities to give and take, verbally and non-verbally, as no other medium does. Some key factors necessary for interview effectiveness include the following.

Have a Clear Purpose

The key question for both the interviewer and person being interviewed must always be: "What am I attempting to accomplish in this communication situation?" Sometimes the intentions differ between the participants. Differing intentions can become barriers to effective interviews, although such differences are normal. For example, in a job interview, applicants want to reveal information that makes them look good and avoid revealing anything that reflects negatively on them. The interviewer wants to discover candidates's strengths and weaknesses. The greater the gap between participants' intentions, the more likely communication barriers will arise.

The purpose of an interview should be clear to both parties.

In workplace communication, interviews are commonly used for hiring, gathering information, reviewing performance, counseling, reprimanding, expressing grievances, and getting feedback when an employee is leaving the organization. To be successful, both parties in each of these kinds of interviews should be well-prepared and clear about their objectives. Defining the context (Step 1 of the Straight Talk Model) is as critical in this form of communication as in any other. We will talk more about this later in the chapter.

In addition to both parties having a clear picture of what they want to achieve, two other key ingredients must be present for a successful interview:

- Ample opportunities for interaction between participants.
- Effective listening.

> The newest computer can merely compound, at speed, the oldest problem in the relations between human beings, and in the end the communicator will be confronted with the old problem, of what to say and how to say it. (Edward R. Murrow)

Create Opportunities for Interaction

The effectiveness of interaction between participants depends in large part on the degree and quality of interactive communication. Interaction means that both parties have ample *opportunity* to participate. If interviewers find themselves talking uninterruptedly for as long as two or three minutes, they are probably failing to maximize this communication medium. Any interview should include a good deal of give-and-take. Thus, creating an environment that is "safe" for interaction is an important task for the interviewer, except in cases where, for example, a criminal is being interrogated. This is accomplished largely by not monopolizing the conversation and by soliciting and encouraging feedback with good listening skills.

Create a safe environment to stimulate participation.

Apply Active Listening

Excellent conversation and interviewing skills arise from *sharing* information, not from *telling*. To share effectively, all parties need to listen. Unfortunately, really good listeners are scarce. For many people, listening means impatiently waiting for a place to jump in with their ideas. Too many people think of listening as something passive—something they *sit back and do* while they wait for their turn to talk. Effective listening requires active mental effort. People who do learn to listen well not only learn a lot, but they build stronger interpersonal relationships, as well. Let's look a bit deeper into listening before we elaborate on interviews and conversations.

The lack of effective listening may be the most common human communication problem. It becomes immediately evident in one-to-one conversations. One of the greatest gifts we can give others is our attention. Everyone wants to be heard, understood, respected, and loved. A lot of us like to talk and very few choose to listen. Therein lies a huge opportunity for distinguishing yourself from the many communicators who are ineffective listeners.

Better listeners are better communicators. Period.

Why is effective listening so tough for so many people? Ironically, of the four basic communication skills—reading, writing, speaking, and listening—only one is not formally *taught*. Elementary schools focus heavily on the first three and assume that students are picking up listening. After all, isn't listening really just a matter of sitting back and letting the talker have his or her say? Well, no, it's not really that passive. Good listeners are active participants in information-gathering.

Look Inside: What Are Your Listening Habits?

How often do you find yourself relying on these ten bad **listening** habits? Check yourself carefully on each one, and be honest (no one is grading you).

Habit	Frequency				
	Almost Always	Usually	Sometimes	Seldom	Almost Never
I get sidetracked by mental distractions (thoughts going on in my head)					
I get distracted by the other person's speech patterns, tone of voice, accent, or noises around me					
Although I try to recall everything the other person says, I don't take notes					
I reject some topics as uninteresting before the other person even gets started					
I fake listening					
I jump to conclusions about the other person's meaning before he/she is finished explaining					
I decide that the other person is wrong before hearing everything she or he has to say					
I judge others on personal appearance and mannerisms, etc.					
I ignore or discount another person's evidence when it sounds wrong					
I don't bother to create a comfortable place for the other person to talk					
Total:					

How to score

Give yourself the following scores for every frequency checked:

For every "Almost Always"	2
For every "Usually"	4
For every "Sometimes"	6
For every "Seldom"	8
For every "Almost Never"	10

Total score interpretation:

Below 70	You need a lot of training in listening
From 71–90	You listen well
Above 90	You listen exceptionally well

In the next few pages we will explain why listening is a critical communication skill, define some common barriers to good listening, and offer some pointers on how to become a more skillful, active listener.

What Contributes to Listening?

Before we can begin to improve our listening skills, we need to understand the demands placed upon our listening capacities. These demands fall into three categories or elements of the listening process: internal elements, environmental elements, and interactional elements.

Internal Elements Affecting Listening

Listening involves the mental process of attaching meanings to words or sounds we hear. Two preconditions you must meet:

- The receiver must hear the words or other sounds used by the message source.
- The listener must possess a set of meanings or referents for these sounds—the words need to make sense.

Trying to hear in a noisy environment, deal with a static-filled phone line, or encounter people who speak too softly are examples of problems with the first precondition. These can cause a breakdown in the ability to receive the message. Overhearing someone speaking an unfamiliar language or with a strong, unfamiliar accent are examples of breakdowns of the second precondition. If the sounds have no referent—they don't refer to anything that makes sense to us—we cannot understand. Listening is the way we put sounds and their meanings together to create understanding.

Listening is a psychological process of associating sounds with meanings.

Environmental Elements Affecting Listening

The listening process is also impacted by factors of the communication environment, which determine what we are able to listen to and what we cannot. These factors can impact our individual ability to listen and our organization's listening capacity, as well. These factors include:

- Our individual listening capacity.
- The presence of noise.

Individual listening capacity

Our listening capacity can be overburdened in two ways: it can be over-loaded with too much information, or it can be under-utilized with too little. In both cases, listening tends to break down.

Think about how many messages clamor for your attention every day. You wake to a clock radio and advertisers want you to listen. You catch a little TV with breakfast and newscasters, politicians, commercials, online messages try to get you to listen to what they have to say. On the way to work or school, more radio ads. At work or in classes we have meetings and idea-sharing and lectures and discussions of all types. You can spend a huge portion of your day listening—or tuning out. Some messages stick while others are never heard or soon forgotten.

Thousands of messages clamor for our attention every day. We choose which ones to listen to.

Listening breakdowns happen when we exceed our listening capacity. We can hear or respond to only a finite number of messages in any given day; we can answer only so many phone calls at one time. We can process or ponder only so many meetings or commercials. Once we reach our capacity to accomplish these tasks, we develop defensive mechanisms for coping. We develop psychological strategies for selecting what we will attend to and what we will tune out.

These selection mechanisms, although often unconscious, are normally based on our individual needs, which, of course, change over time. We do listen to auto ads when we are in the market for a car, for example. When our capacity for paying attention to incoming information is overloaded, the impact on our listening behavior is difficult to predict. Only one thing is for sure: We will tune out some messages.

We make unconscious decisions to listen to some messages while tuning out others based on our expectation that a message may meet our needs.

The opposite problem, where environmental demands cause us to under-utilize our listening capacity, is also widespread. Most people speak at the rate of about 120 words per minute (except for auctioneers or some disc jockeys), yet our normal capacity for listening—assigning meanings to words—is about 500 words per minute. The problem, of course, is that we listen faster than anyone can talk to us, providing ample time for our minds to wander far afield. Listening to others becomes a tedious task, forcing us to slow down our thinking to stay synchronized with, for example, the customer speaking to us. We will fill the gaps with irrelevant or off-topic thoughts.

Since we can listen faster than people can speak, we sometimes drift off.

The Presence of Noise
The presence of noise is another environmental element affecting listening. "Noise" refers to those sounds that are irrelevant to the conversation. It is important to note that noise may be either environmental (the sound of machinery, other conversations, buzzers, bells) or internal (a headache, our dislike of the person to whom we are listening, preoccupation with another problem). Whatever the source, noise distracts us from the business of listening.

Interactional Elements Affecting Listening

In contrast to the environmental elements of the listening process, the inter-actional elements concern internal psychological processes that we do not recognize as easily. Two such psychological elements deserve careful consideration: self-centeredness and self-protection.

Self-Centeredness and Listening
Self-centeredness refers to the degree of "vested interest" we may have in our own point of view. When a difference of opinion arises among people, our

vested interest in our ideas can create a listening barrier. For example, if a salesperson feels particularly strong about selling a particular product—for whatever reasons—she may quite literally not even hear a customer's request for a different product. She will be so personally sold on Product A that she will tune out a customer's desire to buy Product B—even when the customer may be better served with Product B.

It is not hard to understand why self-centeredness occurs. When we have taken the time to formulate an idea, we usually verbalize that idea in the presence of others. In essence, we have made a public commitment to that position, and it becomes awkward for us to change or appear inconsistent. At the same time, the people we are interacting with have also publicly committed themselves to their opinions. In such cases, neither party is effectively listening.

Since listening is a psychological process, based on our individual needs, we think and listen from a self-centered orientation. As a result, we don't listen to *what* the other person is saying; we listen instead to how his or her views alter our position.

We sometimes listen just long enough to formulate our counter-argument.

We sometimes find ourselves listening to other people solely for the purpose of finding the weaknesses in their positions so that we can formulate a convincing response. At that point, we stop listening and begin to plan what we'll say in response. The other person is still talking, and we still hear him or her, but we are no longer listening.

Self-centered listening has a direct impact on the amount of information we receive. Since, in most cases, additional information helps make better decisions, such blocking out of relevant information cannot help but lower the quality of our decisions and our ability to assist customers.

Self-Protection and Listening
Another element affecting the listening process is self-protection. We "protect" ourselves by playing out an anticipated conversation in our own minds before the real conversation ever occurs, to make sure we don't get caught saying something stupid. We figure we know where this conversation is going, so we anticipate what we expect to hear and plan our counter-argument, rather than listening to the actual message. In essence, then, we are practicing by listening to ourselves listen to others.

An old story illustrates this notion of self-protective listening. If you've heard it before, enjoy it again in light of our discussion of self-protective listening:

A fellow was speeding down a country road late at night and BANG! went a tire. He got out and looked but he had no jack.

Then he said to himself, "Well, I'll just walk to the nearest farmhouse and borrow a jack." He saw a light in the distance and said, "Well, I'm in luck; the farmer's up. I'll just knock on the door and say I'm in trouble, would you please lend me a jack? And he'll say, why sure, neighbor, help yourself, but bring it back."

He walked on a little farther and the light went out so he said to himself, "Now he's gone to bed, and he'll be annoyed because I'm bothering him, so he'll probably want some money for his jack. And I'll say, all right, it isn't very neighborly but I'll give you five dollars. And he'll say, do you think you can get me out of bed in the middle of the night and then offer me five dollars? Give me ten dollars, or get yourself a jack somewhere else."

By the time he got to the farmhouse the fellow had worked himself into a lather. He turned into the gate and muttered, "Ten dollars! All right, I'll give you ten dollars. But not a cent more! A poor devil has an accident, and all he needs is a jack. You probably won't let me have one no matter what I give you. That's the kind of guy you are."

Which brought him to the door and he knocked angrily, loudly. The farmer stuck his head out the window above the door and hollered down, "Who's there? What do you want?" The fellow stopped pounding on the door and yelled up, "To *&!%!!* with your stupid jack! You know what you can do with it!"

How does this illustrate self-protectiveness? The fellow had played the scene in his mind and adjusted what he planned to say because of his fear of being hurt or embarrassed. He was being self-protective.

Serious listening problems can arise when we engage in conjecture by listening to ourselves listen to others, by anticipating what *might be said* and by reacting to that instead of to what the other person is actually saying. Actively listen to your colleague or customer before you start making up a dialogue in your head.

Active listening means making sure you understand your colleague or customer before you formulate a response.

Both of these interactional elements—self-centeredness and self-protectiveness—influence the listening process in that they tend to orient our listening behavior toward biased interpretations of messages.

These three elements of the listening process—internal, environmental, and interactional—pose potential problems requiring *active* effort. We must recognize listening as more than something we sit back and do to kill time when we're not talking.

What can we do to improve our listening skills? A good starting point would be to apply some rather simple action tips designed to break bad habits and strengthen some good ones.

Listening Habits to Avoid

Most of us didn't become poor listeners overnight; we learned how over a period of time—we develop poor listening habits. Here are some ideas for avoiding common bad habits.

Talking Too Much

How is your listen–talk ratio? If you are like most people, you talk a lot more than you listen and that can be a problem. You can never become a better listener if you aren't disciplined to be quiet until others have expressed their thoughts fully. Ask other people questions. Then ask a relevant follow-up question that indicates that you listened to the answer. You'd be surprised how popular you can become by letting other people talk!

Being Unprepared

Preparing to listen means you decide to set aside time and other activities so that you can focus on listening. Mentally disconnect from other matters playing on your mind. Look at the people who are talking. Let them know you are now "open for business" to listen to their concerns.

Sometimes this preparation means going to another location where you will not be interrupted, where it's more quiet or comfortable. *Where* we listen can have an impact on *how* we listen. If your organization places physical barriers between you and others, such as a large counter between you and customers or a large desk between you and colleagues, consider inviting them to sit somewhere more conducive to talking. Executives sometimes run the risk of "hiding" behind their large desks, when coming around to sit where the visiting person can comfortably interact makes a better listening environment.

Reduce physical barriers to prepare for better listening.

Faking Attention

Faking attention is an attempt to be polite to someone during a conversation and results in what someone called the "wide asleep listener." This is usually accomplished by looking directly at the speaker when you are really thinking about something else, automatically nodding responses, or even saying "Yes" and "Uh huh" to conversations you have mentally tuned out. When you have agreed to listen to someone, commit yourself to expending the needed effort to listen and give that conversation your active attention.

Failing to be Patient

Changing channels in the middle of an interview or conversation is another unproductive habit. When something appears to be too uninteresting, or too hard to comprehend, or too time-consuming—or if someone starts to tell an all-too-familiar story, the poor listener will tune out. Since we know there is plenty of thinking time between the speakers' thoughts, we figure we can switch back and forth between several conversations without losing any information. This assumption is often incorrect. Let them have their say before "correcting" or debating what they say.

People can't always communicate to you efficiently. Sometimes they don't know the terminology or exactly how to describe their problem. Be patient. Be sure they have had ample opportunity to express themselves fully before you offer additional information or respectful disagreement.

Be patient with others. They may not know your terminology or are less able to express ideas clearly.

Positive Listening Behaviors

Avoidance of poor listening behaviors is only part of the process of becoming a good listener. You also need to take some positive steps to improve your listening effectiveness. Here are some proactive behaviors that lead to improvement.

Use Open-Ended Questions

An open-ended question is simply one that cannot be answered "Yes" or "No" or with a one-word answer. For example, in the following exchange, Tony poses an open-ended question to encourage Tom to speak more about his concerns.

TOM: I really don't think you've treated me fairly, Tony. You seem to give everyone else more opportunities, while I'm still stuck in the same old job.

TONY: I'd like to understand what you're saying. In what ways do you think I've given other people more opportunities?

In interaction with customers, consultants often advise employees to use open-ended questions to assess the quality of the service. For example, employees can replace the typical yes–no query ("Was everything okay?") with open-ended questions ("What could we have done to improve your experience with our product?"). Open-ended questions almost always get more informative responses than closed-ended ones. This holds with all kinds of interactions. Failing to use open-ended questions tends to make an interview sound like an interrogation. Encourage people to open up in their own words.

Listen For More Than the Facts

Much of what people communicate are feelings, impressions, and emotions; the actual facts of messages are often wrapped up in these. For example, an employee came to her manager's office, and in the course of the conversation she appeared quite upset about something. When she explained to the manager that her husband had just been terminated from his job, the manager expressed what he thought was appropriate concern and soon changed the subject. Shortly after, the employee abruptly left the office, apparently angry with the manager. He had listened to the facts of what she'd said, but completely missed her meaning.

From the manager's perspective, these were the facts:

1   Her husband was a very capable young executive who was unhappy with his present employer and had been looking around for another company.
2   This couple was young, had no children, and had few financial burdens.
3   Her husband had recently been offered another comparable position, which he turned down because it paid about the same as he was currently making.
4   Her husband had just lost his job.

In his listening process, the manager associated the new fact (4) with facts he already knew (1, 2, and 3) and concluded that there was no real serious problem. The husband would find a new, and probably better, job soon.

So why did the employee storm out of the office? The manager had listened only for the facts, while the employee wanted to talk about feelings and concerns she had. She wanted him to listen to what she was *not* saying—that she felt threatened by her husband's loss of the job or that she was embarrassed by his termination. What she needed was someone with whom to share these thoughts who might offer some comfort. Many messages convey emotion as well as information. Listening only for the facts is often not enough.

Messages often convey emotion that goes beyond the facts.

Avoid Interrupting

We tend to interrupt people because we get impatient. We want them to get their point across more quickly so that we can jump in and solve it. This, by the way, is a characteristic of men more frequently than women. Women have often been socialized to engage in longer, more supportive sharing of feelings, while men have often been socialized to get to the point and solve the problem. (See the section on male–female communication differences beginning on page 252.)

In the workplace, men tend to interrupt more frequently than women.

Interrupting in the middle of the message can damage a conversation. Yes, you may need to gain clarification of some points, but wait for an appropriate time to ask for that clarification rather than abruptly interrupting. Hold back on frequent use of questions like "What do you mean?" and "Why do you say that?" until you are sure the person speaking is finished. Then, if you need clarification, ask for it.

Use Thoughtful Pauses

When people ask your opinion, it is often wise to pause for a moment before responding. This suggests to them that you are thoughtful and that their questions are worth pondering. And taking time to think before you speak may enable you to offer a helpful and wise response.

Reinforce Others with Positive Non-Verbal and Verbal Cues

Especially in face-to-face interactions, non-verbal behaviors are critical. Appropriate responses such as good eye contact, concerned and engaged facial expression, and encouraging gestures such as nodding are examples of non-verbal behaviors that contribute to better listening.

Use non-verbal gestures or movements to encourage speakers to get their ideas across.

Verbally, we can improve communication by using "continuers" such as "Uh huh," or "I see," or "I can see why you'd be upset." These types of comments tend to let others know that you are listening and to encourage them to fully express their thoughts.

Solicit Clarification

When others are being unclear, it is important that we tactfully let them know it. We sometimes don't do this because:

- We think we will sound uninformed.
- We think we can figure the message out on our own—eventually.
- We don't want to take the time or expend the effort to make sure we understand.

By failing to ask for clarification, we rely too heavily on our own guesses in interpreting messages. When you ask questions about the meanings of a message, any implication that you lack knowledge will be more than made up for by your sincere desire to understand. This is flattering to others. It conveys a regard for people who speak to you. When you solicit clarification, ask open-ended questions, or use a phrase such as, "Help me to understand." For example, "Help me to understand. You felt that the raise you received was not what you had expected." These comments open the door for further description by the employee.

"Help me to understand" is a good phrase to invite people to clarify their ideas without getting defensive.

Shall I Ask or Fake It?

Giles Roberts was an excellent manager. Everyone who worked for him trusted him, which is the highest compliment. He took care of his people, and he took care of business. But way down deep, Giles was a little insecure about his organizational level and knowledge. His academic training and work experience were not always directly related to the company's mission. If he did not feel he knew *everything* about an issue, he would study it on his own until he felt he had the appropriate level of expertise. He wasn't comfortable asking a subordinate to explain operational complexities, fearing that the perception of his credibility might be compromised. As a result, some of Giles's colleagues thought that his decision-making was "slow."

When Giles mentioned his concerns to a communication consultant working with his company, she expressed this professional counsel: nothing bad would happen if you asked a subordinate to "help me understand this" when on unfamiliar turf. After all, as a manager, Giles could not be expected to be the expert on everything.

Giles tried this new approach (yes, with reservations), and he learned that his subordinates were delighted that he trusted them enough to ask and listen to them. Giles's credibility did not diminish. In fact, his ratings as a manager went up.

Repeat Key Ideas Back to the Speaker for Clarification

Repeating has several benefits. It lets speakers know that you are following their thoughts and that you consider it important to understand what they are saying. If you do not understand something, ask the speaker to clarify it. Don't pretend to understand when you really don't. It is better to admit a lack of understanding and receive clarification than to be left in the dark.

Take Notes

Should you take notes when listening to others? There are some real advantages to doing so. Note-taking conveys that you are sincerely interested in understanding. Most people will be flattered that you are taking their input so seriously. In fact, in some corporate cultures, *not* taking notes indicates that you are not listening and that you really don't care about either the speaker or the material. Obviously, this is not the identity you want to project.

Of course, when taking notes, jot down only major ideas and important facts that may help you to listen and remember more effectively. Don't try to write down everything word-for-word. Note-taking can show that you are committed to listening and understanding the speaker. Few people would be offended by such a show of concern.

Most thoughtful people recognize the need for careful listening. We spend more time in listening than any other communication activity. Of all the sources of information we have when dealing with others, listening is the most important. No tool rivals skilled and sympathetic listening for building stronger relationships and affecting better communication.

Understand the Nature and Functions of Conversation

Each culture has unique ways of conversing. One of the problems faced by Luca in our opening story may have resulted from his experience in talking with people whose "rules" are a bit different from his. While he may have felt that his brief, direct responses showed respect to John Bannister, he missed the point. Bannister wanted him to open up and share more information.

When people from different cultures interact, they frequently feel ill-at-ease, and they often misjudge or misunderstand each other. To reduce the communication problems that arise in multicultural organizations, it is helpful if you know something about the communicative styles of the majority of the people with whom you work. (We are not talking just about national cultures as discussed in Chapter 2, but also about subcultures in which people from varying groups apply different communication styles.)

Self-Evaluation: Determining Your Conversation Self-Confidence

The following self-evaluation looks at how comfortable you may be when it comes to making conversation with others. Take the quiz and then prepare a brief response to it. Does the instrument reveal any new information? In what areas might you improve or change your approach to conversations? Be specific.

Circle the number that best reflects your agreement with each statement. Use the following scale: 1 = Strongly Disagree, 2 = Disagree, 3 = Undecided, 4 = Agree, 5 = Strongly Agree

1 I can approach strangers and make them into friends quickly and easily. 1 2 3 4 5
2 I can get and hold the attention of others even when they haven't met me before. 1 2 3 4 5
3 I go out of my way to introduce myself to strangers. 1 2 3 4 5
4 I have several close friends and many good acquaintances. 1 2 3 4 5
5 I enjoy making small talk with all kinds of people. 1 2 3 4 5
6 I am very comfortable in any social setting. 1 2 3 4 5
7 I do not mind using the telephone to contact people I don't know. 1 2 3 4 5
8 Others do not intimidate me. 1 2 3 4 5
9 I can find some common area of interest with almost anyone. 1 2 3 4 5
10 I read a variety of publications and always keep up-to-date on current events. 1 2 3 4 5

My total: _____

Total your score, paying close attention to the items on which you scored the lowest. These will signal areas where you could profit from some changes. Set goals to improve in weak areas as you develop your interviewing skills.

Recognize the Nature of Conversations, American Style

The following are some generalizations about the conversational expectations found in most American businesses. These are, of course, *generalizations*.

■ **Preferred topics.** In casual conversation (what we call "small talk"), Americans prefer to talk about the weather, sports, jobs, mutual acquaintances, and past experiences, especially ones they have in common with their conversation partners. Most Americans avoid discussing politics and religion, especially with people they do not know well, because politics and religion can be controversial topics. In addition, we only discuss with close friends or trained professionals intimate topics such as sex, bodily functions, and emotional problems

By contrast, people in some other cultures are taught to believe that politics and/or religion are good conversation topics, and they may have different ideas about what topics are too personal to discuss with others.

- **Favorite forms of verbal interaction.** In a typical conversation between Americans, no one talks for very long at a time. Participants in conversations take turns speaking frequently, usually after the speaker has spoken only a few sentences. In addition, many American business professionals prefer to avoid arguments. If an argument is unavoidable, they prefer it to be restrained, carried on in a normal conversational tone and volume.

  Americans are generally impatient with ritual conversational exchanges that don't really convey much meaning. Nevertheless, a few expressions are common. For example, "How are you?" "Fine, thank you, how are you?" Or, "It was nice to meet you." "Same here." Or the cliché, "Have a nice day."

  People from other cultures may be more accustomed to speaking and listening for longer periods when they are in conversation, or they may be accustomed to more ritual interchanges (about the health of family members, for example) than Americans are. They may enjoy argument, even vigorous argument, of a kind that Americans are likely to find unsettling.[1]

- **Depth of involvement preferred.** Americans do not generally expect very much personal involvement from conversational partners. Small talk—without long silences that provoke uneasiness—is enough to keep matters going smoothly. In the workplace, Americans rarely discuss highly personal topics, which include financial matters. Many Americans are very uncomfortable if you ask how much money they make or the cost of something they own. Personal topics are reserved for conversations between very close friends or with professional counselors. However, American women tend to disclose more personal information to each other than do American men.

  Some people from other cultures prefer even less personal involvement than Americans do and rely more on ritual interchanges. Others come from cultures where personal information is openly discussed.

- **Tone of voice and non-verbal behaviors.** Most American business people are verbally adept—have a good vocabulary—speak in moderate tones, and use some gestures of the arms and hands. Touching behaviors in normal business communication are usually limited to a handshake or occasional pat on the back.

By contrast, other cultures might be accustomed to louder voices or many people talking at once. Similarly, people from different cultures vary in such things as vigorous use of hands and arms to convey emphasis, more touching between conversation partners, and use of personal space (such as how far apart people stand or sit).

Apply Basic Conversation Skills

Conversing with all kinds of people can be a pleasant experience—and a valuable business skill. The following are some ideas on how to initiate and sustain effective conversations.

Even informal conversation skills can be improved with some simple tips.

- **Have something to talk about.** Good conversation is a process of finding topics of common interest. It stands to reason that the more topics you know something about, the more comfortable you'll be in talking with people.
- **Be well-read.** Regularly read magazines and newspapers. Also, tune into *quality* broadcast programs. Good conversationalists pick up a lot of information from in-depth news shows, documentaries, and quality programming. Public radio and broadcast talk shows can also stimulate thinking and keep us up-to-date. Make it a point to listen to people. Note what they talk about in conversations. Some typical topics you may hear include sports, TV news or current events, magazine reports, organizational changes or news, personal or family news, gossip, entertainment, or politics.
- **Find your conversation partners' interests.** Think about the interests of people with whom you'd like to converse. Identify one or two topics you know that person likes to talk about. You may find, for example, that Bob is a 49ers football fan, Robin loves sports cars, Sharon is active in a support group for women, and Lynn plays drums in a band. Then, try to learn something about their topics. Once learned, mention this information when talking with them. Don't proclaim what you've learned as though you're a new expert, but use what you know to *ask* how they feel about the topic. Then be a good listener. You'll learn more and strengthen your relationship.
- **Practice conversation starters and sustainers.** Learn to make small talk, initiate conversations, and keep those conversations from dying. Use support-listening techniques and open-ended questions such as, "What are your plans for the summer/holidays?" or "How did you first come to know [our host or the new boss?]"

- **Practice conversation closers.** Don't get trapped in endless discussion. Learn ways to end a conversation without being abrupt or rude. Use non-verbal cues to indicate that you need to end the conversation (look at your watch; begin to move away from your partner). Also use subtle verbal cues that you want to end the conversation ("Well, it'll be interesting to see the effects on our market share" or "I'll get back to you if I hear anything new"). Sometimes, however, being direct is better ("Oops, I better get back to my work").

- **Be willing to make time for conversation.** If you don't take time for some social conversation, you may send unspoken messages to others that you are aloof or not interested in them. You may find yourself isolated from the grapevine and out of touch. And remember that a bit of personal data can often explain management or decision-making style. For example, the answer to "What do you do for fun?" might surprise you. The person who talks about competitive sports is likely to manage differently than one who leads with stories about intellectual interests, family, or children.

Avoid Inappropriate Conversation

Other than your closest friends, people don't normally want to hear about your personal problems. (One exception: your supervisor when the problem affects your work.) As a TV talk show host quipped: "80 percent of the people don't care, and the other 20 percent are *glad* you've got problems, too."

Complaints about your boss, co-workers, company, or school may come across as whining or inappropriate griping. Everybody has relationship problems at times. Unless you are seeking advice from a close friend or trusted advisor on how to improve the situation, keep your negative opinions to yourself.

Conversation Topics to Avoid or Apply

The acceptability of topics changes from time to time. For example, years ago hunting would have been a safe topic among many people. Today, with increasing concern about animal rights, hunting talk can create serious controversy. By contrast, some subjects once considered very personal are now more openly discussed. For example, men are far more open about emotions than they were a generation ago. So stay in tune with current issues and controversies.

As a general rule, *avoid*:

- Criticizing, mocking, or belittling others.
- Griping about the company, department, or industry where you work.

- Passing on gossip or hurtful comments about others.
- Using excessive profanity (it loses its emphasis value if overused).
- Stirring up bad feelings among people.
- Making racial, religious, or gender insults.
- Flirting or using comments with unwanted sexual overtones (unless you enjoy being sued).

As a general rule, *do*:

- Make your comments positive and upbeat.
- Be supportive of other people.
- Give others the benefit of the doubt.
- Compliment freely and often.
- Acknowledge people's accomplishments, birthdays, and religious holidays—respectfully.

So, even skills at something as commonplace as everyday conversations can be improved by applying the kinds of approaches we have discussed. The remainder of this chapter goes beyond conversations to a more structured form of interaction: interviews.

Apply the Straight Talk Model When You Interview Others

Interviews are more formalized conversations. Their purpose extends beyond entertainment or relationship building. The Straight Talk Model is clearly useful in improving your interviewing effectiveness. The following sections present ideas about the model's application to this communication medium.

Define the Context for the Interview

As we said earlier, interviews are commonly used in business for hiring, information-gathering, reviewing performance, counseling or reprimanding, expressing grievances, and conducting the so-called "exit" interview. Below is a brief description of the context (situation, audiences, and objectives with those audiences) for each of these types of interview.

- **Hiring interviews.** Hiring interviews call for sharing information about the employer's company and job position and the applicant's ability to fit the needs of the company. The primary audience is typically the interviewee, with hidden audiences potentially being customers, shareholders, or others who may apply for jobs with your company in the future. The objectives are to assess whether the applicant meets the needs of the company and vice versa.

- **Information-gathering interviews.** Information-gathering interviews call for systematically soliciting information from a number of respondents. The data is typically tabulated and used for making decisions. This is common practice in opinion polling, market analyses, or when trying to figure out causes of problems. The primary audience is the person being interviewed. However, when word gets around that you are interviewing people, others who may be polled in the future may be hidden audiences. How you handle today's interview could, for example, influence the responses of future interviewees. If people hear that you are argumentative or are interrogating people, they may have little desire to participate or to be candid.

- **Performance-review interviews.** Performance reviews (or performance appraisals) are periodic evaluations of an employee's work and are common to virtually all organizations. The goal in a performance review is to evaluate employee job performance and agree upon behaviors or goals for future work. The primary audience is the employee being evaluated, with other organizational leaders being secondary audiences. The interviewer's objectives may include motivating the employee, while the interviewee will seek to present a positive picture of his or her work performance. When done well, this form of interview provides a forum for managers to give feedback to employees and for employees to explain past performance.

- **Counseling or reprimand interviews.** Counseling or reprimand interviews occur when a supervisor feels the need to address employee problems. The audiences are similar to those in a performance review; however, the objectives may vary. Often, interviewers want to solve employee problems; the employees may want to defend or explain their behavior and, perhaps, avoid punishment.

- **Grievance interviews.** Grievance interviews are reprimand interviews in reverse. In grievance interviews, the employee feels a need to address a problem, and the supervisor may be defensive about the situation. Audiences will include the supervisor; possible hidden audiences could be labor union leaders or other employees. The objective is to generate change in some problematic situation.

- **Exit interviews.** Human resources professionals conduct exit interviews when an employee leaves the organization. The company or the employee has already made the decision about termination, so the objective of an exit interview is to gather honest information about the employee's experience at the company—to perhaps create some change for the future.

As you can see, the contexts for real-world interviewing in the workplace are many and varied. Defining the context (situation, audiences, and objectives) as prescribed by the Straight Talk Model is an important first step toward interviewing effectiveness.

Defining the context improves interviewing effectiveness.

Consider Your Media and Timing Options as the Interviewer

Your major medium as an interviewer will be verbal, face-to-face communication. (The most common exception to this is when some data-gatherers or employment screeners use the telephone. When using the phone, they forego many non-verbal cues and must rely on especially careful listening to be effective.) Of course, nothing precludes interviewers from using other media. For example, they may support or explain ideas expressed with print materials, tape-recorded information, or even visual aids. However, the primary medium of most interviews is face-to-face interaction.

The timing of an interview can be an issue. When conducting a series of interviews (same general topic, different people), later interviews are influenced by earlier ones. As an interviewer, you will often adjust the questions and base some observations on the earlier responses. Sometimes, you may want to go back to the earliest interviewees in response to ideas you gathered from later interviews. Also, schedule interviews such that you do not get overly tired or overloaded with too much information. Take breaks so that you remain fresh and focused. Back-to-back interviewing can consume a lot of "emotional labor"—the need to stay upbeat even when you are getting tired or frustrated. Allow for some time to digest input or simply space out interview sessions.

Pace yourself when doing a series of interviews.

Select and Organize Information as You Prepare to Interview

The quality of an interview is largely determined by the kinds of questions asked. Prepare key questions in advance that will help to achieve the goal of the interview. As interviewers, you have several types of questions to choose from, each useful under certain conditions. (The term "question" is used here to refer to any comments made to elicit responses from the other party. Sometimes these take the form of statements or commands.) Let's look at some common types of questions.

- **Closed-ended questions.** This type of question allows the respondent little or no freedom in choosing his or her response. Typically, only one or two possible answers exist. Examples: "Did your committee meet last Tuesday?" "Have you completed the Tompkins report yet?" "How long have you been on your present job assignment?"

Use of closed-ended questions permits the interviewer to exercise close control over the exchange. This is, of course, the technique most frequently used by trial lawyers or police interrogators to elicit specific information. This technique's drawback is that it rigidly structures the interview and, while often efficient, may completely miss opportunities for exchanging other relevant information. The interview feels like an interrogation.

One characteristic of closed-ended questions is that they can be manipulative. Respondents may feel frustrated when they must choose between one or two possible answers without an opportunity to clarify. Sometimes, however, these kinds of responses are the most useful to the questioner. But, in most business interviews, other kinds of questions make more sense.

- **Open-ended questions.** Open-ended questions allow the respondent maximum freedom in answering by imposing no limitations on how the question may be answered. Examples: "How do you feel about working with the quality-assurance task force?" "What would be a better way to handle that job?" Often, open-ended questions are in the form of statements such as, "Tell me about your experiences with the new ordering process," "Explain that procedure to me," or "Help me understand how you came to that conclusion."

  The success of this questioning approach depends in large part on the respondent's ability to express thoughts clearly. Often it is necessary for the interviewer to seek additional clarification by using "probes" when the respondent is talking in generalities or using unfamiliar language.

- **Probing questions.** Probing questions ask the interviewee to clarify a response for better understanding. Examples: "Could you give me an example of something that happened in the client meeting that seemed inappropriate to you?" "What do you mean when you say she's ruthless?" "Tell me exactly what happened."

  Probing questions serve to move the language level from the vague or general toward more concrete, specific, and descriptive terms. Probing questions can also determine the intensity of feelings. For example, if a person comments about a project team being disorganized, a probing question may be, "Can you give me an example of why you see the team as disorganized?" The interviewee then has the opportunity to unload some feelings about how frustrating the team has been.

- **Leading questions.** While probing questions lead respondents to elaborate on their own feelings, the leading question typically suggests the response desired. Occasionally this is helpful, but more often it is a block to the emergence of authentic information. Examples: "I'm interested in how well your project team is doing. Did you learn a lot while working with this team?" (Obviously, the interviewer wants the respondent to say "Yes.") "Don't you think it's important for our employees to learn to work in teams?" (Of course. What else could you say?) When the question is prefaced by a remark that suggests the kind of answer the interviewer would like to hear, the range of responses is reduced.

- **Loaded questions.** So-called loaded questions also suggest the desired response to the interviewee primarily through the use of highly emotional terms. Sometimes they are used to determine a respondent's reactions under stress and when a questioner seeks to "crack" a reluctant respondent. The interviewees who are wearing a mask or acting a role may become angry enough to let their true feelings or honest answers emerge.

  Examples: "How can you stand working in such a *mess?*" or "Everybody I've talked to says you are *a pain to work with.* How do you respond to that?" "I've heard reports that you are satisfied with *slipshod* quality. How would you respond to that?" The person hit with a loaded question may respond by attacking. The loaded question, like a loaded gun, occasionally goes off in the wrong direction. Avoid them under all but the most desperate circumstances, and be very careful in both your intention and your choice of words.

- **Hypothetical questions.** Hypothetical questions allow a respondent to express how he or she might handle a particular situation. They are helpful in identifying creativity, prejudices, the ability to conceptualize the "big picture," and other respondent characteristics. Examples: "If you were tasked to lead the reengineering team, what would you do differently?" "Put yourself in the shoes of the sales manager and suggest some approaches she might take to make your client contact more valuable."

Use a variety of types of questions to maintain engagement in interviews.

In a well-executed interview, each question is asked for a particular reason. Participants should think through each question and response rather than babble on with ill-defined and meaningless exchanges that do little to create understanding. Don't worry about pauses in the interview. It is not necessary to fill every moment with the sound of someone's voice.

When the interview is over, the interviewer should summarize briefly and be sure the respondent understands what to do next. There should be a clear agreement about the outcome of the discussion. Often, testing for such understanding is appropriate. You might ask, "Okay, Sarah, now what did we agree must be done next?" Each participant may explain the interview's outcome as he or she sees it. Then, close on an upbeat comment, and express gratitude for the person's participation in the interview.

Deliver Your Ideas Effectively When You Interview Others

An effective interviewer typically uses a variety of questioning formats to generate as much discussion as possible. Remember that leading an interview often emphasizes information-gathering. Therefore, we stress again the importance of listening.

In some contexts, however, we need to deliver information in the interview. For example, supervisors may need to describe how they gathered information used in performance reviews or an employee recruiter may need to explain something about the company. When doing so, apply the same principles as when delivering an oral presentation. Prepare in advance and organize the messages you need to convey to the interviewee. Pay attention to your delivery skills—verbal and non-verbal.

As you interview others, be aware of the non-verbal messages you are sending. An effective interviewer should:

- Focus on the interviewee by maintaining eye contact.
- Avoid interruptions from others that may upset the flow of the interview.
- Create a comfortable physical environment for the interview.
- Set a tone for the interview (formal or informal) with such things as greeting the interviewee, making small talk, using humor, or clarifying the format of the interview.
- Explain the ground rules for the interview. For example: "We'll take the first few minutes to get to know each other a little better, and then I'll ask you some more technical questions."

Evaluate Feedback for Continued Success

Building good interviewing skills requires getting constructive feedback. As in any other communication situation, having someone observe your techniques and critique you can be very valuable. Videotaping practice sessions can be very valuable as well. Identify people who might provide constructive criticism. Also, think about how you could provide such feedback to your associates.

Get feedback on your interviewing just as you would on your presentation skills.

Apply the Straight Talk Model When You Are Being Interviewed

Having discussed ways of being effective when conducting an interview, let's now take a seat across the table and consider what we need to do when we are being interviewed. Again, the Straight Talk Model gives us guidance.

Define the Context for the Interview

As the person being interviewed, you should strive to understand the context and purposes of the interview and anticipate possible questions. Then, practice ways of responding to those questions. If you are unclear about the reason for the interview, look at the descriptions of common interview formats discussed above. As with any communication situation, it makes sense to put yourself in the shoes of the interviewer and anticipate what he or she wants to gain from the interview.

Also, don't forget your hidden audiences and the objectives you have with each audience. For example, if you participate in an information-gathering interview with someone in your company, your performance may be described to others—perhaps your boss. If you participate helpfully, your cooperation may be noticed and your input appreciated.

Don't forget hidden audiences with agenda participants (including you) may have.

Consider Your Media and Timing Options When You Are Interviewed

While media options are often limited in interview situations, you may bring illustrative materials. Prepare visual aids, supporting documents, samples of products or work you have done, or even a video clip if you feel these will help build understanding. Be creative about these possibilities. The interview need not be limited to just what you say. You may also want to *show*.

Consider timing, as well. For example, determine when you would prefer to be interviewed. Are you fresher and more alert in the morning? Do you prefer doing mental work on Mondays and deferring information-sharing until later in the week? Likewise, most people applying for a job prefer to *not* be the first one interviewed. Later candidates allow the interviewer to compare behaviors—hopefully to the advantage of the more recent interview.

Select and Organize Information as You Prepare to Be Interviewed

Determine in advance what information you are willing to share and what you will not. You need not bear your soul or reveal damaging information if such data is irrelevant to the interview's purpose. Practice ways of phrasing your key ideas. Consider what supporting information or materials you may want to use.

In addition, when interviewing for a job, be thorough in researching the company and position in which you hope to work. Be prepared with questions you want to ask the interviewer. (Almost every job interview involves asking the candidates what questions they have about the company.) You can do much of this research on the Internet, although you may also get good insights from people at the company or in similar jobs.

Research the person who will be interviewing you. The more you know about him or her, the more effectively you can connect.

Deliver Your Ideas Effectively When Being Interviewed

When asked questions, answer clearly and decisively. Do not ramble on once you have answered the question. If you don't understand a question, ask for clarification. Always remember that an interview is a two-way communication process. As in any presentation, a good rule of thumb when answering most questions is to:

- Answer the question directly and honestly.
- Provide one supporting example when necessary to clarify.
- Stop talking.

For example, if asked what you felt about working in a taskforce, you may answer this way:

> "Our taskforce has not been very effective." (*A direct, honest answer*)
> "At last week's meeting, only three members had followed through on the assignments to gather more data. Everyone else made excuses about being too busy 'putting out fires.' Without the needed data we could not move toward our project completion." (*One supporting example*)
> (*Stop*)

Be open and willing to discuss your ideas and feelings in an interview. Deliver your point of view objectively, clearly, and honestly. In doing so, you maintain your credibility.

If you don't know the answer to a question, it's okay to say, "I don't know, but I'll get back to you with that information." If you are asked a question that is unclear, you can often rephrase it so you can better answer it. For example,

QUESTIONER: How would you come into the department and shape up the mess?

RESPONDENT: I think what you are interested in is what my first priority would be in implementing some of my ideas. Here is where I would begin ...

For further examples of rephrasing the question, just watch television interview shows. Politicians and other people in the public eye are often masters at this. They "adjust" many questions to give themselves an opportunity to say what they want to say. In fact, they rarely answer a straight yes–no question with a "Yes" or "No." While we don't advocate dodging legitimate questions, in some cases this is an appropriate technique, so long as it is not used to distort information. Listen to any politician when he or she is being asked about the likelihood of running for another office. Unless formally announced, they almost never give a straight answer.

Remember the STARR Approach

Interviews are often an excellent place to apply the STARR pattern of arrangement we discussed at length back in Chapter 4. For example, in a performance-review interview, if you are asked to describe your accomplishments, the exchange might go something like this:

QUESTIONER: Tell me what you see as your most significant contribution to the company this year.

RESPONDENT: I feel best about my work with the Zero-Defects committee. As you recall, our defect rate was running at about 27 errors per thousand (*Situation*) when you asked me to work with this group. I got the team together and we did some extensive analysis of the causes of the problems (*Task*). Based on that analysis, we implemented a three-phase change-management strategy including A, B, and C. (*Action*) Within three months we saw an 87 percent drop in recording errors and 19 percent drop in quality errors. (*Result*) Based on this, I recommended (*Recommendation*) and we implemented an ongoing ZDC process meeting each month, which has achieved the best results we have seen in the history of the company.

Evaluate Feedback for Continued Success

Practicing for interviews can be as important as practicing for giving an oral presentation. Write out possible questions you may be asked. Then practice appropriate responses out loud. If possible, get someone you know and trust to ask you difficult questions and respond to these (this is called "dirty-Q" and can be very helpful in preparing for tough questions). You may never be able to anticipate every question you will receive, but you can guess many of them, especially if you focus on the interview's purpose from the other person's viewpoint.

Get an associate to give you a practice "dirty-Q" by asking you really tough questions.

After an interview, do a self-critique to assess how you did. If appropriate, ask those who interviewed you for pointers about how they responded to your answers. As with any communication skill, feedback can be useful in improving our skills.

In closing, interviews are a powerful medium for information-sharing. They can provide exceptional opportunities for people to build strong work and personal relationships if participants accurately define the context, plan for appropriate media source and timing, select and organize their information, and deliver that information honestly and openly.

The Straight Talk Model Applied

How did our friend Luca, in the opening story, handle his conversation with his boss, Mr. Bannister? Not very well. He came across as insecure, tongue-tied, and perhaps, uninformed. This impression could not serve him well in his career with the company. Bannister asked him a series of open-ended questions—ones Luca could have answered with more than a simple "Yes," "No," or one-word answer. But because Luca had not developed his conversational skills, he missed an opportunity to convey a constructive message to his boss or to project favorable credibility.

Although this encounter was not a formal interview, Luca could have utilized the ideas in this chapter to present himself with greater confidence and professionalism. From making small talk to handling formal interviews, to selecting and organizing ideas and delivering messages with professionalism and skill, one-to-one conversation and interviewing skills like those discussed in this chapter will serve you well in any career. The Straight Talk Model applies as well to such one-to-one communication as it does to more formal speaking or meeting management. Every serious business communicator should seek to develop these skills.

Performance Checklist

After completing this chapter, you should be better able to apply some principles for selecting and organizing information for your message. Specifically, you should now understand that:

- Listening is affected by both internal (psychological) and environmental elements. These can be managed in most cases.
- Avoid poor listening habits and employ constructive listening behaviors to produce "active" listening.
- Conversations have many of the same characteristics as interviews, although they are generally less structured. Some basic conversation skills include: (1) having things to talk about (being well-read and informed), (2) finding your conversation partner's interests, (3) practicing conversation starters, sustainers, and closers, and (4) being willing to take time for conversation.
- Interviews are commonly used in the workplace for hiring, information-gathering, reviewing performance, counseling or reprimanding, and expressing grievances.
- Three key ingredients for successful interviewing are: (1) having a clear purpose for the interview, (2) providing ample opportunities for interaction between participants, and (3) listening effectively.
- The quality of an interview is largely determined by the kinds of questions used. Both interviewer and interviewee should prepare in advance for key questions that will help achieve the goal of the interview.
- Common types of questions used in interviews include closed- and open-ended, probing, leading, loaded, and hypothetical.
- As a general rule, the best way to respond to questions is to answer the question directly and honestly, provide one supporting example when necessary to clarify, and then stop talking.
- The STARR pattern of arrangement (as discussed in Chapter 4) can be particularly useful in responding to open-ended interview questions.
- Prepare for interviews by asking someone to throw possible questions at you (the "dirty-Q") to practice your responses.

What Do You Know?

Activity 8.1: Preparing for a Performance Review

Assume that your boss is going to review your performance in a team in which you participated. He or she has scheduled 15 minutes for an interview with you. How would you prepare to meet with that boss for your "performance review?"

Use the Straight Talk Model to describe your preparation. Write a brief description of how you would define the context, consider your media and timing options, select and organize information to present, deliver your messages, and receive feedback. Then write three questions you would expect to get from your boss and the responses you would give to each question.

Activity 8.2: Being Luca

Go back to the opening story and put yourself in the position of Luca, the new employee. Imagine that you are being asked the same questions by your new boss in a similar situation. How would you respond?

Activity 8.3: Preparing for an Employment Interview

Although only one of many types of business interviews, the job interview is an activity virtually everyone goes through and, of course, it is important. How can you best prepare for such an interview? The best advice we can give is to apply the Straight Talk Model. Consider each step of the model that you have worked with throughout this book, then focus on Step 4, delivering your message, and Step 5, getting feedback, as you practice your approach.

Identify a type of job position or career area you would like to interview for in the future. List five of the most challenging questions you might face in an interview. We have added a few such questions below, but encourage you to check other sources to see what other questions are likely to be used. (The Internet has a wealth of information about job-search interviewing. Do a search using key words such as "job interview questions." Look for sites that provide sample questions and suggested answers.)

Jot down a few notes for each question. Then ask a colleague or experienced friend to do a mock interview with you. Videotape or audio tape your responses and review how you did. Review your answers carefully to be sure you did not convey unintended messages. Make your responses positive and constructive.

Start with a few of these typical questions:

1 Tell me a bit about yourself.
2 In what activities did you participate? Why? Which did you enjoy the most?
3 What jobs have you held? How did you get the job? Why did you leave?
4 How did you spend your vacations while in school?
5 If you were starting school all over, what courses would you take?
6 What are your weaknesses? Specifically, when have you failed?
7 How do your former team members describe you?

8 Do you prefer working with others or by yourself? Why? Can you give me an example?

9 How did previous employers treat you?

10 What interests you about our company or products?

11 Tell me about a time that you had a conflict with a peer at work and how you resolved it.

12 Tell me what you know about our company.

Reinforce With These Review Questions

1 Describe three ways to improve listening skills: (1) _____, (2) _____, and (3) _____.

2 True/False—Conversations and interviews share many common characteristics, although interviews are typically more structured.

3 True/False—Differing intentions between interviewer and interviewee, especially with regard to how much information each is willing to exchange, will create barriers to an effective interview.

4 True/False—Topics for conversation (small talk) are the same across all cultures.

5 Describe three tips for initiating and sustaining effective conversations: (1) _____, (2) _____, and (3) _____.

6 True/False—The timing of an interview can impact on the results in that later interviews may be influenced by earlier ones.

7 While the interview is a communication medium in itself, participants could also supplement it with other media such as _____.

8 Name four types of questions that are used in interviews: (1) _____, (2) _____, (3) _____, and (4) _____.

9 Rehearsing tough questions with a trusted associate is called _____.

10 The three-step rule of thumb we recommend for answering most questions is: (1) _____, (2) _____, and (3) _____.

Mini-Case Study

Aaron had just finished a job interview for a promotion with a major accounting firm and he was pretty disappointed in his performance. "Why did I have to say that!" he chided himself. "I really blew it. They'll never promote me now."

The interview had gone fairly well through the early questions. Aaron was ready for the usual "get acquainted" questions and seemed to be developing rapport with the interviewer, although the older gentleman was a bit more formal than Aaron had expected. This was quite different than communications with his immediate supervisor, who was just a couple of years older than Aaron and related comfortably to 20-somethings.

"Tell me about a time you did something above and beyond the expected on the job," was the question that had Aaron stewing afterwards. "I can't believe I said that!" he thought. The answer he had given described when he worked as a summer intern at a firm in his home town. His example of going beyond was how he "spent some extra time with this little old lady who worked there who had trouble working some of the latest software." He drew a complete blank when it came to examples of work he had accomplished in the last two years!

The interviewer interrupted to ask how old was this "little old lady" was and Aaron replied that she was about 60. From that point on, the interviewer seemed cool to Aaron, and it wasn't tough to figure why: the interviewer himself was in his sixties. "How could I be so stupid?" Aaron kept asking himself.

Questions

1   How could Aaron have avoided this embarrassing mis-step?
2   What pre-interview preparation would have helped?
3   What, if anything, should Aaron do now (assuming he would really like the promotion)?

nine

Evaluate Feedback for Continued Success

The trouble with most of us is that we would rather be ruined by praise than saved by criticism.

(Dr. Norman Vincent Peale)

Why Feedback is So Important

At its most basic level, feedback is crucial to any kind of improvement, and communication is no exception. While positive feedback is nice—we all love a compliment—it's usually the *negative* feedback that helps us the most. Despite people saying, "I always welcome your feedback," most of us need to work to overcome the "feedback hurts" mentality. Of course, it isn't always pleasant to hear negative comments about what we are doing. Sometimes our feelings get hurt, our ego is wounded, or the feedback strikes us as, well, stupid. That said, let's consider a shift in our perspective.

Try this: think about feedback as a form of *coaching*. When we work with a coach, he or she is constantly giving us negative feedback—and we appreciate it. A golf coach, for example, will correct the way you hold or swing the club, and you're delighted to get the negative feedback. In fact, you pay for all these "criticisms."

There is no positive change without negative feedback. We know we need feedback (which often takes the form of criticism) to improve our performance. It makes us better at what we are learning to do. Better communication skills are all about constant learning, and those who provide honest feedback are our coaches. The final step in the Straight Talk Model shows us how to give, solicit, and receive feedback. And finally, we will discuss credibility and how you can learn to evaluate yourself.

Professional Competencies

When you have completed this chapter, you should be able to:

- Recognize the importance of feedback in the process of improving communication skills.
- Enhance your skills at giving, soliciting, and receiving helpful feedback.
- Understand the dimensions of credibility and their impact on communication effectiveness.
- Objectively evaluate yourself with a Credibility Checklist.

The Four Aspects of the Feedback Process

"Feedback" is the term we use to describe any responses, critique, criticism, or comments about the way we communicate. It may take the form of a direct criticism or complaint, but often is subtler, such as non-verbal reactions (a listener dozing off), edited comments on a written document, rejection of an idea presented in a meeting, or, worst of all, simple failure to respond to our communication. If you have ever delivered a briefing or sales pitch and, when inviting audience questions, heard a deafening silence, you'll probably agree with this statement: the worst feedback may be no feedback—when nothing happens after we communicate.

The worst feedback is no feedback.

Feedback comes from two sources, external and internal. External feedback comes from your target audience—your readers and listeners—and trusted colleagues. Internal feedback comes from the process of self-evaluation. Both types of feedback can provide impetus for improvement in communication skills.

You will achieve skill development by applying four aspects of the feedback process—giving, soliciting, and receiving feedback, and then evaluating yourself with the Credibility Checklist. The remainder of this chapter looks at these processes and shows how to make the most of each.

Self-Evaluation: Your Feedback Receptiveness Attitudes

Think back to the last time you received criticism from someone else. Recall a specific event or situation, and describe it in one sentence (examples: "My boss thought I let my staff meeting get out of hand and degenerate into a gripe session" or "My subordinate got indignant when I gave him an unsatisfactory performance review interview").

Now, mentally review the situation with regard to your behaviors and feelings. To what extent did you:

1 Hold back on defending or explaining yourself until the person giving feedback fully expressed himself or herself?
2 Work to understand the criticizer's point of view as best you could?
3 Ask for elaboration or clarification without being overly defensive?
4 Express an honest reaction?
5 Thank the person for the feedback?

For most people, *giving* criticism (even in a constructive way) is risky. When people first offer such feedback, they watch closely to gauge the receiver's responses. The reaction they receive will usually determine whether they will offer feedback again. This means that you have the opportunity to avoid turning off future feedback that could be valuable to you.

Overall, how would you rate your feedback receptiveness in the above situation? What might you change, if anything?

Give Constructive Feedback

Most people enjoy giving feedback if it's positive and complimentary. People like to get compliments, and you are probably glad to dispense positive comments that make others feel good.

However, if you only offer positive feedback and ignore or dilute any negative comments, you are cheating everyone. The communicator will miss the opportunity to learn something about the way the message came across to you. You, as an evaluator, will miss the opportunity to learn from recognizing your own shortcomings that you may see in someone else's work. Without this information, communicators will never know if what the receivers heard mirrors what they meant to say as speakers. In short, there can be no test for efficacy without overt feedback.

Feedback validates the efficacy of a message—it tests to see if communication succeeded.

The most useful feedback points out a need for improvement and offers suggestions for how to make that improvement without discouraging the message sender. How this feedback is given will largely determine whether the receiver will use the feedback. Obviously, tact and clarity are helpful. Truly useful feedback is that which first acknowledges the positive, then points out a need for improvement, and finally offers a suggestion for how to make that improvement without de-motivating the receiver of the feedback. Here are some basic guidelines for giving good feedback. (And, yes, this is an application of the Bad News pattern you learned in Chapter 4.)

- Describe something positive, but be sure that your first statement is not misleading or does not misrepresent your overall intention (such as, "Your ideas made some good points ..." or "I can tell how hard you have worked on this project ...").
- Include a transition (such as, "However, ..." or "At the same time, ...").
- Express constructive criticism in terms of "I" (such as, "I got lost when you were talking about ..." or "I had difficulty understanding your information about ...").
- Give a specific example (such as, "For example, I couldn't see the connection between your description of the market and your solution ..." or "I didn't understand what you meant by ...").
- Offer an option for a solution (such as, "Perhaps if you could show me that information on a chart ..." or "It would help me if you'd define some key terms ...").
- Close with another positive statement (such as, "Your speaking style is good, and with this additional information, your presentation will be excellent ..." or "With a bit more clarification of the budget, I think we'll be ready to make a decision").

Applying these guidelines might sound something like this when giving feedback about a presentation:

Julie, your attention-grabber was really clever. That was a perfect story to introduce the need for improvement in the team. (*Positive opening*)

However (*Transition*),

I had difficulty understanding the explanation of the cost projections for raw materials. (*Constructive criticism in terms of "I"*)

Maybe a story or an illustration of some kind would have made it clearer for me. Perhaps you could use the widget example from Customer ABC. (*Option for solution*)

Since you tell such good stories, I know you can even make the quantitative data simple and interesting for us non-numbers types. (*Positive, motivating close*)

Here is another example applied to a meeting:

I liked your advance preparation for the marketing meeting, Chris. The agenda and pre-work assignments were on target.

But then your agenda seemed to spin out of control. (*Transition*)

From my point of view, it looked like Tara and Andrew pulled everyone off topic with their ideas for their product launch. I got the feeling they were more interested in railroading their pet idea through than looking at other options. (*Constructive criticism in terms of "I"*)

I would suggest that you work to become less accommodating and rein people in when they start to dominate the discussion. Maybe just ask them to hold their fire a minute and then draw in Barbara, our shy-but-brilliant one. (*Option for solution*)

Maybe you could have paused the discussion and used Nominal Group Technique to see where people ranked their ideas. (*Option for solution*)

Sometimes you are such a nice guy that people take advantage of your easy-going manner. Everybody likes you, Chris, but occasionally your meetings suffer because you hesitate to confront those who try to dominate. You can use your natural tact and get better meeting results. (*Positive, motivating close*)

With this organizational pattern, both the giver and the receiver tend to be more comfortable with the feedback process. If you are giving feedback, you should be less reticent to offer constructive feedback because you are also recognizing positive aspects. The person receiving feedback should be less defensive because he/she is also receiving praise.

Use of the feedback organizational pattern makes the process more comfortable.

Feedback for Blamers and Avoiders[1]

There are procrastinators and then there are ugly procrastinators. No, this doesn't have anything to do with personal appearance; it's really about what motivates the behavior of putting off necessary work. Do you ever give feedback to procrastinators?

Procrastination gets ugly when a victim mentality kicks in—when the act of putting off becomes the act of making excuses or placing blame. Sometimes procrastination morphs into outright avoidance—denying that the issue is really a problem and, therefore, avoiding it in hopes that it will go away.

Unfortunately, we all know those self-proclaimed victims who make excuses for their problems, usually by blaming someone else. We also know people who simply won't recognize that a problem exists in order to avoid taking action toward a solution. Sometimes they are family, and you are stuck with them. Sometimes they are colleagues, and you have to work with them.

In either case, you have a communication challenge: how do you convince the Blamer or the Avoider to *get busy and get to work?* This feedback situation is a great place to apply an organizational plan that you have seen before: the Bad News Model. But this time, we're using it to assertively nudge a procrastinator along. The nine steps (expanded a little—assertiveness with Blamers and Avoiders requires extreme measures) should look familiar:

1   **Express recognition.** Tell the person that you recognize his/her feelings. "Recognize" is different from "understand" or even "appreciate," but it does validate that the feeling the person has is real to him/her. You can recognize feelings of anger, frustration, or helplessness.

2   **Transition into the purpose of your message.** "However" works but implies the bad news to come (so it might be the perfect word you want to use). I like "that said" or "on the other hand."

3   **Define the inappropriate behavior from your perspective.** Avoid finger-pointing, which is likely to cause a defensive response. Instead, try something like, "In my experience at work, I have seen many people who ..." or "I am concerned that [a bad thing] is going to happen to you if you continue to ..."

4   **Explain consequences.** Describe those "bad things" that happen to people who behave this way. Don't be generic. Use examples that Blamers or Avoiders can specifically relate to, based on their experience and knowledge base. Be careful to sound objective and rational, not like you are personally threatening them.

5   **Specify required action.** "Specify" is the important word here. Be specific about the necessary actions. Explain exactly what you want the person to do.

6   **Describe potential rewards.** The rewards for action should be as explicit as the consequences for no action. And, of course, the rewards should personally relate to the needs and desires of the Blamer or Avoider, *not* to what sounds great to you (remember that their work ethic does not equal yours, so their reward system is different).

7 **Offer help.** Do not, however, offer the Blamer or Avoider an opportunity to off-load the work onto you. No one buys into a solution or a process unless he/she participates in the decision or the effort. Suggest baby steps—actions that are reasonable and possible from the Blamer or Avoider's perspective. Don't convey the sense that it will be easy for them—they will perceive your disregarding the difficulty as insulting. (Even if you are so frustrated that you don't care how insulted they are, remember that insulted people will not take the action you want.)

8 **Imply expected response.** Do *not* say: "So, what are you going to do about it?" Rather, try a statement that expresses your belief that the Blamer or Avoider will actually follow through. Try something like: "When we meet tomorrow, I'll be happy to look at your first draft."

9 **Close with motivation.** Compare this challenge to something the Blamer or Avoider has overcome in the past: "I know you can do [this] because you did [that.]"

Let's look at an example: the team member who won't carry his weight. He's an Avoider. We'll call him "Clark."

Clark, I recognize that you think that this project is useless busy work. (*Express recognition*)

That said, (*Transition into your purpose*)

... we all need to work on it as a team and finish by Friday, (*Define inappropriate behavior*)

... or we could lose this client. (*Explain consequences*)

I need for you to do the research and write your piece of the plan by tomorrow. (*Specify required action*)

If we do this well, we will get a larger budget next quarter, and we'll be able to do some very cool work for this client that will look good for all of us in the long term. (*Describe potential rewards*)

The project we did for Client ABC is similar, if you need a template or some ideas. (*Offer help*)

When the team gets together tomorrow, we can pass around the individual pieces and edit each other's work. (*Imply expected response*)

I remember how you wrote the XYZ proposal on your own practically overnight, so I know you can pull this off. (*Close with motivation*)

Another example: Judy the Blamer, who doesn't like her job. She's your colleague and friend. Note the nine steps:

1 Judy, I hear you talking so often lately about how you don't like your job since you have a new manager.

2   However,

3   ... I am concerned that your unhappiness might be affecting the quality of your work.

4   If your customers get negative vibes from you, they are going to have a bad experience in our [store, office] and that's going to affect how much money they spend—which ultimately is going to affect your performance reviews.

5   I think you need to request another assignment or look for another job ...

6   ... so that you can use all your skills and work in a better environment for you. And you'll probably make more money because you'll be doing something you like.

7   There are some great websites with job search information, and every company has a Web page for potential employees. I'll help you identify them.

8   Why don't you see what's out there and then bring some pages and your resume when we have lunch next week?

9   You have so much experience that I know you can find a position that you would find fulfilling.

Summarizing the Steps

Nine steps are a lot, but Blamers and Avoiders probably haven't responded to simpler communication and require a more complex strategy:

1   Express recognition.
2   Transition into your purpose.
3   Define inappropriate behavior.
4   Explain consequences.
5   Specify required action.
6   Describe potential rewards.
7   Offer help.
8   Imply expected response.
9   Close with motivation.

Keep in mind that everything you *say* must be based on *their* wants and needs—not yours. Also remember that *your goal* is to get the behavior *you* want and need. Of course, reaching *your* goal is also in *their best interest*. You might feel guilty of a little manipulation, but then, don't feel *too* guilty. It's *benevolent* manipulation. *They* are the Blamers and Avoiders. *You* have to do what's necessary. This feedback approach and a little courageous assertiveness may be all it takes.

Solicit Feedback from Others

Now let's look at feedback from the other side of the table. To grow as effective communicators, we need to reach out for feedback. "Feedback is our friend" or certainly our coach. Okay, sometimes it's a friend we would rather not hear from, but virtually any feedback can be useful. Below we will discuss ways to maximize the benefits of feedback by knowing who, when, and how to ask.

> To improve as communicators, we need to reach out for feedback.

Identify Whom and When to Ask

Solicit useful feedback following these two simple guidelines:

- Identify people you respect and trust—people who can provide you with the feedback you need. Don't just ask friends you know will validate you. They may make you feel good but will be less likely to give you the beneficial information. Look for people who are experienced and effective communicators.
- Ask people *in advance* to evaluate *something specific* about your presentation, interview, or meeting participation. An example of a simple request may be: "Terri, I would sure appreciate it if you would … ("listen to my sales pitch for any times that I sound tentative," or "look at the way I participate in our group meeting and let me know if I make sense when I speak up," or "ask me some interview questions and give me some pointers; I am looking for ways to differentiate myself from the competition").

Some organizations have formalized mentoring programs. Others retain communication consultants or advisors. If such people are available to you, take advantage of their expertise.

Customer Feedback Builds Stronger Businesses

The field of customer service provides a strong rationale for organizations getting feedback, and most successful companies actively seek such input. Why? Because a complaining customer—one who gives negative feedback—can be a company's best friend. Without complaints (feedback), organizations could never know how to improve. Without improvement, they would stagnate and eventually fail. Yet many companies make it hard for customers to complain—to give needed feedback.

Why should we want to make it easy for customers to complain? Because successful handling of customer complaints can be a gold mine of repeat business. While 63 percent of unhappy customers who do not complain will *not* buy from you again, of those who *do* complain and *have their problems resolved*, only 5 percent will *not* come back. You have a 95 percent chance of saving unhappy customers if you hear their complaints—in other words, if you get their feedback.

Other studies have shown that customers whose complaints are heard and acted upon are actually *more likely to continue being loyal* to you than those who do not have a complaint in the first place—even if you cannot fully fix their complaint. The first step, of course, is to hear their concerns—get feedback.[2]

Now, apply this reasoning. Gather feedback on your communication effectiveness.

Know How to Ask for Feedback

The way you ask will have considerable impact on the quality of the feedback you get. Closed-ended questions are rarely the best type for getting people to express their true feelings. If you ask a yes–no question such as, "So, how'd I do?," you may hear "Great!" or "Fine" and feel better, but you won't get the information you need to learn and grow. Instead, ask open-ended questions that avoid single-word responses. The following are some possible open-ended questions you could use to get good feedback:

- How relevant was my material to my audiences? How do you think my target listeners responded?
- How did you interpret what I wanted my receiver to do at the end of my message? What specific action step did you hear?
- How can I improve this message?
- Which techniques that I used seemed to help my listeners get the main objective of my message?
- What would you suggest for me to improve my interviewing (or meeting or presentation) skills?
- I'm concerned that my visuals aren't interesting enough. It seems like my slides are just lists of words. How could I improve them?

Remember, in addition to using open-ended questions, ask people to look at specific areas where you think you could improve. For example, you may say, "Raul, I have been trying to cut back on filler words when I speak. Would you look for those and point out when I say, 'Ah,' 'Um,' and 'Ya know?'" Or, you may ask for feedback on vocal style. For example, you may say, "Saleen, you're really good with delivery of your messages. Would you give me some ideas on how to use my voice better?"

Ask for suggestions, not just yes–no responses.

Receive and Process Feedback

How you respond to feedback will largely determine whether you will continue to get it. People will not keep giving you feedback if you overreact emotionally (display anger or hurt), disregard (imply that the evaluator's idea is unimportant), or blame others ("Ted messed up the computer"). None of these reactions will help you improve as a communicator.

Express appreciation for feedback, even if you don't totally agree with it.

Remember, the people giving you feedback are doing you favors. (Granted, it may not always feel that way, but they could easily avoid giving feedback and deny you its benefit.) Be appreciative, even when you may not agree with what they are saying.

Look closely at your attitudes. Hopefully, your ego is not so enlarged that you fail to recognize the value of good feedback. Apply the following positive attitudes and behaviors to receiving feedback:

- Develop feedback-receptiveness—be open to and appreciative of good feedback. We cannot improve without it. (Sorry to seem redundant, but the fact bears repeating.)
- Listen carefully to comments, display non-verbal cues (eye contact, nodding, "Uh huh") to indicate that you are listening. Try to take notes, which lets the person giving the feedback know that you are taking his/ her input seriously.
- Ask for specific information and examples in a non-defensive way, then repeat these back to the person giving the feedback for clarification. Don't challenge or interrogate the person, but do be sure you are clear about what they are describing.
- Notice non-verbal messages from your audience. For example, when giving a presentation, observe audience eye-contact, nodding agreement, looks of confusion, or restlessness. These can tip you off as to how well you are *really* doing.
- Correct in the direction of the evaluation—don't overreact. A person's critique of your communication may be disconcerting or even hurtful. But within almost any feedback is at least a grain of truth. You need not

accept all feedback as valid, but you will often find something of value in almost any feedback.

- Accept responsibility for any needs and changes. Ultimately, you will sort out the valid and valuable feedback from all you receive. When you identify the best insights, accept the responsibility for applying suggestions to your future communication.

- Recognize that whatever your audience perceives, accurate or not, is very real to them—show appreciation for their point of view. Say "Thank you!"

The more you are willing to accept responsibility for your actions, the more credibility you will have. (Brian Koslow)

Evaluate Yourself with the Credibility Checklist

Giving, soliciting, and receiving external feedback from other people is critical to communication improvement. Without knowledge of how our listeners react to us, we would be unaware of ways to improve our communication. However, another source of feedback can be equally valuable: the internal feedback of honest self-evaluation. Self-evaluation looks inward at the most important element of your communication strategy: your ability to project *credibility*.

Credibility. We know it's important. We'd like to have it—lots of it, actually. But exactly what *is* credibility, and how do you get it? Simply put, your credibility is your target audience's perception of you. The only *reality* is what that audience, the people to whom you speak or with whom you interact, perceives. Your *intention* doesn't count. Credibility is in the eye of the beholder.

Therefore, we might agree that the most important overall goal of your personal and professional communication strategy is the perception of credibility. If your audience perceives that you are credible—if they believe you, trust you, have confidence in you—you will be persuasive. And if you are persuasive, you will get what you want: you will achieve the objectives of your presentation, of your interview, of your chance encounter in the hall—and of your emails, reports, and memos, as well.

Projecting credibility may be your most important communication task.

Your credibility is based on your audience's perception of four key characteristics—your goodwill, expertise, power, and confidence. These four characteristics make up the Credibility Checklist, which we will show you later in the chapter. This checklist is your way of confirming your decisions throughout the Straight Talk process.

- **Goodwill.** Your audience's perception of your focus on them and concern for them—their perception of *what you think of them.*
- **Expertise.** Your audience's perception of your education, knowledge, and experience—their perception of *the facts about you.*
- **Power.** Your audience's perception of your status, prestige, and success—their perception of *what other people think about you.*
- **Confidence.** Your audience's perception of how you present yourself, how sure you are of yourself—their perception of *what you think of yourself.*

Let's take these one at a time: each dimension is a step toward gaining the credibility you need for professional success.

Establish Goodwill

This one is not only first, but if you don't pull it off, you won't have a chance with the other three. Goodwill is your audience's perception of what you think of them. This dimension is about *them*, not about *you*. Goodwill is their perception of how much you care about them—how unique they are, how special they are, how important they are to you or your organization.

You will achieve the perception of goodwill from carefully selected information based on analysis of your target audience. So, obviously, if you haven't thought carefully about the people hearing your presentation or participating in your meeting, you won't be successful on this dimension of credibility. You should consider personal and professional facts, cultural backgrounds, attitudes, and the consistent concerns that they have expressed to you in the past. Once again, context analysis is paramount.

Effective context analysis can help you project goodwill.

For example: if you are speaking to a group of new hires, you will show concern for them and focus on them by recognizing their first-day enthusiasm (and the confusion of getting around in this building!) and by acknowledging their impressive backgrounds or education.

Demonstrate Expertise

This second dimension is your target audience's perception of the facts about you. You will achieve the perception of expertise through examples that demonstrate your knowledge, education, and experience. It's your chance to share the facts about yourself.

The good news, of course, is that facts are objective. The bad news is that *perception* of facts is often *subjective*. Use the information you learned in your audience analysis to select the most relevant facts to share, based on each particular audience's interests and concerns. What impresses one person might not work at all with someone else.

Expertise is also tricky because you don't want to come off as cocky or arrogant. (In an ideal world, we would all be eloquently introduced by someone else!)

Show your expertise by tactfully describing your accomplishments.

For example: back to the new hires. Build credibility with your "been there, done that" examples. Tell a great story about your first days on the job. Don't tell the "stumble around in the halls" story; talk about how your communication skills enabled you to meet the VP who later recruited you into your present position. Share examples of education, knowledge, experience—all based on the interests of your target audience.

Reveal Your Power

You will achieve the perception of power with material that refers to your rank and illustrates your successes. Remember that this is the audience's perception of what other people think about you. It's your opportunity to mention any recognition that would be *meaningful to this audience*. What rewards or recognitions have you achieved that *they* care about?

Example: those pesky new hires again. They are likely to be interested in what you did to be promoted—particularly, what you did to get good performance reviews, especially in your initial six-month evaluation.

In addition, power is nebulous to specifically *define*, so we expand the definition of power to include personal power (ability to control your own environment), interpersonal power (ability to influence other people), and corporate power (ability to mobilize resources). Depending on what you know about your audience, you can find many examples to increase the perception that you are powerful and therefore credible.

Perceptions of your power can come from several sources.

All that said, however, keep in mind that an individual's status, prestige, and success may be perceived differently depending on the specific culture of an organization or industry. Be prepared to explain your examples in context, so that your target audience really understands how powerful (and credible) you are.

Express Confidence

The confidence dimension of credibility is the audience's perception of how you present yourself—how sure you are of yourself and what you are saying and doing. Remember, this is their perception of what you think of *yourself*.

You will achieve the perception of confidence through excellent communication skills, which always include doing your homework and preparing messages based on your audience's needs and concerns. Once the material is right, it's easier to feel confident. But you have to look confident, too.

So consider these tips for appearing confident and in control (even if you don't *feel* that way):

- Focus (be *where you are* while you're there).
- Stand (or sit) tall and "square off" with your audience.
- Look them in the eyes.
- Talk with them (not *at* them).
- Mirror their non-verbal behavior (casual, formal, etc.).
- Take your time.
- And, of course, smile.

If you project confidence, your target audiences will automatically perceive you *higher* on the other three dimensions of credibility.

You can project confidence with appropriate verbal and non-verbal cues.

The Credibility Checklist

So, how's your credibility? Take some time to carefully consider this checklist to find out:

Goodwill. The audience's perception of my focus on them and my concern for them.

What do I do to show my target audience that I care about them?

Expertise. The audience's perception of my knowledge, education, and experience.

What knowledge, education, and experience do I have that might impress my audience?

What have I accomplished that I am really proud of?

Power. The audience's perception of my status, prestige, and success.

What is my rank in my current organization, and how might this impress my audience?

What awards or recognition have I received that might impress my audience?

What is the source of my personal power (my ability to control my own environment)?

What is the source of my interpersonal power (my ability to influence other people)?

What are examples of my organizational power (my ability to mobilize resources)?

What relationships give me "power by association?"

Confidence. The audience's perception of how I present myself—how sure I am of myself and my message.

What are some examples of how I exhibit confidence in my verbal and non-verbal behavior?

Apply the Credibility Model for Internal Feedback

In summary, if you want the people to use the term "credibility" when they describe you, follow these steps:

1   Do your homework. Learn about your audience, then focus on them and talk about their concerns.
2   Talk about yourself—how your experience relates to their needs and concerns. But be humble and clever; if you sound like you're bragging, you'll *lose* credibility.
3   Give examples of how your previous successes have been recognized by other people.
4   Present all of this with confidence.

When you do, you will have achieved the most important overall goal of your personal communication strategy. Your audience will perceive you as credible, which means they believe you and trusts you. You will be persuasive. You will meet with success. You will get what you want.

Performance Checklist

After completing this chapter, you should be better able to apply some principles for giving, receiving, and soliciting feedback, and then for evaluating yourself. Specifically, you should now understand that:

- People cannot improve on their communication skills if they continue communicating the same way over and over.

- Communicators can take advantage of the opportunities for continuous improvement by applying four aspects of the feedback process—giving, soliciting, and receiving feedback, and evaluating themselves with the Credibility Checklist.
- The most useful feedback is that which first acknowledges what was done well, then points out a need for improvement, and finally offers a suggestion for how to make that improvement without de-motivating the speaker.
- If your audience believes you, trusts you, has confidence in you, you will be more effective and persuasive as a communicator. The success of any communication attempt depends heavily on the message receiver's perception of the sender's credibility.
- Writing specific and full answers to each item on the Credibility Checklist can generate internal feedback and a realistic assessment of what your audience thinks of you and your message.

What Do You Know?

Activity 9.1: Get Internal Feedback with the Credibility Checklist

Consider an upcoming communication task you face. This may be a speech, participation in a meeting or class, an interview or performance review, or simply a discussion with a friend, co-worker, or family member. Complete the checklist below in the context of that task. Be as specific as you possibly can be. Don't be bashful!

Communication Task _____

Goodwill. The audience's perception of my focus on them and my concern for them.

What do I do to show my target audience that I care about them?

Expertise. The audience's perception of my knowledge, education, and experience.

What knowledge, education, and experience do I have that might impress my audience?

What have I accomplished that I am really proud of?

Power. The audience's perception of my status, prestige, and success.

What is my rank in my current organization, and how might this impress my audience?

What awards or recognition have I received that might impress my audience?

What is the source of my personal power (my ability to control my own environment)?

What is the source of my interpersonal power (my ability to influence other people)?

What are examples of my organizational power (my ability to mobilize resources)?

What relationships give me "power by association?"

Confidence. The audience's perception of how I present myself—how sure I am of myself and my message.

What are some examples of how I exhibit confidence in my verbal and non-verbal behavior?

Activity 9.2: Create a Feedback Board of Advisors

We all go to other people for advice and suggestions. For many people, this is an occasional and haphazard process. But many successful people are recognizing the important of a more formalized process of soliciting feedback and advice.

Identify the key people you would go to for each of the following requests. Then describe briefly the characteristics of these people that make you interested in their advice. How do they measure up on the Credibility Checklist in your eyes?

Advice Topic	Whom You Would Contact	Why? (Their Characteristics)
How to approach your boss with a request that will cost a significant amount of money		
How you should structure a meeting, retreat, or training session you are in charge of		
How to better promote your career advancement		
How to make the most of new-hire interviews (as interviewer or interviewee)		

Add other topics and sources of feedback. Record your ideas about a board of such advisors. How could this be beneficial to you? What could you do to reciprocate? How might you contact them about "serving on your board?"

Reinforce With These Review Questions

1 Name the four aspects of the feedback process: (1) _____
   (2) _____, (3) _____, and
   (4) _____.

2 True/False—One helpful technique for giving feedback is to express criticism in terms of yourself. For example, "I had trouble following ..." instead of "You were not clear ..."

3 True/False—Closed-ended questions are often the best way to get people to express honest feedback.

4 True/False—How you respond to feedback will largely determine if you get more of it.

5 The four elements of credibility are: (1) _____,
   (2) _____, (3) _____, and
   (4) _____.

6 True/False—"Goodwill" refers to how much your audience agrees with your point of view.

7 Your audience's perception of what other people think about you is your
   _____.

8 True/False—The way you ask for feedback will have a large impact on the quality of feedback you receive.

9 True/False—As a general rule, feedback is essential to any improvement.

10 Customers who complain and have their concerns addressed are (more/ less) likely to do business with a company than customers who never have a problem.

Mini-Case Study: Feedback and Coach Roy

The biggest obstacle to knowing what people really think about us is fear. We fear they'll tell us our product or service stinks, that we're horrible people, and that we should never have set foot on Earth.

Danica, a newly-appointed marketing manager for a mid-sized technology firm, read this opening paragraph in a trade publication article and nodded. *That's so true!* she thought. *We have got to get more proactive about getting and using good feedback. Too many of the people on my new team seem to be afraid of feedback. They seem to be tuning out any awkward or painful comments. I get that. It seems to be human nature, but this is a tough business. If we are all so concerned about being "nice" to each other, I really worry that we are holding back on criticisms.*

That afternoon, she jotted some notes in her planning system:

- Need to change our culture.
- Get people comfortable giving and getting feedback if we are going to compete and grow this business.
- How?

The following weekend, Danica, who was a good amateur golfer, stood on the first tee at her local course. That's when it dawned on her: coaching. *That's what I need to initiate in the company!*

She knew the value of coaching. Her game had improved dramatically since she had hired a coach, a rather crusty fellow named Roy who was quick to point out when she was doing something wrong. Sometimes Roy could be annoying—such a stickler for detail—but he had helped her improve her game to a single-digit handicap. *That's it*, Danica thought, *maybe I need to take a Coach Roy-approach to get my people communicating better—with each other and our customers. Too bad Roy doesn't know squat about technology.*

Questions

1 How does this case reinforce the ideas in this chapter? How is feedback like coaching?
2 Since Danica is a new leader in the department, what can we assume about her credibility (positives and negatives)? How likely is it that her subordinates would agree to change behaviors regarding feedback? What resistance might she be likely to face?
3 Develop a draft of an action plan for improving internal feedback regarding communication behaviors in her department. Be specific about the processes, policies, or incentives you recommend.

Reference Tool

Recognizing Gender Differences in Workplace Communication

The following material can be particularly important in raising your awareness of gender differences that can impact on communication effectiveness. In recent years, such gender differences have been a popular area for communication research. This reference tool is designed to give you an overview of the most critical findings in gender-communication tendencies.

Scientists, cultural anthropologists, social psychologists, and other researchers agree that the perceptions and realities of men and women constitute separate cultural paradigms. When these different cultural perspectives manifest themselves in workplace communication, we find two resulting behaviors:

1 Men and women communicate *differently*.
2 Men and women communicate the *same* way but are *perceived differently* by audiences of both genders.

As you read this reference tool, note that we have based our application of the Straight Talk Model on American men and women with roots in European cultures, which is where researchers have focused most of their work.[1] However, much of the information is applicable to individuals with roots in African, Latino, and Asian cultures, as well. Also keep in mind that we based *everything* we say on *tendencies* of men and women as cultural groups.

Individuals may exhibit any combination of male or female behaviors. In fact, most people do, on occasion, exhibit behaviors normally associated with the opposite sex. This does not mean that the man is effeminate or that the woman is manly. Indeed, both sexes can benefit from an ability to utilize communication propensities of the other. For example, men who are responsive, open, sensitive, and interested in nurturing behaviors often get "bonus points" from women who appreciate the consideration. Similarly, women who take charge or relish a competitive environment may be demonstrating more commonly masculine behaviors and may be excellent communicators.

In addition, many successful professionals have adopted situation-specific communication behaviors that we normally attribute to the opposite gender. A male psychologist, for example, may use some "feminine" communication tendencies, while a female firefighter may use direct communication tactics normally associated with men.

In this reference guide, as an application of the Straight Talk Model, we offer suggestions and options for *guidance*, rather than as absolute, definitive solutions. Our intention is to heighten your awareness of different gender tendencies so that you can better adjust your approach for better communication.

Define the Context

The context of your communication includes the existing situation, the target audiences, and your objectives with those audiences. Your thorough understanding of all three forms a basis for your communication process, regardless of the cultural background of your audience. However, the unique differences of male and/or female target audience may determine how you analyze the situation and your objectives. We will begin this application of the Straight Talk Model with audience analysis.

Define Your Audience

Individual traits and behaviors vary greatly. As you identify your potential audiences and learn specific details about them, consider your context analysis to facilitate a thorough examination of each to help avoid assumptions and resulting miscommunication.

Identify Your Three Potential Audiences: Primary, Hidden, and Decision-Makers
After you identify your audiences, investigate and learn about them. These audiences can overlap, and there may be no hidden audience at all. Look beyond the obvious as you focus on facts, attitudes, wants, and concerns of each.

FACTS
Researchers have identified hundreds of facts about potential differences between the male and female individuals who may comprise your multiple audiences. We are focusing on the information that impacts on communication. Remember that this information is based on countless studies of the tendencies of men and women as groups. These are not absolutes, and every man or woman you know may not display these behaviors and characteristics. You might choose to add "probably" or "is likely to" in your head as you read.

If your receiver is a *man*:

- He has been socialized to perform aggressively and to boast of his successes. (Note here, for example, that men in some cultures, such as Finns or Asians, are very uncomfortable talking about themselves. So remember, all of these points are *tendencies of people as groups*.)
- His childhood games taught him that competition is fun and winning is good. He continues to be motivated by competition.
- He views conflict as impersonal, a necessary part of working relationships.
- He has traditionally been afforded attention-getting roles, as reflected in his interest in personal benefit and use of the word "I."
- He is impressed by power, ability, and achievement.
- His left-brain orientation yields problem-solving skills that are logical, analytical, factual, and hierarchical.
- He tends to focus on one thing at a time.
- His friendships are built on mutual activities and goals. He builds trust based on actions and accomplishments.
- He may only hear your literal words and miss your underlying emotion. He is not likely to express his true feelings through facial expressions.
- His communication style tends to be direct.
- When he succeeds, he attributes it to his ability. When he fails, he attributes the failure to outside circumstances, or he blames someone else.

If your receiver is a *woman*:

- She has been socialized to work cooperatively and to be modest about her successes. Her childhood games taught her to compromise and collaborate, and she continues to be motivated by affiliation. She competes primarily with herself (that is, with her own expectations of what she should be able to accomplish).
- She takes conflict personally. (Note: women with roots in East-European Jewish, Italian, and Greek cultures, however, tend to view conflict as a positive function of a close relationship.)
- She has traditionally been afforded attention-giving roles, as reflected in her interest in the wider needs of the corporate community and use of the word "we."
- She is impressed by personal disclosure and professional courage.
- Her right-brain orientation yields problem-solving skills that are creative, sensitive, and non-hierarchical.
- She has the ability to focus on multiple projects simultaneously. She is probably accustomed to balancing the demands of work, family, home, school, and/or community issues, and thus applies these skills to her job.
- Her friendships are based on personal closeness. She builds trust by sharing both secrets and herself.
- She may be proficient at decoding non-verbal meanings and is likely to display her feelings through facial expression and/or body language.

- Her style will tend to be indirect, except with other women of equal rank.
- When she succeeds, she may believe she was lucky. When she fails, she blames herself.

ATTITUDES

The gender of both the sender and the receiver affects your audience's attitudes about you, about your topic, and about being there to receive your information. First, consider your receivers' attitudes about you. If you are communicating ...

- Man to man, he may afford you instant credibility based on similarity.
- Man to either man or woman, you may start off with a higher perception of credibility than your female counterpart has, especially in terms of expertise, status, and power.
- Man to woman, she may expect that you will not really listen to her. She may also surmise that your idea or plan is based on your independent thinking and that it is an inflexible decision with little opportunity for compromise.
- Woman to woman, she may expect you to be friendly, nurturing, and concerned. She may afford you instant credibility based on similarity.
- Woman to either man or woman, you should expect to have to demonstrate better skills and more experience than your male counterpart does to be perceived as equal to him in credibility.

Woman to man, there are two major issues to consider:

1   He will expect you to be friendly and nurturing, even passive-dependent. Aggressive behavior and other deviations from his expectations can cause discomfort, confusion, and even negative responses.
2   He may simply disregard you.

Men and women may have different initial reactions to and attitudes about your topic. Your female audience member's greater psychological resilience makes her more agreeable to change, which is, of course, an element in most persuasive messages. Your male receiver may only accept your message if he immediately perceives personal benefit.

Finally, men and women may respond differently to actually being your audience. That is, they may have different attitudes about being there to hear your presentation or attend your meeting. Your male receiver is more likely to be an autocratic problem-solver. He may resent interrupting his schedule to hear your message, unless the other audience members are hierarchically superior, and thus inclusion is a compliment. He will assume that your presentation of a problem is a direct request for a solution. Your female receiver, often a team player who is motivated by acceptance and affiliation, is more likely to appreciate being included in your audience. She will respond to your presentation of a problem with support and reassurance, and she will offer to share experiences and jointly discuss the solution.

In analyzing attitudes, remember that your audience may prefer to be somewhere else, doing something else, with someone else. However, it is likely that the women to whom you write and speak will be more receptive to you, your topic, and being there than a male counterpart. Recognize that your audience might share these perceptions about you, your topic, and being there to receive your message. Plan carefully in order to establish a more accurate understanding of your intentions and yourself.

WANTS

The next step in audience analysis involves your determination of what information your audience wants to know. Avoid confusing what they want to know with what you believe they "need to know." Until you tell them what they *want* to know, they may not be receptive to what they *need* to know.

A man is likely to want to know the benefit for him and just what he has to do to win. He may be thinking, "What's in this for me?" and "What's the bottom line?" He will want to know how your plan will help him compete, both as an individual and as an organization. A woman is likely to want to know the benefit for the individuals in the organization and what she should do to facilitate the process. She may be thinking, "What will be the impact of this plan on the working relationships of the people involved?" She will want to know how your "winning" plan will allow her to provide a win–win situation for everyone, rather than a loss for someone else.

CONCERNS

Finally, your audience's fears—the consistent concerns that your male and female audience members express—exhibit a summary of gender differences. Again, a caveat: *do not assume* that *every* man and woman will exhibit each gender-specific trait. In fact, many men and women have adopted situation-specific, successful behaviors of the opposite gender. You may expect, however, that a careful review of these traits will enhance the depth of your understanding about your audience and therefore increase the probability that you will select the appropriate persuasive information. Remember:

- Men tend to be most concerned about *winning*. They will work as hard as necessary to win against their standard of comparison, usually other men. They fear defeat. They are interested in how the facts affect the bottom line.
- Women tend to be most concerned with *relationships*. They work to do their best; their standard of comparison is their personal ideal of their abilities. They fear that their successes mean someone else's defeat. They are interested in how the process affects the organization as a whole.

Analyzing your audience may be the most important component of your entire communication process, because every decision you make depends on your accuracy and detail at this point. Remember:

1   Identify your primary, hidden, and decision-making audiences.
2   Discover personal and professional facts, avoiding generalizations.
3   Be aware of their attitudes about you, your subject, and being there to receive your message.
4   Determine what they *want* to know, over and above what they *need* to know.
5   Recognize consistent concerns.

Define Your Situation

The next part of defining context involves a close look at the problem that has created the need to communicate, the external environment in which that problem exists, and the corporate culture that influences the problem.

Identify and Limit the Problem

Isolate the decision that now requires you to communicate a message to a particular audience.

1   What is the distinct cause for the message you are preparing?
2   What are the specific parameters that reduce the situation to manage-able proportions?

Both your gender and that of your audience can affect the definition of the problem. A man may define a problem in terms of outcome. A woman may define the same problem in terms of the people affected. Be certain that your definition of the problem is consistent with that of your male or female receiver and that you anticipate a mixed audience of both men and women.

Evaluate the External Climate

If your audience is male, they may tend to be more broadly focused on what is going on in their industry and related industries than are female colleagues, who may focus more specifically on internal issues.

Evaluate the Corporate Culture that Impacts on the Problem

A woman may be more sensitive to the nebulous attitudes and norms shared by members of an organization. Therefore, a female audience member will recognize if your plan, idea, or behavior is consistent with that of the corporate culture. Male audience members, while acutely recognizing the presence or absence of "fit," may not attribute the reason to the effects of corporate culture. In spite of their sensitivity to culture, however, women may not be as involved in office politics, which may reduce their comprehensive under-standing of the *overall* culture.

Define Your Objectives

Most messages, no matter how simple or apparently insignificant, encompass three objectives: an overall goal, a specific purpose of the communication, and your hidden agenda. The overall goal, based on the mission statement of the organization, should be inherent in any corporate message and may appear to be an objective guideline. However, men may take the actual words of the mission statement literally, while women may broadly apply the intention and allow for a more liberal interpretation. On the other hand, men may assume the corporate mission statement does not apply to them, if they do not see the immediate or specific benefit to their projects or themselves.

The specific purpose of the communication depends on your needs and on your analysis of the target audience. Also consider your own gender tenden-cies. Men tend to overestimate their potential for success, while women tend to underestimate it. As you assess your audience's level of knowledge about your topic, you may expect that your male audiences will allege more know-ledge than they actually have, while your female audiences may underplay their knowledge.

And finally, consider your hidden agenda, the personal objective(s) to which you are aspiring. *Everybody* has hidden agenda, including the members of your audience. Men's goals are likely to be competitive; women's goals may be affiliative. (Note: men may even interrupt when they notice chances to offer information that fulfills their hidden agendas. Women may be more indirect and wait for an opening.)

Choose Your Media and Timing Options

After evaluating your situation, audience, and objectives, you can explore the communication options available to you: how you should send your message (medium) and when you should send it (timing).

Note: we are considering *you* as the *source* throughout this Reference Tool, but after reading, you might realize that both your gender and that of your audience can influence your success. As we discussed in Chapters 1 (Overview), 2 (Context), and 3 (Options), sometimes you might need to ask someone else to make an initial introduction and help you establish your credibility.

Define Which Medium is Most Appropriate for Your Message

As you assess your options for how your message should be sent to your intended receiver, base your choices on the wants and needs of your target audi-ence, rather than on your own. Table A.1 presents additional considerations.

TABLE A.1 Differences Between Male and Female Reception of Messages

Male Receivers May	Female Receivers May
■ Never hear a message circulating on the **grapevine**, particularly if there are women in this communication network.	■ Receive your message from the grapevine quicker than you want them to, particularly if there are other women in the communication network. (Depending on the number of people who repeated the message on its way, what they hear may be distorted.)
■ Expect to discuss important information in a casual conversation, especially if you are a man.	■ Appreciate information received in informal conversation.
■ Be defensive about being called to a formal interview, especially if you are a woman.	■ Be intimidated by a formal interview, especially if they are subordinates who are "summoned" to your office. They may expect that your purpose is negative—that is, that they have done something wrong.
■ Be annoyed by a phone call that interrupts them, particularly if the caller is a subordinate who does not make the benefit clear.	■ Sound hesitant in response to your phone call that caught them off-guard or unprepared.
■ Pay little attention in a meeting or formal presentation, unless they understand the immediate personal benefit and recognizes that their superiors are included as well.	■ Appreciate being included in a problem-solving meeting. They may offer their attention and positive non-verbal feedback to your formal presentation. Do not overestimate their approval, however.
■ Appreciate the technology involved in a teleconference.	■ Appear uncomfortable in a teleconference where technology alters the perception of non-verbal behaviors.
And here are some additional notes, even though this is a book about oral communication	
■ Not recognize the personal energy involved in a personal note.	■ Appreciate the thought and effort that went into a personal note or a greeting card that recognizes a special occasion.
■ Prefer the brevity of a text message, short email, or memo.	■ Feel short-changed by the brevity or terseness of a text message, short email, or memo.
■ Appreciate a letter or longer email that they can read at a time of their own choosing.	■ Try to read the hidden meaning in a letter or longer email.
■ Read only the executive summary and selected sections of a report.	■ Be impressed by the detail you include in a report.
■ Be impressed by your title on your business card.	■ Recognize the creative aspects of your business card.

Determine When the Message Should Arrive

When deciding message timing—when the message should arrive—consider the needs of your audience in conjunction with your own communication objectives. Too often, we communicate at our own convenience, which may not be consistent with the timing needs of our male or female audience.

Male receivers are more likely to be rigid about the deadline they have set for you, even though they may be more relaxed about their own deadlines. Female receivers are more likely to be considerate of your needs in adjusting a deadline, but they are probably very concerned about keeping theirs.

Select and Organize Information

Ineffective communicators too often jump to this stage of the communication process before thoroughly working through Steps 1 and 2 of the model—defining the context and considering medial and timing options. If, however, you have given careful thought to the first two steps, you are in a position to select and organize information that is especially effective—and that will work best in connection with your audience's gender mix. Below are some examples of ways you can bring gender consideration into play as you create your message.

Plan a Beginning, a Middle, and an End

For your male receivers:

- Emphasize *personal* benefit in the introduction.
- Be succinct with your introduction (but do not delete it!), so that you can quickly make your point.
- Re-establish personal benefit in the conclusion.

For your female receivers:

- Emphasize the benefits for her department or team in the introduction.
- State the organizational plan for your presentation and stick to it.
- Confirm a win–win situation in the conclusion.

Limit Your Information

Remember that most communication experts recommend no more than three main points. Then, for your male receivers:

- Be direct with your main points.
- Include issues concerning long-term impact on the organization's bottom line.

For your female receivers:

- Consider an indirect approach to your main points. (Note here, for example, that professional situations and experience often diminish gender differences. Most business professionals respond best to a more direct approach.)
- Include issues concerning short-term impact on individuals and teams.

Enhance Your Message with Visual Aids, Numbers, and Examples

For your male receivers:

- Illustrate your points with numbers that impact the bottom line.
- Avoid personal disclosure to illustrate professional points, especially if you are a woman.
- Avoid attempting to impress your male audience with sports, war, or other male-specific metaphors, unless you fully understand them yourself.

For your female receivers:

- Employ personal anecdotes.
- Be careful about sports or war metaphors, especially if you are a man, unless you are certain that your audience will appreciate them.

Tailor Your Message for Each Individual Audience

Remember: these are guidelines, not absolutes! You can never assume that any individual is going to think or behave a certain way simply because of gender. However, allow this information to expand your thinking and broaden your considerations as you select the most appropriate and effective material for conveying each message to each audience.

Deliver Your Message

Now that you are armed with well-selected, organized, and supported information, you may confidently present that information to your target audiences using your chosen medium. As you do so, consider these gender-relevant approaches.

Deliver Effective Messages

If you are a man speaking to men:

- Express your confidence through direct eye contact (but do not expect them to reciprocate).

- Expect interruptions and appreciate them, since they indicate that your male audience is listening.
- Avoid being overly dramatic or demonstrative about your topic.

If you are a man speaking to women:

- Warm up your facial muscles to enhance your ability to express yourself through facial expression.
- Make direct eye contact with each individual.
- Allow enough space for your female receivers to be comfortable. Watch for signs such as stepping away or sitting back in their seats that indicate you are too close.
- Encourage feedback during your presentation, since they may be hesitant to interrupt you.
- Develop and communicate a transition from their thoughts to yours, rather than ignoring their comments and just changing the subject.
- Show passion for your product or idea. Your female audience may interpret a non-enthusiastic style as uncaring.

If you are a woman speaking to men:

- Warm up your voice to achieve the deepest, most well-projected sound that is possible for you. Your male audience will expect you to have excellent vocal skills.
- Warm up your body so that you will be more comfortable using whatever space is available for you.
- Express your confidence through direct eye contact. Do not look down or at the ceiling.
- Avoid reading or even appearing to read, which reduces the perception of your confidence and therefore your credibility.
- Remove physical barriers that diminish your size, such as lecterns. Try to stand, if your audience is sitting. If you must sit, try to use a seat that puts you at an equal or higher eye level than that of your male audience.
- Employ natural, broad movements to convey confidence. Relax; a perception of nervousness will damage your credibility.
- Avoid tag questions, that is, phrases attached to statements that change the statement to a question ("This is a great idea, *don't you think?*"). Your male receivers may perceive that you lack confidence about your statement.
- Anticipate interruptions as normal male communication rather than personal attacks or even negative feedback.
- Recognize that you may receive little if any active listening, such as smiles or head nodding. This does not mean they are not listening.

- Control your energy and focus your enthusiasm. If you are too dramatic, your male audience may enjoy your performance but miss your message.

If you are a woman speaking to women:

- Warm up your facial muscles so that the smile your female audience is expecting will look natural and so that you can freely express the emotional content of your message in your facial expression.
- Reduce space barriers to a minimum by getting as close as you can to your large audience, and by sitting on an equal level with an individual or small group.
- Take advantage of your female audience's tendency to be able to read the true emotional context of your message by using your face, hands, and body to express yourself.
- Understand that the active listening and non-verbal feedback you are likely to receive may be more polite than positive.
- Express your enthusiasm sincerely and personally.

Finally, for everyone: *be yourself*. Remember that most people are comfortable one-to-one but believe that they have to become someone different when they address a group. The suggestions above should help you become more adaptable to multiple communication situations, not to change you into someone else.

Evaluate Feedback for Continued Success

The differences in the way men and women receive feedback tend to be so substantial and obvious that even cartoonists lampoon them. Differences regarding giving and receiving feedback center on the ways in which men and women:

- Listen.
- Attribute success and failure.
- Accept responsibility and blame.
- Filter positive and negative information.

Understand Listening Behavior

In general, a man who is actively listening is likely to look directly at the speaker without moving or speaking. A positive response from him indicates "Yes," not just "I'm listening." When a woman listens, she usually offers an active response—that is, she nods her head or says "Um-hum" to indicate her attention.

Understand Attribution of Success and Failure

When a man succeeds, he often believes it is because of his ability. When he fails, he may believe that the situation was simply beyond his control (that is, his assistant didn't prepare the correct report, the client wasn't ready to buy, or the deal wasn't meant to be). When a woman succeeds, she often believes that she was lucky, had an excellent support team, or was in the right place at the right time. When she fails, she may believe that she simply lacked ability.

Understand Accepting Responsibility and Blame

Men tend to have a difficult time understanding that assuming responsibility does not mean accepting blame. If a man does not disassociate responsibility and blame, he might refuse both. He additionally may allow the blame to fall on whoever is willing to accept it. A woman may be quick to say, "I'm sorry," meaning that she regrets that something happened, not that she regrets she did it. However, she may find herself not only responsible, but at fault, by her own admission.

Understand Filtering Good and Bad News

Male defense mechanisms are usually better developed than those of women, which means that men tend to be better at shaping reality to their own advantage. As a result, men tend to focus on positive information and filter out the negative, which results in positive self-esteem but little improvement. Women, on the other hand, tend to focus on negative information and filter out the positive, which offers them greater potential for improvement, but continues to challenge self-esteem.

Apply the Guidelines for Soliciting and Evaluating Feedback

The following are some guidelines, in addition to those discussed elsewhere in this book, to facilitate your ability to solicit and evaluate feedback:

If you are a man *receiving* feedback:

- Avoid interrupting; this is your time to listen, not to talk.
- Write down negative comments with the same detail that you note positive comments.
- Ask for examples of negative comments, not just positive ones.
- Look for non-verbal messages along with literal ones.
- Avoid rejecting information with which you do not agree, recognizing that there is some truth in every perception.
- Accept responsibility. You are being held accountable, not being blamed.

- Plan some change in behavior as a result of this feedback.
- Express sincere appreciation for all the feedback, not just the *positive* part.
- Leave the evaluator with the perception that you understood all of the feedback, both positive and *negative*.

If you are a woman *receiving* feedback:

- Expect interruptions from the men to whom you are speaking.
- Write down positive comments with the same detail that you note negative comments.
- Ask for positive comments in writing.
- Avoid over-interpreting non-verbal information. Pay attention to the actual words, especially if the sender is a man. If the sender is a woman, her non-verbal cues are important, but they should not lead you to exaggerate their meaning.
- Avoid overreacting. Plan a minimum of correction in the direction of the evaluation (your minimum response will probably be perceived as a large behavioral change).
- Avoid apologizing, justifying, or giving reasons. Focus on solutions.
- Express appreciation for all the feedback, not just the *negative* part. Leave the evaluator with the perception that you understood all of it, both negative and *positive*.

Evaluate Yourself with the Credibility Checklist

Your effectiveness as a communicator depends in large part on the target audience's perception of your credibility. But your goal here is not just achieving credibility, which you will accomplish by applying the Straight Talk Model. Rather, your concern should be that men and women who exhibit the same behaviors and who are equal in terms of training, rank, and experience are often not *perceived* as equal by their target audiences.

Establish Goodwill: Your Focus on and Concern for Your Receivers

Women have traditionally been afforded attention-*giving* roles, and men have traditionally been afforded attention-*getting* roles. As a result, both male and female receivers expect that a woman will focus on them more than on herself. However, if a man offers the same kind of nurturing and attention that is expected of a woman, he receives "extra points." The woman who does not meet expectations loses credibility. While women may benefit from initial expectations that they will show goodwill, if they do not behave accordingly, receivers will judge them more harshly than they would men who behave exactly the same way.

If you are a woman, you may want to meet expectations that you will nurture your subordinates and show concern for your many audiences. If you are a man, you should exceed expectations by expressing concern for your many audiences.

Demonstrate Expertise: Your Education, Knowledge, and Experience
Researchers have discovered that even when a man and woman possess equal expertise, both male and female receivers perceive the man as being the more-qualified expert. If you are a man, do not exaggerate your knowledge and experience at the risk of becoming unbelievable. Receivers will perceive your modesty as charming and persuasive. If you are a woman, do not diminish your expertise. Receivers might perceive your humility as an actual lack of knowledge and experience.

Display Power: Your Status, Prestige, and Authority
Rank should correlate with perceptions of status, but researchers have found that when men and women have equal rank, audiences afford higher status to men. Success translates into others' perception of your power as well, but both men and women attribute a man's success to his ability and a woman's success to hard work and an easy task.

In addition, audiences often perceive typically "masculine" behaviors, such as interrupting, controlling conversation, and occupying large amounts of space, as being more powerful. However, women who employ "power behaviors" may confuse or alienate their target audiences. On the other hand, behaviors such as smiling and lingering eye contact often send mixed messages, as well. One audience may perceive smiling women as expressing warmth. Another audience may assume that the same women are allowing domination when they smile, maintain eye contact (perceived as gazing adoringly), and admit invasion of their space.

If you are a man, expect to perform to the high level of expectation of your audiences. If you are a woman, expect to work harder in order to be perceived as equal to your male counterparts.

Express Confidence: the Way You Present Yourself and Your Message
The confidence with which you demonstrate your skills is the most important factor in the perception of your credibility from your audience. Men are socialized to be comfortable in front of groups, yet women's language skills are often more developed. Confidence in communication is a *major* expectation in the corporate arena.

Reality and personal experience teach us that being confident is not always easy. However, audiences tend to perceive women who do not appear confident as lacking ability. An uncomfortable man may be perceived as endearing, particularly by a female audience. (A male audience may not notice at all.)

If you are a man, your confidence and extemporaneous abilities should not preclude careful preparation. You must select and organize information based on thorough audience analysis to maintain credibility. If you are a woman, prepare and practice so that both your skills and your confidence in demonstrating those skills are the best that they can be.

A Final Thought

The problems that arise from differences in the perception of the credibility of men and women in the workplace are complex. So are the solutions. The first step is to recognize that this is not a woman's issue; it is a *corporate* issue. Men, women, organizations, and businesses will benefit if men and women of equal rank, training, and expertise are afforded equal credibility.

On an individual level, we must recognize that men and women have been socialized to behave in particular ways and to expect certain behaviors from others. As male and female business communicators, we all have behavioral tendencies. As male and female audiences, we all have biases. If you believe differently, you need to raise your awareness.

Finally, as members of organizations, we have responsibilities. We must recognize both our strengths and weaknesses, and those of others to create the greatest possible perception of personal and corporate credibility.

Notes

1 Introduction to the Straight Talk Model: Discovering a Strategic Approach

1   An earlier version of the Straight Talk Model (then named the "Strategic Communication Model") described in this chapter was originally published in Sherron Bienvenu and Paul R. Timm, *Business Communication: Discovering Strategy, Developing Skills* (Upper Saddle River, NJ: Prentice Hall, Inc., 2002).

2 Define Context Before Speaking or Participating

1   www.kwintessential.co.uk/cultural-services/articles/crosscultural-blunders.html.
2   http://money.cnn.com/galleries/2007/biz2/0701/gallery.101dumbest_2007/index.html.
3   http://money.cnn.com/galleries/2007/biz2/0701/gallery.101dumbest_2007/2.html.
4   http://money.cnn.com/galleries/2007/biz2/0701/gallery.101dumbest_2007/41.html.
5   http://money.cnn.com/galleries/2008/fortune/0812/gallery.dumbest_moments_2009.fortune/20.html.
6   Stephen P. Robbins and Timothy Judge, *Essentials Of Organizational Behavior*, 9th edition (Upper Saddle River, NJ: Pearson Prentice Hall, 2008), p. 248.
7   Adapted from G. Hofstede, "Cultural Constraints in Management Theories," *Academy of Management Executive* (February 1993), p. 91.
8   Denise Wymore, marketing consultant, "Marketing to the Generation Formerly Known as Generation X," presented to Credit Union Executives Society (CUES) conference, Waikoloa, Hawaii, December 2004.
9   Don Tapscott, *Grown Up Digital* (New York: McGraw Hill, 2009), p. 162.
10 Interview by Robert C. Ford, "David Neeleman, CEO of JetBlue Airways, on People + Strategy = Growth," *The Academy of Management Executive*, 18, 2 (May 2004), p. 141.
11 This is published in Jeffrey Abrahams' book, *101 Mission Statements From Top Companies* (Berkeley: Ten Speed Press, 2007), p. 40.

3 Consider Your Media, Source, and Timing Options

1   This classic, early study was found in T.L. Dahle, "An Objective and Comparative Study of Five Methods of Transmitting Information to Business and Industrial Employees," *Speech Monographs*, 21 (1954), pp. 21–28.

2   D.A. Level, "Communication Effectiveness: Method and Situation," *Journal of Business Communication* (Fall 1972), pp. 19–25.

4 Select and Organize Your Message Content

1   Family Practice Notebook. www.fpnotebook.com/Psych/Exam/DsrgnzdSpch. htm.
2   "What's in it for me?"

5 Enhance Your Message with Powerful Support Material

1   Chip Heath and Dan Heath, *Made to Stick: Why Some Ideas Survive and Others Die* (New York: Random House, 2007).
2   Heath and Heath, p. 209.
3   *Hollywood's Peter Guber: Spinning Memos into Tales*, June 24, 2009, Knowledge@ Wharton.
4   Source: University of Minnesota/3M Study reported online at www.plu. edu/%7elibr/workshops/multimedia/why.html (accessed November 20, 2000).
5   Stephen Michael Kosslyn (2006) *Graph Design for the Eye and Mind* (Oxford: Oxford University Press), p. 126.
6   Neither author is an attorney and this information does not purport to be legal advice. It is based on wide experience, however, and is intended to provide some commonsense guidelines.
7   See, for example Scott Tambert, *How to Use Images Legally* (Washington, DC: Scott Tambert). Tambert is a specialist in public-domain images research. He is not a lawyer, and you should always seek competent, professional counsel on legal matters (www.pdimages.com/web9.htm).
8   Excerpted from Abhay Padgaonkar, "PowerPoint, Warts and All: Relearning to Communicate," *Marketing Profs*, August 14, 2007 (www.marketingprofs.com/7/ powerpoint-present-danger-next-slide-please-padgaonkar.asp).

6 Deliver Your Message with Confidence and Impact

1   Michael Waldhold, "Here's One Reason, Uh, Smart People Say 'Uh'," *Wall Street Journal*, March 19, 1991, p. B1.
2   This time-tested approach was discussed in the classic speech text by Harold P. Zelco and Frank E. X. Dance, *Business and Professional Speech Communication*, 2nd ed. (Austin: Holt, Rhinehart and Winston, 1978), pp. 77–79.
3   Originally published in Dr. Sherron Bienvenu's online Communication Solutions newsletter, September 2004.

7 Contribute to Effective Meetings

1   Based on a true experience of one of your authors. The names (of people and the organization) have been changed to reduce embarrassment.
2   *BusinessWeek* online, September 25, 2006. Reprinted with permission of The McGraw-Hill Companies Inc.

8 Participate in Effective Conversations and Interviews

1 One of our favorite books on cultural differences in conversations is Terri Morrison and Wayne A. Conaway, *Kiss, Bow Or Shake Hands*, Adams Media Corp, © 2006.

9 Evaluate Feedback for Continued Success

1 Adapted from Dr. Sherron Bienvenu, Communication Solutions online newsletter, February 2006. See: www.ChinUp.net.
2 Paul R. Timm, *Customer Service: Career Success through Customer Satisfaction*, 5th Edition (Upper Saddle River, NJ: Pearson Prentice Hall, 2011), see Chapter 8.

Reference Tool

1 Research on gender differences in workplace communication predominately includes American men and women with European backgrounds. However, we have excluded three types of gender research:

    1 Studies of senior executives—fewer than 3 percent of whom are women—which conclude that no differences exist.
    2 Studies of freshman and sophomore college students in controlled environments.
    3 Studies of intimate relationships.

The first is unrealistic for the overwhelming majority of the workplace population; the second and third have little relevance to the corporate environment.

For current insights into communication issues relevant to women in the workplace, see Sherron Bienvenu's Web page: www.ChinUp.net.

Index

accent, speaking with 144
ANSA pattern, persuasive messages:
  1-attention, gaining audience 96–7;
  2-need, developing 96, 97; 3-solution,
  offering 96, 98; 4-action close 96,
  98–9; example 99; worksheet 104
anxiety management: public speaking
  138; relaxation 155; stage-fright, as
  normal 155–8; symptoms,
  overcoming 156–7
area charts 121, 122
attention grabbers: anxiety management
  158; effective meetings 178–9;
  introductions 78; persuasive
  messages 86, 97; stories as 109–10
audiences: attitudes 37; concerns,
  consistent 38; context analysis 4,
  8–19, 28, 32–42; decision makers
  33–4; facts, personal/professional
  34–7; gender differences 253–7;
  hidden 33, 34, 224; hidden agenda,
  acknowledgment of 41–2;
  identifying all potential 32–4;
  learning about each 34–7; meaning
  of 3; needs of 12–13; notes, making
  37; objectives with each, defining
  38–42; primary 32–3, 34; 'wants' of,
  versus your 'needs' 37–8, 68, 256

bad-news messages: alternative,
  offering 90, 93; ANSA pattern
  96–9; apology, avoiding 92, 93;
  buffer, neutral or mildly-positive
  91; clarity 89–90; communication,
  effective 88; de-emphasis 90, 92–3;
  direct versus indirect approach 90;
  empathy 88–9; goodwill 88;
  message example 91; optimistic
  close, using 90, 93; 'quick-and-
  dirty' 90, 94–9; reasons 90, 92;
  STARR pattern 94–6; transition 90,
  91–2
Baker, Stephen 168
balance theory 97
bar charts 121
big idea 76, 82, 87
brainstorming 189; action, from ideas
  180; competitiveness, appropriate
  181; extended benefits of 181;
  facilitation skills 181; fear, living in
  180; ideas, combining and extending
  180; individual 180; rules, following
  181

Chandler Harris, Joel 74
clip art 128–9
Coca-Cola Company 39–40

computer-mediated (CMC) communication 58

conclusions 77; action step 80; final statement 80, 81–2; Q&A session 80, 81; summary 80; writing up 183

confidence: Credibility Checklist self-evaluation 244, 245–6, 247, 266–7; message delivery 17, 153–4; preparation/rehearsal 154–5; visual aids 112

content, message: bad-news messages 88–93; big idea 76, 82, 87; body 77; conclusions 77, 80–2; Context Analysis Worksheet 76; informative presentation activity 100–4; introductions 77, 78–80; longer messages 99; mini-case study 105–6; Outline Worksheet 81, 100–4; performance checklist 100; persuasive messages 83–7; repetition, reinforcement of 75–6; review questions 104–5; routine request, and informative messages 82–3; schizophasia (word salad) 75; select-and-organize approach 76–7; tangential speech 75; way it is scenario 75–6

context analysis: audience, defining 4, 8–19, 28, 32–42; communication success 25; corporate culture 5, 6–7, 51–2; external climate 5, 6, 30, 257; gender differences 253–8; information-gathering 4–5, 42–6; interviews, effective 218–20, 224; meetings, effective 170–3, 186–8; mini-case study 53–4; peer as audience activity 22–53; problem, limiting 5–6; review questions 52–3; situation, defining 4, 5–7, 28, 31–2; strategy, communication without 26–8; way it is scenario 26–8

Context Analysis Worksheets 29; activities 22–53, 50–1; audiences 33; blank 48–9; content, message 76; example 46–7; peer as audience activity 22–53; situation, defining 29

conversations: cultural differences 213, 214–16; *versus* interviews 199–200

copyright 123

core values 39–40

corporate culture: adapting to 158–9; aggressiveness 31; attention to detail 31; context analysis 5, 6–7, 51–2; gender differences 257–8; innovation/risk-taking 31; outcome orientation 31; people orientation 31; stability 31; team orientation 31

counseling interviews 219

Covey, Stephen R. 4

Credibility Checklist: audience perceptions 243; confidence 21, 244, 245–6, 247, 266–7; expertise 20–1, 244–5, 246, 266; feedback self-evaluation 233, 243–9; gender differences self-evaluation 265–7; goodwill 20, 244, 246, 265–6; persuasion 20; power 21, 244, 245, 246–7, 266

criteria-setting 182, 189

cultural differences: audience, failure to consider 26–7; conversations 213, 214–16; gender differences 252–3; individualism *versus* collectivism 32; long- *versus* short-term orientation 32; power distance 31; quantity *versus* quality of life 32; uncertainty avoidance 32

customer complaints 240–1

Deep, Sam 197

delivery, of message: anxiety management 138, 155–8; confidence 17, 153–4; corporate culture, adapting to 158–9; enthusiasm 153–4; feedback, and constant improvement 160; gender differences 261–3; 'how-to' presentation activity 164; listeners, needs of 159–60; mini-case study 166–7; performance checklist 161; personality, expressing 158–9; platform-management skills 146–9; presentation evaluation worksheet 165; presentations, common 140–1; review questions 166; sales pitch activity 165–6; self-inventory activity 161–3; straight talk skills, development of 17; success, audience's desire for your 159; success factors 16–17; successful speaker evaluation activity 164; team presentation activity 164; way it is scenario 139–40; yourself, being 18, 158–60

delivery skills: accent, speaking with 144; clear speech 141–2; expressive speech 142–3; eye contact 149; physical control 151–3; professional image 149–51; timing, attention to 143–4; verbalized pauses, minimizing 145; vocal patterns, distracting 144–5

design consistency, of visuals: background (templates) 124–5; bullet points 127, 128; capitalization 127; enumeration 127; fonts 125–7; illustrations 128–9; parallelism 127; PowerPoint™ features 128, 129; spacing 128; structure 127

dress 150–1

email messages 64, 65
empathy 88–9
exit interviews 219
eye contact 149

face-to-face (FTF) communication 58, 64
fax messages 64
feedback: appreciation, expressing 242; attitudes and behaviors, positive 242–3; blamers and avoiders 236–9; board of advisors activity 249; changes, responsibility for 243; as coaching 232–3; consequences, explaining 237; customer feedback 240–1; examples 238–9; feedback-receptiveness 242; gender differences 263–7; giving constructive 18–19,

234–9; help, offering 238; how to ask for 241–2; inappropriate behavior, defining 237; internal *versus* external 233, 247; interviews, effective 223, 226–7; listening 242; meaning of 233; meetings, effective 185–6, 191–2; mentoring programs 240; mini-case study 250–1; motivation, closing with 238; negative, usefulness of 18–19, 232; non-defensiveness 242; non-verbal messages, noticing 242; organizational pattern for 235–6; overreaction, avoiding 242–3; performance checklist 247–8; positive 18–19, 234; potential rewards, describing 237; procrastinators 236–7; purpose, transition to 237; receiving and processing 242–3; recognition, expressing 237; required action, specifying 237; review questions 250; self-evaluation, Credibility Checklist 233, 243–7, 243–9; soliciting 240–2; thanking 244; whom and when to ask 240

fillers, speech 145
flipcharts 113
fonts 125–7
formal report 64

Gallagher, Carol 55
Gantt charts 121–2
gender differences: audience, defining 253–7; context, defining 253–8; feedback 263–7; hidden agenda 258; information, selection and organization of 260–1; media and timing options 258–60; message delivery 261–3; objectives, defining 258; self-evaluation, Credibility Checklist 265–7; situation, defining 257–8; workplace communication 252–3

Goizueta, Roberto C. 1
Gramm, Phil 28

grapevine 63
grievance interviews 219
grooming 150
group decision-making: advance
    preparation, assignment of 177–8;
    advantages of 174–6; agenda,
    distribution of 178; brainstorming,
    rules of 179–81; conclusion, writing
    up 183; criteria-setting 182;
    disadvantages of 176–7;
    introduction, starting with 178–9;
    nominal group process (NGP)
    182–3, 194
groupthink, avoiding 183–4
Guber, Peter 110

handouts: full-page slides 115; notes
    pages 115; PPT, Tufte's war on
    115–16; three-to-a-page 115
Hargadon, Andrew 180
hiring interviews 218–19
Hofstede, Geert 31

information, selecting and organizing:
    audience, tailoring message for 261;
    context analysis, review of 15; gender
    differences 260–1; information
    limitation 260–1; interviews,
    effective 220–5; main points,
    limiting 16; meetings, effective
    188–9; organizational patterns,
    selection of 15–16see also content,
    message; support material
information-gathering: interviews 219;
    listening 42–4, 52; observation
    44–5; secondary sources, reading
    45–6
information overload 117
Internet 45–6
interviews, effective: agenda participants
    224; closed-ended questions 220–1;
    context, defining 218–20, 224; versus
    conversations 199–200; counseling
    interviews 219; employment
    interview preparation activity
    229–30; environment, safe 201; exit

interviews 219; face-to-face
    communication 220; feedback,
    evaluating 223, 226–7; grievance
    interviews 219; hidden audiences
    224; hiring interviews 218–19;
    hypothetical questions 222; ideas,
    effective delivery of 223, 225–6;
    information, selecting and organizing
    220–5; information-gathering
    interviews 219; information sharing
    199–200; interaction, opportunities
    for 201; leading questions 221–2;
    loaded questions 222; media and
    timing options 220, 224; mini-case
    study 230–1; non-verbal messages,
    attention to 223; one-to-one
    communication 197, 199; open-
    ended questions 221; pacing self
    220; pauses 222; performance
    checklist 228; performance-review
    interviews 219, 228–9; practice
    sessions, videotaping 223; probing
    questions 221; purpose, clear 199;
    questions, rephrasing 226; reprimand
    interviews 219; review questions
    230; situation 224; STARR approach
    226; summarizing/closing 222–3;
    way it is scenario 198–9see also
    listening
intonation 144–5
introductions 77; attention-grabbers 78,
    79, 86; audience benefits 79, 80;
    content preview 79, 80; group
    decision-making meetings 178–9

Jowett, Benjamin 14

laser pointers 131
letters 64
line charts 120
listening: active listening 190, 201,
    208; alertness 44; content reflection
    43, 44; environmental elements
    affecting 44, 204–5; 'go on'
    comments 43; importance of 223;
    interactional elements affecting

205–8; internal elements affecting 203–4; listening capacity 204–5; listening skills activity 52; message reflection 43; noise, presence of 205; non-verbal encouragement 43; notes, taking 44; opportunities, recognizing 44; retention listening 44, 190; self-centeredness 205–6; self-protection 206–8; support listening 42–4; and visuals 111–12

listening behaviors: attention, faking 208–9, 212; clarification, soliciting 211–12; cultural differences 213, 214–16; emotions, listening for 210; interrupting, avoiding 210–11; key ideas, repeating back 212–13; listen-talk ratio 208; listening habits checklist 202–3; notes, taking 213; patient, failing to be 209; preparation 208; questions, open-ended 209–10; reinforcement, verbal and non-verbal 211; thoughtful pauses, using 211 see also conversations

media options: communication overload 59; efficiency-versus-effectiveness 59–61; employee motivation 66; feedback capacity 61–2; formality 62–3; gender differences 258–60; hard-copy availability 62; job-related messages 66; management choices 66–7; media capabilities 61–3; media characteristics and costs 64; media choices activities 71, 72; media combinations 63–6; media groundrules activity 72; media richness theory 57–8; message intensity and complexity 62; mini-case study 73; one voice, speaking with 66–7; performance checklist 71; receiver expectations 58–9; review questions 72–3; speed 61; upward feedback 66–7; way it is scenario 56–7

media richness theory 57–8

meetings, effective: advantages and disadvantages activity 193–4; audiences, defining 171–2, 187; buck-passing 176; commitment 175–6; context, defining 170–3, 186–8; control, loss of 176; costs of 177; decision-making meetings 189; delegation 174; differences, resolving 174; feedback, evaluating 185–6, 191–2; follow-up 185–6; groups versus teams 176; ideas, monitoring of 174, 183; individual dominance, avoiding 174, 183–4; information, selecting and organizing 188–9; information delivery, monitoring 183–5; information meetings 188–9; judgments, relative versus absolute 175; listening, active 190; media, source and timing options 174–7, 188; meeting purpose 174; meetings, communicating in 169; mini-case study 196; mini-presentations 191; objectives, defining 172, 187–8; optimism 189–90; organizational culture 171; participant rating activity 194–5; participation, active 189–91; performance checklist 193; retention listening 190; review questions 195–6; risky shift phenomenon 185; rules, participating within 191; self-evaluation checklist 173; selling versus participating 187; situational factors 170–1, 186–7; solutions, testing 186; status differences 183–4; synergy 174–5; timing factors 174; way it is scenario 169–70, 192 see also group decision-making

memos 64, 65

mentoring programs 240

message content see content, message

message delivery see delivery, of message

mission statements 39–40

missstatements 26

Murrow, Edward R. 197

Nardelli, Robert 25–16
Neeleman, David 39
nominal group process (NGP) 182–3, 194
non-verbal messages, observing for 192
Northwest Airlines 27
Norvig, Peter 115–16
notes, making 37, 44, 146–7, 213
notes, sending 64

open-ended questions 209–10, 221, 241
oral presentations 64, 65, 100–6, 140–1, 164–5
organizational charts 121, 122–3
overhead transparency projectors 114

Padgaonkar, Abhay 129
pauses 122, 143–4, 145
performance-review interviews 219
persuasion continuum 41
persuasive messages: as action-oriented 83–4; activity 100–1; agenda 86; ANSA pattern 96–9; audience objectives 40–1; big idea 87; buy-in, generating 84–5; decision-making model 87; emotions, involving 84; features and benefits 85–6; indirect approach 86; introduction 86; objections, anticipating 85; persuasion continuum 87; persuasive stories 84; problem-solution order 86–7; real-life examples 85; Rule of Threes 85; stories, using 84
physical control. body movement, appropriate 152; facial expression 152; gestures, spontaneous/natural 151; hand positions 152; physical space, use of 153; smile 152; weight distribution 153
pie charts 119–20
platform-management skills: notes, use of 146–7; questions, handling 147–9; script, reading from 146–7; visual aids, management of 147
politically incorrect statements 26
politicians, blunders of 28

PowerPoint™ 113, 126, 128, 129
preparation: opening/concluding remarks 154; practice, videotaping 155; self-consciousness, as self-destructiveness 155; timing options 70, 154
presentations 64, 100–6, 140–1, 164–5
professional image 149–51
props 114

questions: closed-ended 220–1; hypothetical 222; leading 221–2; loaded 222; open-ended 209–10, 221, 241; probing 221; Q&A session 80, 81

rehearsal 154–5, 170
repetition 75–6
reports 65
reprimand interviews 219
request and informative messages: big idea 82; cause-effect order 83; chronological order 83; completeness 82; directness 83; problem-solution order 83; topical/spatial order 83
retention listening 44, 190
risky shift phenomenon 185
Robbins, Stephen P. 31
role plays 114–15
Rosenblum, Kim 25

self-centeredness 205–6
self-protection 206–8
simulations 114–15
situation, defining: Context Analysis Worksheet 29; corporate culture 31–2, 257–8; cultural differences 31–2; external climate 5, 6, 30, 257; gender differences 257–8; information overload 30; meetings, effective 170–1, 186–7; problem, limiting 30, 257
sketches 114–15
slides (PowerPoint™) 113
Smith, Hyrum 109
sound/video clips 114

source options: audience perceptions
67–8; audience 'wants' *versus* your
'needs' 68; credible source, choice of
13–14, 67–8; hidden agenda,
acknowledging 68; source, meaning
of 56
speech: clarity 141–2; expressiveness
142–3; fillers 145; tangential 75
STARR pattern, informative messages:
1-situation 94, 95; 2-task 94, 95;
3-action 94–5; 4-result 95, 96;
5-recommendations 95, 96;
interviews, effective 226; worksheet
103
stories, use of 84, 109–12
Straight Talk Model, introduction to:
communication culture activity 23;
message planning 1; mini-case study
24; model, rationale for 23; review
questions 23–4; strategic process
3–21
support listening 42–4
support material: bar chart preparation
activity 133; copyright 123; design
mistakes activity 133; examples, use
of 110; major points, individual
visuals for 116–17; message
stickiness 107; mini-case study
136–7; performance checklist 133;
permissions 123–4; photos, use of in
slides 123–4; review questions 136;
selling activity 134–5; stories
110–12; type/design concept, use of
appropriate 117; way it is scenario
108–9

Sussman, Lyle 197

telephone conversations 64
templates 124–5
timing, and message delivery skills
143–4
timing options: audience needs 14, 69,
71; gender differences 260; meetings,
effective 174; message effectiveness
69; message sequencing 14, 70;
postponing, judicious 70;
preparation 70, 154; rehearsing 70
Tufte, Edward Rolfe 115–16
typefaces 125–7

'up-speak' 144–5

visual aids: audience perceptions 112;
communication effectiveness 112;
delivery of 131–2; efficiencies,
improved 112–13; feedback on 132;
formats 117–23; listeners, and
visuals 111–12; and message
comprehension 109–11; misuse of
130–1; options 113–16; speaker
confidence 111, 112; visual aid
preparation activity 135*see also*
design consistency, of visuals
voice improvement exercises 156
voice mail 64

Wal-Mart 27
Walton, Mark S. 84
Will-Harris, Daniel 10
word charts 117–18, 119